Library and Information Studies in the Digital Age

Library and Information Studies in the Digital Age

Anurag Ghosh

RANDOM

RANDOM PUBLICATIONS

NEW DELHI (INDIA)

Library and Information Studies in the Digital Age

ISBN 978-93-5111-557-1

Published in 2015 in India by

RANDOM PUBLICATIONS

4376-A/4B, Gali Murari Lal, Ansari Road
New Delhi-110 002
Phone : +9111-43580356, 011-23289044, 011-43142548
e-mail: sales@randompublications.com,
info@randompublications.com, randomexports@gmail.com
Reprint 2021

Type Setting by : Friends Media, Delhi-110089
Digitally Printed at : Replika Press Pvt. Ltd.

Preface

Information and technology literacy represents a content area in Net Gen students' education that has not been fully addressed. Separate but related is the "style" issue of how best to deliver this educational content and provide information and technology services to Net Gen students. Net Gen students work in information environments, and a very important one in college is the course management system.

The term digital library is diffuse enough to be applied to a wide range of collections and organizations, but, to be considered a digital library, an online collection of information must be managed by and made accessible to a community of users. Thus, some web sites can be considered digital libraries, but far from all. Many of the best known digital libraries are older than the web including Project Perseus, Project Gutenberg, and ibiblio.

Libraries should develop tutorials, exercises, and guides that can readily be embedded in course materials within course management systems, and some are already doing this. They can develop games to teach these skills; TILT, the Texas Information Literacy Tutorial developed by The University of Texas at Austin libraries, is an early example. Simulations such as Environmental Detectives can incorporate information-seeking skills into the game, reinforcing Net Gen students' interest in figuring things out and working in groups. Libraries should explore blogs as a mechanism for students to exchange information on valuable information resources they find for particular course assignments.

Today's technological transformations are intertwined with another transformation, globalization and together they are creating a new paradigm – the network age. These transformations expand opportunities and increase the social and economic rewards of creating and using technology. They are also altering how and by whom technology is created and owned, and how it is made accessible and used. Technology is not inherently good or bad the outcome depends on how it is used.

The book will be highly useful for students, teachers and all those concerned.

I would like to thank my team for standing beside me throughout my career and writing this book. My special thanks go to "Random Publications" who have published the book.

– Anurag Ghosh

Contents

Preface .... *v-vi*

1. **Introduction** **1**

Federated Search 2
Advantages of Federated Search 3
Selection of Federated Search Engine 4
How Federated Search Works 6
Drawbacks of Federated Search 8
Need and Purpose of Federated Search Tools 9

2. **Management Information Systems in Library** **30**

Introduction 30
A Modern Digital Library System 31
Development of Management Information Systems 35
Workplace Environment in the Digital Era 38

3. **Digital Geolibraries and Digital Collections** **68**

Linking Digital Library Resources to Related Resources 71
National Data Infrastructure 78
Databases, Web Services, and Internet GIS 80
Co-usage of Documents in a Large Digital Library 82

4. **Information Communication Technology and Digital Storage in Libraries** **114**

Introduction 114
Impact of Information Technology on Information Professionals 118
Role of Storage Devises in Digital Library Environment 134
Preservation and New Technologies 140
Selection for Preservation 143
Needs for Digitization of Library: Technology and Supporting Format 146

5. **Collections and Organizations of Digital Libraries** **168**

Introduction 168
Collections of Resource Descriptions 169

Measurement of use and Performance Indicators in the Digital Library 170
Document Representation of Digital Library 175
Digital Archives 181
Distributed Services Architecture in dLibra Digital Library Framework 183
Semantic Query Routing and Processing in P2P Digital Libraries 187
Publish/Subscribe Functionalities for Future Digital Libraries 190

6. Development from Traditional to Digital Libraries 194

Introduction 194
Advent of Information Technology 194
The Challenges of Digital Preservation 195
Digital Preservation Requirements 198
Areas for Research and Development 203
Management Tools 206
Development of IT Skills for Information Professionals 208

7. Digital Library Evaluation 213

Introduction 213
Collection Evaluation 215
Context of Evaluation 217
Criteria for Evaluation 218
ICDL: Evaluation Method 220
Federal Initiatives: Digital Libraries and Others 221
Evaluation of Digital Libraries and their Services 226
Preservation Microfilming 228
The Digital Libraries Universe: A Three-Tier Framework 231
Exploring Digital Libraries through Visual Interfaces 241

8. Digital Librarians: Safeguard the Past, Looking Advance 252

Introduction 252
Characteristics of a Digital Library 262
Definition of Digital Libraries 264
Digital Library Projects on Digital Reference Services 266
Teach about Digital Libraries 270
Preservation Planning 278
Predominant Approaches in Long-term Digital Preservation 285

***Bibliography* 291**

***Index* 293**

1

Introduction

In the electronic information environment one of the responses to the problem of bringing large amounts of information together has been for libraries to introduce portals. A portal is a gateway, or a point where users can start their search for information on the web. There are a number of different types of portals, for example universities have been introducing "institutional portals", which can be described as "a layer which aggregates, integrates, personalises and presents information, transactions and applications to the user according to their role and preferences".

A second type of portal is a "subject portals". A third type of portal is a "federated search tool" which brings together the resources to a library subscribes and allows cross-searching of these resources. They work using the Z39.50 protocol used by database suppliers to enable communication between computers. This protocol is not always effective because database suppliers have not always adopted it consistently so other protocols are also used such as HTML, XML and SQL. Since, these tools access resources that the library pays for, some type of authentication is required to ensure. Well before the launch of the World Wide Web, librarians recognised the need for establishing a common interface to search multiple sources. The ANSI/NISO gives the international search-andretrieval protocol, Z39.50, which was originally proposed in 1984 as a standard means of interrogating bibliographic databases. Since, then it has gone through three versions, the latest of which was issued in 1995. Federated search compliments the Z39.50 facility, it offers the ability to extend search beyond the online catalog virtually to any electronic resources that can be authenticated at the point of access. This means that users no longer need to jump from one search interface to another.

Information integration over distributed sources is an urgent problem to be solved for providing access to a variety of Digital Libraries through a common search interface and portal. Federated or cross-database search tools now available on the market are the correct solution for unifying access to a variety of information resources.

These tools can search not only library catalogs but also commercial abstracting and indexing databases, web search engines, and a variety of other databases, while often merging and de-duplicating results. Federated searching started in 1998 when Webfeat Team took the initiative to connect any or all of their databases at the same time through a simple, common user interface and turned this idea into a product called Webfeat.

WebFeat, the original federated search engine, used by over 15,000 leading public, academic, government and Global 1000 libraries and information centers — including over a third of the largest 100 U.S., public libraries, 18 statewide library systems, and 2 out of every 10 Association of Research Libraries (ARL) institutions, brings you the next frontier in federated search technology.

Originally founded in 1992 as an information technology consultancy. The WebFeat concept is simple: search any or all of your library's databases simultaneously with a single intuitive interface. WebFeat can search any database, including licensed databases, free databases, catalogs, Z39.50, Telnet, proprietary databases, anything! And with SMART, WebFeat's next generation usage tracker, you can report detailed database usage within your library with just a few mouse clicks.

FEDERATED SEARCH

Federated search is the simultaneous search of multiple online databases and is an emerging feature of automated, Web-based library and information retrieval systems. It is also often referred to as a portal, as opposed to simply a Web-based search engine. It is sometime termed as broadcast search, parallel search, cross reference search, etc. Various terms are used to refer to these tools in the literature including: metasearchers, crosssearchers, cross-database searchers, portals, broadcast searchers or parallel searchers.

The term metasearcher is particularly prominent and is the term adopted by the United States National Information Standards Organisation (NISO), which has developed a Metasearch Initiative. However as Fryer explains, the term metasearcher can cause confusion due to its association with web Metasearch engines such as Metacrawler which function in a different way to federated search tools. The term federated searching is the function of search tools, which search a number of databases, particularly subscription databases, simultaneously with one interface. The content searched by federated search tools is content that could not normally be searched via a web search engine.

DEFINITIONS

Researcher defines federated search as, "Transforming a query and broadcasting it to a group of disparate databases with the appropriate syntax, merging the results collected from the databases, presenting them in a succinct and unified format with minimal duplication, and allowing the library patron to sort the merged result set by various criteria". In simple words, Federated searching will be defined as a search system using a common interface that enables the simultaneous searching of databases from a variety of vendors.

Federated search technology enables users to search multiple information resources simultaneously through one search query. Users can then view search results in a single integrated list. In other words, users do no longer need to consult each information resource individually.

Instead, they can search multiple library catalogs (OPACs), Web sites (*e.g.* Amazon.com, Google, etc.), subscription and citation databases all at once. Federated search technology is an integral component of an Information Portal, which provides the interface to diverse information resources. Once the user enters his or her search query in the search box of the Information Portal, the system uses federated search technology to send the search string to each resource that is incorporated into the Portal.

The individual information resources then send the Information Portal a list of results from the search query. Users can view the number of documents retrieved in each resource and link directly to each search result. Metasearch, this word is synonymous to federated searching, people find no difference between federated searching but there is slight difference between federated and meta searching.

ADVANTAGES OF FEDERATED SEARCH

There are certain advantages of using Federated Searches. Some of them are as follows:

- The reduced time it takes to do a basic search is benefit enough.
- Unified access to diverse content sources.
- Simultaneous searching across all sources.
- Ability to Simple search as well as advanced search.
- Integrated results which are easy to view and use.
- Direct links to the native source for further searching.
- Ability to filter, sort, save, print, export and e-mail search results

SEARCH MODELS

Search on data bases starts with simple search formulation using single keyterm and combinations of terms. The search results thus obtained can be listed in simple predefined format or using user customised format to get desired information. Various search models indicate the interactions of users search formulations and its interface with databases in a Library or online web access to aggregated databases.

OLD SEARCH MODEL

Without a federated search tool, each database requires its own unique search tool - significantly complicating and slowing the search process for patrons. In this kind of search model user submit their search query to individual database or search engines etc and individually they get their required information.

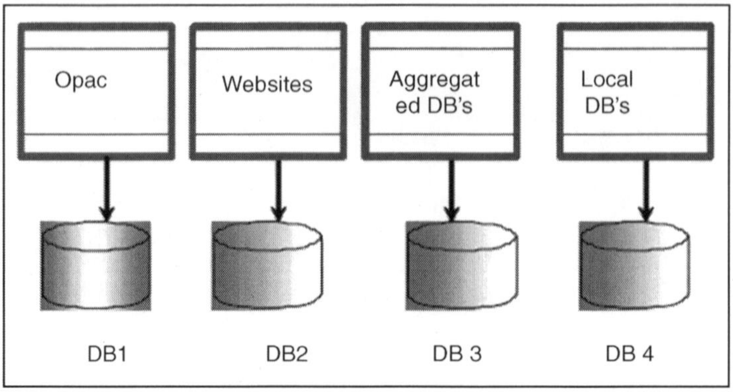

Fig. Old Srearch Model.

This kind of search tools are very time consuming and most of the time user didn't get their desired information.

FEDERATED SEARCH MODEL

Using federated search, a single tool searches and accesses all databases with one, easy to use interface.

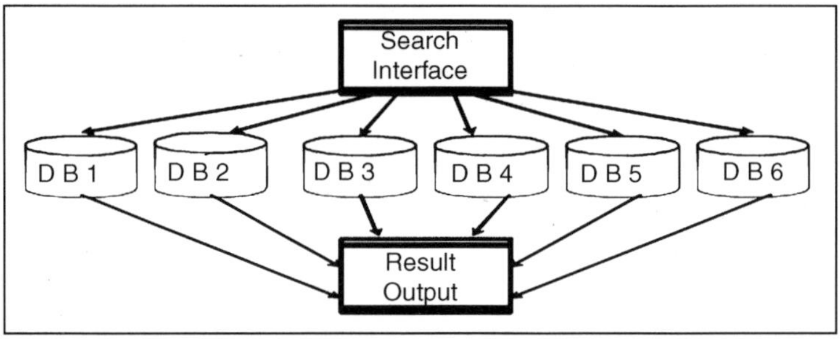

Fig. Federated Search Model.

It provides opportunity to the users that they get their desired information from various databases, search engines, etc.

SELECTION OF FEDERATED SEARCH ENGINE

In selecting a Federated search engine, one needs to bear in mind the following:

- The maximum number of resources the software can include
- The ease of setting up resource targets
- Availability of simple search options
- Speed of search results
- Limiting and refining searches
- Ranking results by relevance
- Export options, *i.e.,* print, e-mail, download
- Adequate statistics and reporting features

STANDARDS AND DEVELOPMENT

NISO – (US) National Information Standards Organisation launched and continue to develop initiatives in order to develop and adopt standard search and retrieval protocols for federated searching. XML – Web protocol and SOAP (Single Object Access Protocol)

ACCESS ISSUES WITH FEDERATED SEARCH

Verification, authentication and certification can be difficult for the federated search vendor. Since, federated search engines don't hold the data locally, *i.e.,* the engines perform the search, and send the results back to the portal.

The federated search engine must be able to access multiple passwordprotected databases behind the scenes, or IP validate all at the one time, and show users their results in one easy navigable interface.The challenge for federated search vendors is to provide only licensed users access to databases, as specified for each license agreement that is in place for the organisation.

AUTHENTICATION

Authentication sets federated search engines apart form other expensive and highly sophisticated search software such as Verity and Autonomy. The latter usually restricts searches to internally generated information, ignoring subscription databases that enterprises have bought in-house. All the user needs with federated searching is ID, password or IP validation along with files to be searched, and the federated search engine do the rest..

THE SET–UP PROCESS

The set up process is lengthy and time consuming for both the Library and the vendor. This is not the end of the process either! It continually evolves as databases change, or new resources are acquired and links are added to the federated search portal.

INTERFACE ISSUES

We need to decide how much time is to be devoted to design, who is the audience and should this audience be able to perform multiple searches, without having to do more than input their ID and password or IP authenticate, and type in the search query.

REMOVING DUPLICATES (DE-DUPING)

Most federated search engines will de-dupe some only when requested. However this opens up a Pandora's Box about how the results are returned. User habits indicate that the end user views only the first ten hits or results.

How do the vendor and the interface designer ensure that the highest hits are returned? This area is continually evolving, and it is up to the federated search engine provider, to provide what they can, to the best of their technological ability in this regard.

HOW FEDERATED SEARCH WORKS

Federated search computer programmes allow users to search multiple data sources with a single query from a single user interface. The user enters a search query in the portal interface's search box and the query is sent to every individual database in the portal or federated search list. Access details for the individual databases must be preset in the portal by its owner.

Federated search systems either rely upon vendors to create commercial portal systems, or they rely upon government or other organisations to provide open access portals. How federated search is implemented depends upon which of the two types of organisations is providing the portal. Federated search portals, either commercial or open access, generally search public access bibliographic databases; public access Web-based library catalogues (OPACs), Web-based search engines like Google and/or open-access, government-operated or corporate data collections.

These individual data sources send back to the portal's interface a list of results from the search query. The user can review this hit list. Some portals will merely screen scrape the actual database results and not directly allow a user to enter the data source's application. More sophisticated ones will de-dupe the results list by merging and removing duplicates. There are additional features available in many portals, but the basic idea is the same: to improve the accuracy and relevance of individual searches as well as reduce the amount of time required to search for resources.

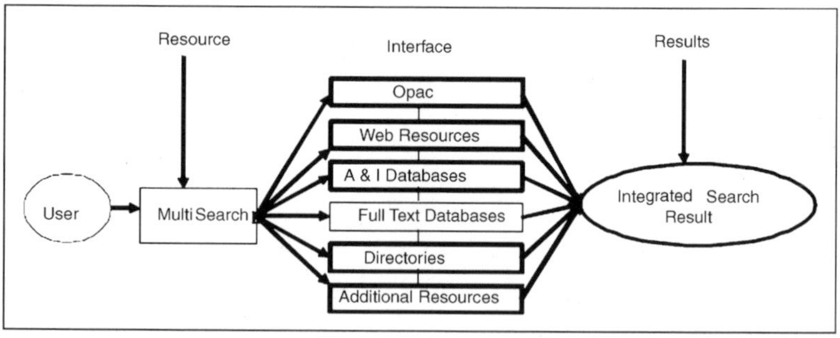

Fig. Diagrammatic Representation of Federated Searching.

In federated searching, a wealth of information is incorporated into a single repository that can be searched. In this model, the information is processed prior to the user's search. From the enduser's point of view, federated searching and metasearching may seem similar, because both provide a single interface to multiple resources, but they actually differ in many respects.

The pre-processing taking place in a federated searching environment, which we can describe as just-in-case processing, offers new opportunities regarding search methodologies and the presentation of results. For example, a ranking algorithm can be applied to each data element stored in the repository, unrelated to any future user query. Such an algorithm can take into account the number of times that an article has been cited, the number of articles that the author has published, the number of times that a book has been borrowed, a journal's impact factor, and other parameters.

A federated searching system can use the calculated rank to better evaluate the relevance of the specific item once it has been retrieved as the result of a query.The system searches a local repository that was created earlier through the accumulation of data from numerous resources. Looking back a few years, we can see that the need for a single search interface to multiple resources arose some time ago, and, in fact, metasearching and federated searching have been available for quite some time.Such systems originated in a variety of environments; for example, Elsevier, a publisher offering numerous journals, created a federated search mechanism enabling its users to search all its e-journals through its ScienceDirect service.

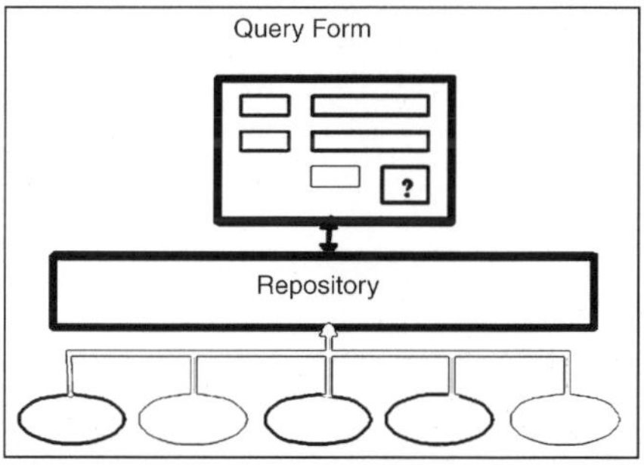

Fig. Diverse in Form Mation Resources.

As Elsevier acquired other publishers, it was able to add their journals to the same platform. Database vendors developed similar mechanisms. For example, Ovid provides a single interface to a few hundred databases that it publishes, and still retains them as separate databases.

Commercial organisations were not the only ones that addressed the need for a single search interface; several large research institutions created a local environment based on federation.

For example, the Los Alamos National Laboratory and the Ohio Link consortium in the United States, the University of Toronto in Canada, the Technical Knowledge Center of Denmark (DTV), and the Max Planck Society in Germany all offer large, diverse collections of e-journals that they store locally. These institutions have implemented federated searching to provide a single search interface across their electronic collections. However, not all organisations have the resources to adopt this just-in-case approach.

Furthermore, with the rapid increase in the number of heterogeneous resources that institutions offer their users, a single federated searching system can serve only as a partial solution.

IMPLEMENTATION

When a federated search engine is implemented at a particular library, it then becomes a unique service. Federated-searching software allows customisation, so no two implementations are exactly the same. For example, a library may choose to include all of its online resources as targets for a federated search engine or it may choose to create subject groupings first, each of which leads to a federated search service for a narrow topic.

Gerrity, Lyman, and Tallent discuss implementing a federated search system at Boston College, where they promoted the new service as "MetaQuest".

One application of federated searching is the metasearch engine; however, this is not a complete solution as many documents are not currently indexed.

This is known as the deep Web or invisible Web. Many more information sources are not yet stored in electronic form.

'Google Scholar' is an example of a project trying to address this.When the search vocabulary or data model of the search system is different from the data model of one or more of the foreign target systems the query must be translated into the each of the foreign target systems.

This can be done using simple dataelement translation or may require semantic translation.

DRAWBACKS OF FEDERATED SEARCH

Limitations of the current generation of federated search engines. These include:

- The lack of a uniform authentication standard means that some databases are inaccessible to federated search engines.
- True, full, deduplication is impossible because databases download results in small sets and metadata standards vary by resource.
- Relevancy ranking is limited by the quality of the metadata, which usually does not include abstracts or full-text information.
- Although federated search systems are fundamentally software, they must be implemented and managed as a service, which takes a great deal of resources.
- Federated search engines cannot improve on the native interface in terms of search accuracy and precision.
- Federated searching is not for power searching needs. Just as with searching metasearch engines, only basic Boolean commands can be used.

The federated search has some other issues as well. First, it cannot cover all online library resources. The goal of one-stop shopping cannot be achieved completely by any federated search.

There are various reasons for this:

- Some databases do not work with any federated search at all, such as SciFinder Scholar. SciFinder Scholar does not use a web browser but rather requires its own internet client. Neither MetaLib nor WebFeat can cover SciFinder Scholar.
- If databases require a login, they will not work with the federated search.
- Some databases work with one federated search product but do not work with the other. MetaLib cannot search LexisNexis databases because LexisNexis does not allow Z39.50 or XML gateway access. WebFeat cannot search databases that do not have a search box on their front page because WebFeat counts on the search box on the native interface to search.
- Many libraries have databases on a pay-per-search basis, and libraries normally do not want them to be searched by a federated search for budgetary reasons.
- Some databases have a limited number of concurrent users, and if these databases are included in a federated search, the limited seat(s) is/are taken immediately whenever someone logs into the federated search, and no other users can use these databases. Libraries normally do not want to include databases with a very limited number of concurrent users in the federated search.

It may not make sense to add to a federated search menu the very specialised databases that most general users would not be interested in, or the databases that require special software. One example is Inter-university Consortium for Political and Social Research (ICPSR) that requires statistics software such as SPSS to view data.

NEED AND PURPOSE OF FEDERATED SEARCH TOOLS

The need and purpose of the federated searching are as follows:

- The growth of different types of databases, produced by different suppliers, with numerous interfaces and logins means that library users can find it confusing when attempting to access information;
- Library OPACs and web-pages have been alienating users with their use of library terminology and by including long lists of databases that users find it difficult to select from and search;
- The needs and expectations of library users, particularly students using academic libraries. The growth of different types of databases, produced by different suppliers, with numerous interfaces and logins means that library users can find it confusing when attempting to access information.

There are certain purposes which can be served by the federated search are as follows:-

- Transforming a query and broadcasting it to a group of disparate databases with the appropriate syntax.
- Merging the results collected from the databases,
- Presenting them in a succinct and unified format with minimal duplication,
- Providing a means, performed either automatically or by the portal user, to sort the merged result set.

In traditional search engines such as Google, only sources that have been indexed by the search engine's crawler technology can be searched, retrieved and accessed. The large volume of documents housed in databases is not open to traditional Internet search engines because of limitations in crawler technology. Federated searching resolves this issue by the technique described above and makes these deep Web documents searchable without having to visit each database individually.

FEDERATED SEARCH TECHNOLOGIES

There are mainly four technologies used for federated searching.

- Screen scraping or HTTP
- Z39.50 protocol
- ZING - SRW protocol
- XML gateway

SCREEN SCRAPPING OR HTTP

"Hyper Text Transport Protocol" - HTTP is the single most important technology that drives the web and yet remains virtually transparent. Without this protocol HTML and XML via the web would not be able to perform the myriad of tasks that we put them to daily.

The Hypertext Transfer Protocol (HTTP) is an application-level protocol for distributed, collaborative, hypermedia information systems. HTTP has been in use by the World-Wide Web global information initiative since, 1990. The HTTP protocol is a request/response protocol.

A client sends a request to the server in the form of a request method, URI, and protocol version, followed by a MIME-like message containing request modifiers, client information, and possible body content over a connection with a server.

HTTP communication usually takes place over TCP/IP connections. TCP guarantees that packets arriving to and from the web server are error free and in the right order. It doesn't however guarantee that packets arrive no matter what the network conditions are. When communications are congested or unavailable web page delivery is slow and can time-out.

Z39.50 PROTOCOL

Z39.50 is an American national standard for information retrieval. It is formally known as ANSI/NISO Z39.50-1995 - Information Retrieval (Z39.50): Application Service Definition and Protocol Specification.

This document specifies a set of rules and procedures for the behaviour of two systems communicating for the purposes of database searching and information retrieval. As a network application standard, Z39.50 is an open standard that enables communication between systems that run on different hardware and use different software The Z39.50 standard was developed to overcome the problems associated with multiple databases searching such as having to know the unique menus, command language, and search procedures of each system accessed.

Z39.50 simplifies the search process by making it possible for a searcher to use the familiar user interface of the local system to search both the local library catalogue as well as any remote database system that support the standard. In libraries, the Z39.50 protocol is most often used for searching OPAC sources.

The important facilities offered by Z39.50 are as follows:

- *Browse*: Allows the client to scan the contents of wordlists or indexes on the server. This can be particularly useful in the case of controlled keyword lists or facets.
- *Access and resource control*: Allows authentication of users, and cost control and online charging for commercial services.
- *Sort*: Allows the client to request different orderings of query results, eg. relevance ranking, sorting by date or version number, etc.
- *Explain*: Allows the client to interrogate the server about a number of details about its contents and its level of support for the application profile.
- *Item Order*: Allows offline ordering of materials in cases where they cannot be delivered electronically, or where per-unit charging (eg. online charging) is required. Such services are being supplied in an ad-hoc fashion by online Web-based component repositories such as ASSET. The item order service provides a ready-made and semantically standardised version of this service.
- *Item Update*: Permits an authorised client to update the contents of the remote database.

SRW (SEARCH/RETRIEVE WEB SERVICE)

Search/Retrieve Web Service is a new HTTP-based information retrieval protocol providing broadly the same facilities as Z39.50, but by means of very different technology. SRW is designed to be a low barrier to entry solution to performing searches and other information retrieval operations across the internet. It uses existing, well tested and easily available technologies such as SOAP and XPath in order to perform what has been done in the past using proprietary solutions. The protocol has two ways that it can be carried, either via SOAP or as parameters in aURL.

This second form is called SRU – Search Retrieve by URL. Other transports would also be possible, for example simple XML over HTTP, but these are not defined by the current standard. The primary function of SRW is to allow a user to search a remote database of records. This is done via the search Retrieve operation, in which the client sends a search Retreive Request and the server responds with a search Retrieve Response. The request has several parameters, most of which are optional. The response is primarily a list of XML records which matched the search, along with the full count of how many records were matched.

XML (EXTENSIBLE MARKUP LANGUAGE)

XML stands for EXtensible Markup Language. XML is a markup language much like HTML and was designed to carry data, not to display data. XML tags are not predefined. You must define your own tags. XML is designed to be self-descriptive and it is is recommended by the World Wide Web Consortium. It is a fee-free open standard. XML is not a replacement for HTML. HTML is about displaying information, while XML is about carrying information. In simple words, XML is a software and hardware independent tool for carrying information. It is used both to encode documents and serialise data.

It supports Unicode, allowing almost any information in any written human language to be communicated. XML is now as important for the Web as HTML was to the foundation of the Web.

XML is everywhere. It is the most common tool for data transmissions between all sorts of applications, and becomes more and more popular in the area of storing and describing information. XML simplifies data sharing as in the real world; computer systems and databases contain data in incompatible formats. XML data is stored in plain text format. This provides a software- and hardware-independent way of storing data. This makes it much easier to create data that different applications can share.

THE HYBRID DIGITAL LIBRARY

I shall propose some reflections upon the open access topic which is at the heart of our meeting, focussing upon its implications in the domain of cultural heritage. I will insist especially on the transition of museums in the web. When compared to the scientific production published in books and journals, the transition of museums into the cyberspace poses different challenges both in the production and organization of digital information and in the modalities of granting it access.

I shall first focus upon the way in which the virtual museums should be conceived in the web. In the second part of my presentation I shall then introduce my view of the compromise we will have to accept when dealing with museums in the perspective of an open access policy to cultural heritage. I am obviously aware that it is extremely daring to formulate a long-term vision of the transition of cultural heritage in the web, and that I risk being engaged in an exercise of purely wishful thinking.

Visibility on the web is today one of the major concerns for museums the world over. Many efforts are devoted to web presentations of Museums and their collections and of cultural heritage at large. The transition of museums in the cyberspace is still largely conceived as a linear development of traditional procedures. This means that the style and traditional conception of documentation and information tends to exhibit a strong inertia in the new medium.

As a consequence of this inertia, the museum world seems still to be a long way from having fully exploited the potential of the web revolution. In this new dimension it becomes ever more difficult to accept the constraints which characterize the traditional activity of documentation and information. Let me schematically remind you of two of the basic constraints which are at work in the documentation strategies of the museums of the real world:

- Catalogues are conceived as rigorously confined to the objects preserved by individual museums.
- Objects are treated as isolated items; only limited attention is devoted to the cultural and social context to which they pertain, and to enhance their conceptual genesis and meanings.

It may be worth recalling that Museums, libraries and archives of the real world are the result of a process which began many centuries ago. Museums started out in 16th century Europe as promiscuous bodies where art objects, instruments, artifacts of various nature, natural items, books and documents were intrinsically integrated and displayed alongside one another.

The conceptual glue of what we would today rate as a promiscuous ensemble was the exceptional character and the uniqueness of all the collected entities and the curiosity that they aroused in the visitor. Later evolution of museums might be portrayed as a story of ever stronger specialization. First, the separation of art collections from scientific collections (during the Enlightenment).

Then art collections underwent a further process of specialization with the separation of paintings (this marks the origins of the Pinacotheca) from sculpture (sculpture galleries), from drawings (print and drawing rooms) and from minor arts (decorative arts departments). The same process took place with regard to scientific collections. After their separation from art collections, specialization progressed through the division of mathematical and physical objects from natural history items; moreover, in the mid- 19th century, technological and industrial collections gave rise, under the impulse of the Universal Exhibitions, to new independent museums. Later on, new institutions devoted to the preservation and presentation of bio-medical and ethnoanthropological collections were founded.

This evolution has produced a fragmentation of cultural documentation and cultural heritage according not only to disciplines, but also to the various categories of objects (books, documents, drawings, paintings etc.) and to their different material supports (canvas, marble or stone, paper, fabrics, timber, metal etc.). This specialization and fragmentation process has placed all museums in a difficult position, when it comes to making explicit to visitors the value of the collection they preserve. The same holds true for libraries and archives.

These limitations derive from the fact that objects are presented in museums atomized and de-contextualized. This makes it almost impossible for visitors to grasp their real meaning and to perceive their importance. When dedicating our energies to the digital conversion of cultural heritage, we have first of all to avoid the mistake of reproducing the fragmentation of objects and records in the different containers of all real world, and their isolation in specialized and totally unrelated structures (as museums, archives and libraries are today).

The new format of the humanities in the digital Age will have then to coincide with the re-composition of what the material history of cultural patrimony has fragmented. Once the information has been processed and transformed into a digital entity, it has no more to follow the fate of its physical support.

There is thus no reason to store it according to the same systems used to preserve the object it emulates. The logical consequence of what I have been saying is that we can finally re-arrange the records which digitally mirror the real objects in a totally new orderly architecture. We will thus build new hybrid repositories.

Hybrid not in the sense that this adjective has in the librarian jargon (where hybrid library means a combination of digital and analogical contents), but hybrid because the web repository is heterogeneously populated by a variety of different digital objects, which represent material objects, preserved in different containers. In recent years, growing use has been made of information technology especially through the development of so-called virtual museums model. The idea of the virtual museum which seems to be asserting itself, is, in fact, the idea of the digital clone of the real museum, accepting all of its structural features. To have meaning and utility, the "virtual" museum of the web should rather be constructed with a radically different configuration from the 'real' museum. In cyberspace the real museum should constitute only the point of departure and return of journeys that are confined neither to the internal perimeter of the museum, nor to the same typology of items or the same discipline or genre to which it relates. The visitor should be permitted explorations not only of objects, but also of ideas and persons, of places and events, of books and documents, whenever this information is preserved.

The transition of cultural heritage in the cyberspace has thus to be conceived as the creation of a totally new architecture of knowledge: a meta-museum/library/archive, with no walls nor physical separations.

A totally different construct from the way in which cultural heritage is arranged in the real world. In order to make this vision of the future of virtual museum to come true, the keywords and guidelines to keep in mind will thus be *hybridisation, re-composition*, and *systematic enhancement of the network of meaningful connections* among the items of the cultural heritage.

On the sociological ground, one of the corollaries of this new vision of the future web of cultural heritage is that the traditional division of labour will have to be rebalanced. There is no question that in the cultural institutions of the real world (in museums, above all) curatorial concerns have played a crucial role in shaping the physical organization of the heritage.

The understandable priority of the curatorial vision has also deeply affected the development of traditional documentation and communication strategies, with their strong selective emphasis upon the patrimony preserved in individual institutions. In the cyberspace the documentation and communication strategies can be finally conceived independently of the curatorial priorities and vision. The autonomy of documentation activity from curatorial concerns will permit to stress the connections and conceptual relations among items of cultural heritage which in the real world are preserved in different places and containers.

In the long run, this new perspective will produce an unheard of integration of knowledge, thanks to the enhancement of the enormous multiplicity of threads which connect the various digital items stored in the immense repository of the web. All this obviously implies the establishment of new forms of programmatic cooperation among content providers. It will obviously be necessary to offer the possibility of vertical exploration of collections preserved in individual institutions.

But the crucial step is represented by the possibility of an effective horizontal navigation in the endless virtual shelves of the web repository. We have vertical exploration often at hand in the actual web. Much more challenging appears the solution of the problem of an effective horizontal navigation among the digital surrogates of cultural heritage items in the web space. In order to achieve this goal, a strong change of paradigm in the standard procedures of web content production has to be put into practice.

Only the adoption of common standards of classifications on the part of content providers – which is still a rare phenomenon – will permit the user to navigate among data stored in different archives. Today interoperability among different digital archives is guaranteed on a large scale only by search engines; that is by a third party (the other two being content-providers and users), which has no role in the content production. Search engines work from the outside, ignoring the conceptual structure of data that they filter.

As everybody well knows, search engines use above all statistic methods and string search. Because of their extrinsic filtering procedures, search engines cannot guarantee content-driven search. I fully agree with Jürgen Renn presentation in our conference and with the ECHO Network Agorà vision that the schizophrenia between content and link providers is one of the major limits of the actual web. It represents a serious obstacle to the exploitation of the web as a universal and hybrid repository of cultural heritage.

We need then first of all to integrate and tune these two crucial functions. Moreover, in order to be really satisfactory, especially in the cultural heritage, links among the documents which are disseminated in the web should adhere to the representation of knowledge embedded in them. Search engines filter the web using words and strings, that is textual elements.

But textual search is very inadequate in order to filter conceptually coherent content in a federal digital repository, like the web. First of all, it is ambiguous, suffering the misleading effects of word polisemia (both in queries and in answers); moreover, it is almost impossible to effectively manage the multi-linguistical character of the web; finally, it is not appropriate to represent and filter extra-textual documentation (sounds, images, audiovisual materials etc.), which constitute an ever growing dimension in the web.

Even if some of these limits can be overcome by the adoption of community multilingual controlled dictionaries, textual classification and search in the web repository remains inadequate if we look for content-sensitive linking. In fact content-sensitive linking constitutes a fundamental challenge for the development of a web of cultural heritage intended as a universal and hybrid repository. In order to achieve this goal we will have to shift emphasis in document description and hyper-linking from words and textual elements to meanings.

It is at this very point that the semantic web comes appropriately into play. In the scenario which I have sketched of the future web as a universal hybrid metarepository of cultural heritage, the shift from textual elements to associations based upon meanings has to be considered as a crucial step.

The re-composition and recontextualization of the fragmented items of cultural heritage in the cyberspace implies in fact the systematic production of content-sensitive hyperlinks. The latter will be fully effective only if they are based upon semantic relationships.

Ontological system of classifications, shared by the specific web community involved in cultural heritage exploitation - a community formed by subjects who are, at the same time, users and providers, clients and servers - will guarantee both the rational construction of a universal hybrid repository and the possibility of effective navigation in it.

Ontologies will serve both as content-sensitive search engines and as effective representations of the structures of knowledge embedded in the web repositories, thus paving the way for their use as tools for e-learning activity and giving the users the possibility of designing personal itineraries.

Users will also have the chance of improving the efficacy of ontologies, by producing standardized descriptive metadata which will become shared knowledge for the community. They will not simply access data provided by others, but will be able to create added value to be exploited by the community. Content-sensitive hyper-linking is a need strongly felt by members of the international community who work in the humanities and in cultural heritage.

This crucial need inspires the vision of the ECHO Network project, with its strong emphasis upon a shared service infrastructure to help intelligent and interoperable implementation of the web of Cultural Heritage. I come now to my second point. Once we have been able to effectively promote in the web the heritage preserved in the museums, will it be possible to grant open access to it? It is obvious that the vision of the web of the virtual museums which I have schematically outlined presupposes a largely open access to the web of cultural heritage.

The fantastic cumulation of knowledge in the shared environment of the web produced by different actors would be much less productive and profitable within the framework of commercial copyright or in the so-called "deep web" model. This is certainly true, but we cannot utopically remove the economical dimension of the complex process with which we are dealing.

We are in a phase in which everywhere – and very strongly also in Europe – national policies (and also European Union policy) are insisting upon the need to reduce public investments in the preservation and promotion of cultural heritage and upon the necessity of involving private entrepreneurs in the management of museums in order to obtain the best commercial exploitation of cultural patrimony.

In this conjuncture a radical emphasis upon open access policy might turn out lacking a firm grounding and appear without concrete prospects. We cannot simply ignore these political trends and the reason and expectations behind them. So, in my view, we have to work in order to find a way of integrating our open access vision with a strategy of cultural, educational and touristic services provided on payment by museums through the web.

One of the possible strategic directions might thus be that of granting free per view access to the information published by museums in the web, providing payment services for advanced interaction with the published content (like unloading images, publishing unloaded material for commercial purpose, e-learning activity and so on).

I have no detailed proposal to advance here, but I want to stress once more that the view of a fully open access policy to cultural heritage in the web will have very little chance of imposing itself, unless we find a balanced solution between the moral duty of granting universal access to cultural heritage and the need of at least partially recovering the costs of producing, maintaining, updating and integrating the digital representation of cultural heritage in the web.

This is, to my mind, a crucial point. I fear that we will not cover any distance by simply contrasting the present commercially driven national and communitarian policies for the promotion of digital cultural heritage through information technology with our noble vision of open access. We have to operate in order to find an acceptable compromise and a sustainable economic model between these diverging opposite conceptions.

Otherwise, we might well obtain good results in our battle for open access to research papers and journals in the web, but we will receive little satisfaction in the crucial area of museums - especially of the great art museums – where commercial interests, due to the enormously superior number of potential customers, are much stronger. In this area we will have to guarantee the user new services, opportunities and creative access strategies without a commercial approach, even if this will involve some fair form of payment.

I would like to go back, in my concluding remarks, to the vision of the virtual museum of the future which I have sketched in the first part of my presentation. The real world museums, archives and libraries tell us incomplete, fragmented and often incomprehensible stories. The items that they preserve are organized according to extrinsic criteria (format, physical supports, typological categories, state of preservation, and so on) which do not help to catch their conceptual value and relationships.

In the future web of cultural heritage museums will have to be, at the same time, individual entities (that is faithful representations of the real museums) and global and hybrid repositories.

Global, in the sense that the items they preserve will be linked to all conceptually connected items. *Hybrid*, because those connections will not be limited to items of the same typology but will include all kinds of documentation.

If the cultural heritage in the web does not look something like this, let us say, ten years from now, and if we will not have been able to guarantee a fair level of open access to this shared repository, we will have to candidly acknowledge that the revolutionary potential of the transition of cultural heritage in the cyberspace has not been fully exploited.

I am personally convinced that the vision of the future of museums in the web which I have proposed will prove to be more than wishful thinking. This vision will represent a real cultural revolution, on condition that we are able to avoid the risk both of ignoring the concrete economical constraints and of passively accepting the transferral of the pay per view model to the web of cultural heritage and research.

DIGITIZATION PERSPECTIVE OF MEDIEVAL MANUSCRIPTS

Medieval Manuscripts are rich sources of tradition, history and culture. These ought to be preserved, organized and disse-minated to make them available to the world at large. The western countries have taken a lead in starting digital initiatives to preserve the manuscripts but such initiatives in India are either poorly organized or in primitive stage of development.These rich treasures of our country are distributed in private and public institutions in variety of media (parchment, vellum, palm leaves, paper etc.), languages, scripts, collection sizes and in different conditions. Hence there is a scope to address the problem and focus it from different dimensions to suggest solutions. The information technology has come with a promise to develop digital initiatives for manuscripts for preservation, dissemination and delivery.

It is further desirable to initiate digital libraries for medieval manuscripts (DLMM) to achieve following goals:

- A cost effective bibliographic control of manuscripts.
- An unhindered access to contents over computer and communication network without any barrier (political, geographical, social etc).
- The effective retrieval is possible in digital format because surveying and cataloguing them manually has not been carried out in a scientific, systematic and uniform way and that has resulted in their poor recall and precision etc.
- The medium, generally paper, used in these manuscripts is old and not of superior quality. Most of the manuscripts are moth eaten, torn out, water stained etc. Thus digitization is a viable alternative to enhance the longevity of its life and preserve them from different hazards.
- The digital format can serve as an electronic archival copy accessible in the network from where users can make multiple copies at different points.
- Modern times witness new weapons of warfare and destruction coupled with escalating terrorism having inbuilt tendency to devastate treasures of culture and scholarship. Therefore, it is significant to address the problem and use image technology advances to preserve the manuscripts from such hazards.
- Manuscripts are not fully exploited by the scholars and researchers and to make them available in digital form around the globe via internet and fully searchable through search engines will make their diffusion much wider and give more visibility to cultural heritage of ancient and medieval scholarship.

- The revival of culture, moral values and traditions eroded by technological and industrial developments is desired these days. Hence, MMDL may help to rediscover it by making manuscripts (containing rich culture and traditions) more transparent, accessible to one and all. The attention of world towards rich past will help to have better understanding of each others values and traditions and will generate a fresh quest for knowledge among scholars who are already well set for making increasing use of computers and communication networks.

DIGITIZATION PROCESS

The main focus of digitization is preservation and access of manuscripts. The digitization confronts many problems and requires utmost caution and research and exploration.

The project chain normally consists of:

- Instigate the project
- To assess and select the material
- Prepare for digitization
- To digitize
- Edit
- Delivery
- Support

Most archival programme begin as an idea which may stem from a new funding opportunity or it may be a part of institutions overall strategy in managing its rare collections. Thus the initiative can be either reactive digitization in response to external request or proactive digitization when authorities target an archive of manuscripts. In reality, many institutions in India operate in reactive manner when catching a new call or opportunity for sponsorship. This immediately follows to perform an initial assessment of the manuscripts under consideration and select material from it which could be digitized.

The medieval manuscripts are normally copyright free but need adequate information about the manuscript for its retrieval which involves expertise of orientalis, scholars, codocoligists, linguists etc at one or the other stage of the project. However, 'cherry-picking' is acceptable proposition (*i.e.* focusing a sized item within chosen archive when funds are limited and extended when funds are available) by using a matrix covering all varying categories by which an item can be assessed. This matrix needs to devise to meet diverse situation when many such examples can be located.

Digitization is the core of an archival project which need source item, capture device, computer with required storage to house the digital image and necessary software interface. The picture is clear when one focuses on three components *i.e.* anatomy of image, image formats and digitization hard-ware and software. The anatomy of dots, pixels, resolution, bit depth, shade etc effect the quality of image. For example one major problem arise when resolution concerning the size of the image scanned compared with the original dimension of the manuscript but the resolution at which one chooses to scan is not always the "effective" resolution. This creates more problems especially in surrogate like microfilm but technology seems to remedy such problem in future.Bit depth and dpi are probably important factors which influence quality and dynamic range (Dmax-Dmin) all depending upon the hardware used. However it will be everyone's interest to opt for high quality though affected by many constraints and pressures. The most frequently cited reason for not choosing maximum resolution is resulting file size.

Simple formula for calculating the file size is:

- Resulting file size= dpi x dpi x bit depth x dimension/8

Let us assume one page of 10 inch square item scanned at 24-bit colour at a resolution of 600 dpi Applying formula it comes to:

- 600 x 600 x 24 (10 x10)/8
- = 864,000, 00/8
- =108, 00,000 bytes
- 108,000 Kb or 108 Mb

It clearly shows the file size extremely large—equivalent to 75 floppy disks and nine such images would fill 1 GB hard drive. There could be other reasons as well for sacrificing higher quality for better speed. However, one solution to the balancing of quality versus size is to employ some form of compression using encoding/decoding algorithm to make it much smaller. Ideally this would mean no loss of information but many file formats provide 'lossy' compressions although not necessarily obvious to human eye, do involve degradation in quality. Therefore TIFF is generally used for master images of bi-tonal documents for being 'lossless'.

Interpolation is also used in connection with compression but it is best to avoid it in capturing or resizing to maintain quality true to its original. Good number of file formats (.TIFF;.JPG;.GIF;.PCD;.PNG;.PIC;. BMP;.PDF;.DJVU; AND PYRAMID File) have their relative qualities and limitations but still TIFF is widely used as cross–platform and archiving format for high quality images to be saved without any loss in original capture but alone not tied to any particular scanner or displayed and conversion from TIFF to other formats is relatively straight forward.

However JPG and GIF prove ideal for displaying via web in all browsers. The others may have advantage for compression, printing etc but remains to be seen how far these may go. The digitization process has complexity in deciding about many problems of utmost importance which influences are curatorial concerns on how source material is to be digitized.

For example, handling of a rare and delicate item like manuscript or painting may be restricted regardless of digitization, one could not be able to run ones' fingers across an original copy and therefore certain types of scanning will be prohibited and this contact digitization (using flatbed scanner with bright light from CCD) is often prohibited for handling fragile manuscripts, as against non–contact digitization (like camera) at a distance with employing facilities (ultraviolet or infrared) illumination for controlling light to reduce heat.

So a survey of digitizing hardware (flatbed scanner; sheet feeders; drum scanners, slide scanners; microfilm scanners; different variety of digital cameras; oversized document scanners and scan backs) need to be undertaken so to arrive at right type of software for different types of manuscripts. Outsourcing to the reputed and well established firms can be another alternative for bigger archives, of course, with extreme care and vigilance.

The digital software (covering capturing, processing and delivery of images) is required though much hardware comes bundled with a range of imaging software but as referred to earlier, many decisions are to be undertaken regarding file formats etc. Processing may involve many things like cropping, fine tuning, colour schemes, applying filters etc and creating of derivatives. After understanding hardware and software requirements, the archival body responsible for digitization should be able to perform digitization assessment as under:

- Suggest digitization procedure to meet objectives of the archive/library and satisfy needs and recommen-dations of curators/conservation experts
- Establish digitization from original material/or surrogate
- Place of digitization: In-house or out sourcing
- Establish cost of conversion (*i.e.* unit cost for digitizing each unit)

The next step is in the practical issue of actual digitization and steps involved therein before capturing image are:

- Material is to be checked and prepared
- Sample shots taken to allow for accurate bench-marking (process at the beginning of digitization project to set levels in the capturing process to ensure that the most significant is captured. It is a dual process involving not only the study of the source document itself but also sample shots and the bench marker should have full knowledge of present/future needs of the user)
- Cameras calibrated accordingly when digitalization is under way.
- Quality Assurance (Different from Benchmarking being post process check to verify decisions made earlier were right ones) checks to be undertaken to assure digital files match all applications.

ORGANISATION

Without a brows-able or searchable catalogue, end users will struggle through to find manuscripts in the collection they may seek. This descriptive information attached to digital archiving may be commonly referred to as metadata. This needs to be a thorough understanding and debate as one third of overall cost of a project of digitization is involved in it. Text based cataloguing provides most straightforward approach to recording of information about digital manuscripts and the director/manager has to decide the structure of its catalogues and its resultant format–an appropriate metadata system which should meet the current and future requirements of the library and its users.

Metadata as term crept into standard Vocabulary of IT related projects has invited much discussion, confusion and problems that a single accepted standard have not evolved and yet user requirements are eluded out of sight. However a successful metadata system should satisfy needs of cataloguers, users, technical experts and administrators. Thus it should be flexible, extensible and forward looking which allow easy searching and browsing by the user at different points of access to collection preferably as a part of online catalogue. Many large digital projects looked elsewhere leaving MARC or Dublin Core and RDF systems out strapped to cope up with the complexities. The solution that has been adopted is that of SGML/XML. However RDF is also used in combina-tion and has proven more logical and practical policy. The findings of the CEDARS (The CURL Exemplars for Digital archives) are extremely influential on future digital initiatives. Like many other projects, CEDFARS has recognized the need for a comprehensive metadata system and currently looking at open archival system.

JIDI (JISC image Digitization initiative) project has set out a lengthy set of definitions for metadata categories and has segmented cataloguing into five levels via Collection, Work, Visual document, Person and Organization. But RLGs working group on preservation issues on metadata has taken 16 categories under which digital image should be recorded. The CEDARS/JIDI/RLG is extensive, complex and overlapping and XML approach seems to offer best possible solution for the present.

Assuming that one accepts XML as the metadata system of choice, the next step is to decide the Flavour of XML i. e. which DTD is used. One may write ones own DTD, though most digital imaging project select an off the shelf DTD and at present two DTD that are greatly used are TEI and EAD. The Text Encoding Initiativer (TEI) was established in 1987 and reviewed in 1998 as TEI-lite. Besides its complexity, people have looked to other DTDs for their projects on account of the literary and linguistic background of TEI. The notable example being of EAD (Encoded Archival Description) seems to be attractive to both curator and librarians as it emanated from background of archival description.

Most digital archival projects chose TEI flavour (DTD) of XML; EAD occasionally or a combination of both. Some are started to embed Dublin Core metadata or others with XML and write their own DTD. The other aspect is describing content, file naming and creation of metadata. The knowledge about a manuscript, its relation with traditional knowledge, history and scholarship, lack of standard terms in vocabulary tools are problems which crop up very significantly and may affect the retrieval system especially at delivery stage.

The uniformity, consistency and expertise of the cataloguers under the supervision of orientalists well versed in different languages will be of utmost importance. However, secondary tools (descriptive catalogues/Directories etc) will be of immense help at this stage especially in varied cultural and linguistic diversity of Asian subcontinent. One may have to follow different extremes—simply dealing with broad description of the manuscript and other to decipher the depth matter about the nature, significance and importance of the document.

The file naming of manuscripts is very useful especially if Meta get lost and thus should be meaningful and/or mnemonic conveying information about file and its relation to other files besides persistent and consistent. The first one need to convey is some form of meaning to a file name. The most obvious example would be using a file naming system that reflects the shelf mark/accession numbers of the volume under digitization *e.g.* The filename "ms25fir.jpg" would suggest that it is an image of folio one, recto from manuscript number 25.

Similarly.jpg suffix may indicate that this is derivative of master image (.TIF). Some users are frequently frustrated by the fluid state of WebPages and their sudden disappearance, rendering URL obsolete. It is therefore important that the identifiers one uses for digital file are persistent-hence the notion of persistent URLs (PURLS).

DELIVERY AND DISSEMINATION SYSTEMS

Flat–file Browsing (series of Linked files) can be a quick and easy solution to many programmes but it is also extremely unsophisticated from both cataloguers and users perspective. Complicated searches are not available besides updating the site is always cumbersome. The structured approach is seen as desirable and database programme can be used to store the metadata and link it to image files. The simplest way is to use a standard desktop database system such as Microsoft access link aging images and can interface relatively easily with the web (using Microsoft ASP).

The second option is to choose a system designed specifically for image database—an option that has been chosen for many projects. These have limitations due to high cost, lack of interoperability and focused on museums and galleries. A third option is SGML/XML route to treat the catalogue as a text base. It will allow one to catalogue all the material in XML, place XML file or files on a server and allow user search the texts. The user would probably do this in web form. Then, through CGI scripts the system could convert the users input (i. e search or browse) to syntax usable by XML search engine on the server. This search engine in turn would analyse the catalogue files and return the hits; with further set of scripts converting material back to HTML for web display (although with XML this intermediate conversion process will eventually will not be necessary). Experience shows that the solution works well and is customizable to such an extent as to satisfy the most demands of users.

This, however, needs knowledgeable and experienced staff. The first digital image the user sees is the thumbnails image-*i.e.* a small derivative of around 100 pixels high created from a larger image. The thumbnail is usually small enough (PFG file of up to 40:1 compression) to allow to download quickly and convey at the same time meaningful graphical information about full image. From Thumbnail, the user could be allowed to download an image of sufficient resolution (say 72 dpi–a screen resolution) to fit a low end monitor of 640x480 resolutions.

Some difficulty arises when one considers the next level of image for advanced analysis or study (e. g. 150-200 dpi). The files would be larger in terms of file size (and slower to network) and one may not be keen perhaps to allow such images to be freely available. Besides creating, delivery of the full text has invited decisions to choose between transcriptions or by OCR. Having done so, it is surrounded with some form of structural make–up using a recognized SGML/XML DTD, with level of encoding to be chosen by the project management.

Future copyright decisions, if any and image protection decisions are to be made at an institutional level. It will vary from collection to collection and importance and policy of the parent institution. However employing banners and water-marks may cut right across the image and always be visible and defeat the entire purpose of the programme of digitations. The dissemination programme can be offline using CD_ROM technology and need to save as a backup for future use and transfer to other media keeping the life span of the medium in consideration.

However to make the cultural and historical assets more visible on-line access will be the viable solution but proper organization and management is to be taken into account in keeping large size of the collection in view in each country of Asia. It is reported by National Commission of Manuscripts in India that there are 50 million manuscripts about India available in many media, languages and scripts. Thus such diversity in a particular country can't be managed by a single organization but needs to be organized according to the region, language, script and available expertise in the institution etc.

However coordinating bodies in particular country can coordinate and monitor in order to achieve possible unifor-mity, consistency and maintaining of accepted standards so that overlapping is avoided and interoperability is achieved in a cost effective manner. This will also solve the web-hosting problems to a greater extent and a Portal can be maintained by the coordinating agency so to serve a Gateway for important resources of Asia with links to global digital archives in the coming future.

DIGITIZATION INITIATIVES

Western Countries

Western countries have taken a lead in undertaking digital library projects for medieval manuscripts resulting in development of various lists, union catalogues of manuscripts in various libraries in the region or country. These have evolved into OPAC's of the manuscripts with many fields for their retrieval and displaying images of manuscripts with different resolutions.

The prominent among them is the prestigious programme of Laurentius digital library of the Lund university, MASTER (Manuscript Access Standards for electronic Records), "Medieval manuscripts of Bodleian Library", The Digital scriptorium, Oxford university manuscripts, Medieval Manuscripts Of Syracuse University Library, The Bibliotheque National De France, "Medical Manuscripts in NLM", "European Manuscript server Initiative" (EMSI), "Unesco Memory of World", "The Humanities Text Initiative (HTI)" and "Manuscript digitization Demonstration Project of LC". These projects have used photographic and digital methods to develop a full or partial archival copy of the manuscripts available on-line using different software with JPEG format for image processing in association with different metadata initiatives. These attempts could be very useful in evolving a common strategy for digitization of vast manuscripts resources.

Indian Initiative

Khuda Baksh Oriental Public Library

It is one of oriental libraries having rich collection of Persian, Arabic, Urdu and other language manuscripts. The descriptive catalogue is in 30 vols which appeared in 1923 and reprinted in seventies, besides other catalogues and publications compiled by different authorities. Now the institution has launched a web site and a link is given to the whole catalogue of the library in a tabular form. The table has hyperlinks to different volumes of the catalogue which can be browsed as JPEG files and browsed from as a file from top to bottom. The whole project has been undertaken by National Informatics Centre. It has not introduced any retrieval mechanism as the document is treated as collection of image files in JPEG format. The catalogue, ironically, can't be accessed under metadata or any useful descriptor.

Raza Library, Rampur, Uttar Pradesh

The library developed under the patronage of "nawabs" contains a collection of about 10,5000 vols. has appeared recently on the web with an interface for the manuscripts. It displays information of two manuscripts on a single screen, giving brief bibliographic information in Romanized form along with a folio of the manuscript scanned. However the collection is limited to few manuscripts only and further work is in progress. The retrieval engine for the data is missing as they have not structured the data nor made use of any digital library software.

Kashmir University Project

The Department of Library and Information Science, University of Kashmir, Srinagar, JandK has undertaken a project sponsored by the UGC for designing a database of medieval manuscripts available in Kashmir. The work is in progress and is made accessible on web after proper test and assessment.

ISSUES

- High band communication with computer networks which support efficient image document transfer
- Data storage
- Data compression and interpolation
- Scanning and conversion technologies
- Planning and execution (in house, outsourcing, financial implications, funding etc)
- Data image file format(.TIF..JPG.GIF..PCD.PNG,and others like.PIC..PDF.BM)
- Text encoding initiative (TEI)
- Single interchange standard for both First level (abbreviated)and full description of the manuscript
- Development of the software for simple descriptive records and provide means for fully detailed records
- Link manuscript images and full text transcript
- Adaptation of Unicode for different scripts and languages and research thereof for developing multilingual databases.

FEDERATED SEARCH PROVIDERS

Individual institutions have their in-house Federated option and other institutions uses global federated search options, following are the popular federated search providers:

- Google Scholar
- Scopus
- Liberty

GOOGLE SCHOLAR

Google Scholar is seen as the competition for both campus institutional repository systems (at least in terms of search and discovery) and academic library federated searching. Google Scholar provides a simple way to broadly search for scholarly literature. From one place, you can search across many disciplines and sources: peer-reviewed papers, theses, books, abstracts and articles, from academic publishers, professional societies, preprint repositories, universities and other scholarly organisations.

Google Scholar helps you identify the most relevant research across the world of scholarly research.

FEATURES OF GOOGLE SCHOLAR

- Search diverse sources from one convenient place
- Find papers, abstracts and citations
- Locate the complete paper through your library or on the web
- Learn about key papers in any area of research

Google Scholar gives various option to the user so that they can search according to their equirements, such as time period, author wise search, subject wise, publication, institution wise etc and after giving the key term by the user, it searches that key term to various databases, search engines, journals etc and display the result on interface with name of author along with its full bibliographical description and it also provide citation information.

SCOPUS

Scopus is the largest abstract and citation database of research literature and quality web sources. It's designed to find the information scientists need. Quick, easy and comprehensive, Scopus provides superior support of the literature research process.Scopus is updated daily and it offers 15,000 peer-reviewed journals from more than 4,000 international publishers, over 1000 Open access journals, 500 Conference proceedings, over 600 trade publications and over 125 Book series. It also covers 33 million records, out of which, 16 million records include references going back to 1996 and 17 million pre-1996 records go back as far as 1869.

LIBERTY: QUEST

Liberty is a total web based library automation software which allows federated searching. In Liberty federated searching refers as "Quest" it capitalises our investment in online databases by providing library users with a single search point from with in Liberty.

Benefits of Quest:

- *Single Search Point for Multiple Databases*: Include databases that your organisation subscribes to in your Liberty3 search. Quest simplifies searching and access for your users.
- *Easy to Use*: Quest offers basic or advanced searching options, interleaves search results, and represents search results graphically. Quest allows a number of refine and sort options including sort by relevancy.

- *De-duplicate Searches*: Easily remove duplicates from search results by title or URL.
- *Customisable*: Quest offers you the option to include the library catalogue in the federated search. You can also select the databases you wish to search in your federated search.
- *Local Soft link Support and Service*: Quest is supported locally and hosted on Soft link servers. There is no need for you to worry about installation or maintenance.
- *The biggest players* in the federated searching industry are MuseGlobal (Muse Search), Fretwell- Downing (Zportal), and Webfeat (Knowledge Prism). These product offerings allow a user, regardless of vendor, to access multiple databases through one search interface. Endeavor (ENCompass) and ExLibris (MetaLib) are also in the federated search engine.
- Scirus, Wikipiedia, Pub med central, these are public domain site which provide federated searching.
- Publishers offering numerous journals created a federated search mechanism so that users are able to search their all journals. A good example is Elsivers Science Direct. As Elsivers acquired other publishers, it was able to add their journals at the same platform.
- Database vendor develop the same mechanism such as Sliver Platter provide a single interface for more than 300 databases that they published SCOPUS, etc.
- Proquest, Ebsco, Gale Cengage and Elsevier etc are such databases who offer federated search. In Gale Cengage "federated search" refers as "Power Search".
- The NISO Metasearch Initiative seeks to develop industry standards for one-search access to multiple resources that will allow libraries to offer portal environments for library users offering the same easy searching found in Webbased services like Google.
- Many public and academic libraries also utilise Auto-Graphics' federated search solution AGent Search.

2

Management Information Systems in Library

INTRODUCTION

Three libraries claimed that they had management information systems in their institutions and libraries. One library had a partial system in both the institution and the library, and was trying to develop a comprehensive one in library. One had a partial system in the library, and was attempting to have a comprehensive one, even though there was no management information system in its institution. Of those who did not have management information systems in their libraries, three librarians offered the explanation that this was because there was no management information system in the institution. One commented that its attention was concentrated on selecting and introducing a reliable turnkey automated system. All librarians mentioned that user friendliness and inexpensiveness are priorities in establishing their management information systems.

Apart from the library which has decision support systems, current automated library systems are not fully used for formal management information systems, even though these could perhaps provide enhanced information for performance measurement and could contribute to the establishment of a more comprehensive evaluation of the achievement of the libraries' objectives. In terms of the ability of their automated system to support a management information system, all the libraries stated that existing systems were generally helpful in data processing. However, they produced output data which is crude and which has to be further manipulated before it can be interpreted.

Seven of the libraries' computer systems produce quite complete operational data such as statistics of cataloguing, circulation, etc., but no system provides statistical data on reference services. One university library struggled to collect even crude data since its turnkey system has limited capabilities. It produces only data on circulation and stocks, and lacks compatibility with any other automated system in the library or the institution. Therefore, in order to have data in usable form and when needed, all libraries must at present manipulate them. Two libraries, however, had microcomputers which had no downloading facilities: they first had to print out the data from larger computers and manipulate it manually before inputting it into a microcomputer to be used with other information. Others did have microcomputers with downloading facilities, and could use them to process the crude data into usable outputs. All the libraries thus employ workable methods of producing management information, but they lack immediacy, and are expensive to operate. The forms of output vary. Those libraries which had formal management information systems had facilities to examine them online, but mostly data is presented in hard copy. Libraries which had informal and/or partial management information systems tended to rely on on-demand reporting. Although most libraries stated that the outputs are easily read, analysing the outputs of the system depends mostly on the abilities of the users to interpret them.

Outputs provide information for junior, senior and chief librarians. Graphical presentations were available to make numerical data understandable in a very short time. Apart from the information provided for junior management, the outputs of management information systems are generally discussed in senior staff meetings on a weekly or monthly basis. With regard to decision making in the areas of library planning and evaluation, in particular budgeting and resources allocation, two chief librarians stated that management information systems had made a great impact in the sense that all decisions were made based on the information from their systems. This is due to the comprehensiveness of the information made available. Their systems can provide only crude data, but it can be interpreted easily so that it assists in answering very specific questions.

A MODERN DIGITAL LIBRARY SYSTEM

Invenio is an integrated digital library system originally developed at CERN to run the CERN Document Server, currently one of the largest institutional repositories worldwide. It was started over 15 years ago and has been matured through many release cycles. Invenio is a GPL2 Open Source project based on Apache/WSGI + Python + MySQL architecture. Its modular design enables it to serve a wide variety of usages, from a multimedia digital object repository, to a web journal, to a fully functional digital library.

The development strategy used to implement Invenio ensures it is flexible in any layer. Being based on open standards such as MARCXML and OAI-PMH 2.0 its interoperability with other digital libraries is guaranteed. Being originally designed to cope with the CERN requirements for digital object management, Invenio is suitable for middle-to-large scale digital repositories. Records can be of any nature. This presentation will introduce the different features of Invenio, their usage in the CERN context and how other institutions and projects are also driving some of its development.

USAGE

Besides being used to run the CERN Document Server, Invenio has also been chosen by several other big institutions or projects. Among them it is about to be used to serve the SPIRES High Energy Physics information through the recently launched INSPIRE service, that will become the repository of reference for high energy physics. It is used by the EPFL. ADS has expressed interest to move to an Invenio-based platform, while starting a collaboration at the data level between astrophysics and high energy physics worlds. For example in Spain Invenio is already used by the *Dipòsit Digital de Documents* (DDD) and by the "Repositorio Digital de la Universidad de Zaragoza". Recently the European Commission has chosen Invenio to become part of two important projects D4ScienceII, and OpenAIRE, with the latter having the goal to set up a portal where all the EC funded research project documents will be available.

FEATURES

Let us demonstrate the key Invenio features by following the lifetime of a record in the system, from ingestion to dissemination. As an integrated digital library, Invenio is built to allow the management of digital objects and the meta-data associated with them. Meta-data are stored in the MARCXML format, which has the flexibility to store any kind of information and which can be easily converted, thanks to XML style-sheets to any other meta-data format.

INGESTING RECORDS

Data and Meta-data can enter into Invenio powered repositories through different ways. They can be manually deposited by an author, through custom and fully configurable web interfaces, backed by an equally configurable work-flow architecture, that lets the submission administrator set up any kind of procedure triggered by a deposition. Meta-data and data can as well be harvested regularly from OAI-PMH compatible repositories. Data can also be input into the system from any non-standard format by writing ad-hoc conversion scripts either in XSLT or in the proprietary BibConvert's language. Users also have the possibility to upload records by sending e-mails that will be parsed automatically. The system can be configured to accept submission by robots thanks to the availability of a simple web API.

DIGITAL OBJECT MANIPULATION

Fully fledged tools to integrate and manipulate digital objects are available. In particular Invenio can manage multiple formats for the same document, multiple revisions, automatic conversions between formats, automatic stamping of PDF documents with watermarks, creating icons, automatic text extraction to allow for full-text searching, automatic meta-data extraction and many more. Data consistency is also ensured by MD5 checksum being continuously verified.

INDEXING AND RANKING

All the new records ingested into the system and their modifications are indexed by a very fast indexing engine that has been developed in-house. All the indexing stages are configurable; which metadata fields to index, how to extract tokens, which language is expected in order to apply stemming and removing stop words, and so on. A plug-in based ranking engine takes care of creating special indexes to be used at search time for sorting results based on word similarity, citations, download statistics, and to present citation networks.

CURATING RECORDS

Curators have powerful web-based tools to manipulate records, whilst maintaining change histories, auto-completion of fields based on fully configurable knowledge bases, multi-record modification, assisted duplicate record finding and an efficient AJAX-based record merging tool, and so on. Curators can also exploit flexible tools to perform meta-data compliance checks against configurable rules. Automatic tools are also available to extract citations and references from scientific papers and to extract keywords based on a given ontology, to enrich the available meta-data. Distributed curation activities can be instantiated through integration of Invenio with RT, one of the most famous open source ticketing systems.

DISPLAYING RECORDS

Bibliographic records can be displayed in any format, thanks to an easy and fully-configurable formatting layer, which allows creation of record-based rules to choose which representation of a record to use, while each representation can be fine tuned to fit any particular need. Thus any kind of content can be hosted and properly displayed, such as multimedia documents, books, address book contacts, and so on. Records can be organized in a flexible hierarchical structure using real and virtual collections. Each collection can in turn be customised to choose the look and feel and the kind of features enabled. The whole web appearance of Invenio can be fully customised thanks to an integrated templating system, thus facilitating integration of Invenio into an existing institutional portal. Since Invenio is being developed in an international environment it supports internationalization and comes translated already in 25 different languages.

SEARCHING AND BROWSING RECORDS

A powerful search engine resides at the core of Invenio. Supporting a Google-like syntax, it can be used to dig into the repositories in a very easy way, while allowing the more experienced users to take advantage of many advanced features such as regular expressions, range queries, selection of meta-data, and many more. Results can be clustered by collections and ranked with respect to word similarity, number of citations, downloads based rankings, and any other pluggable algorithm.

Any search query can automatically turned into an RSS feed to add to a personal news aggregator.

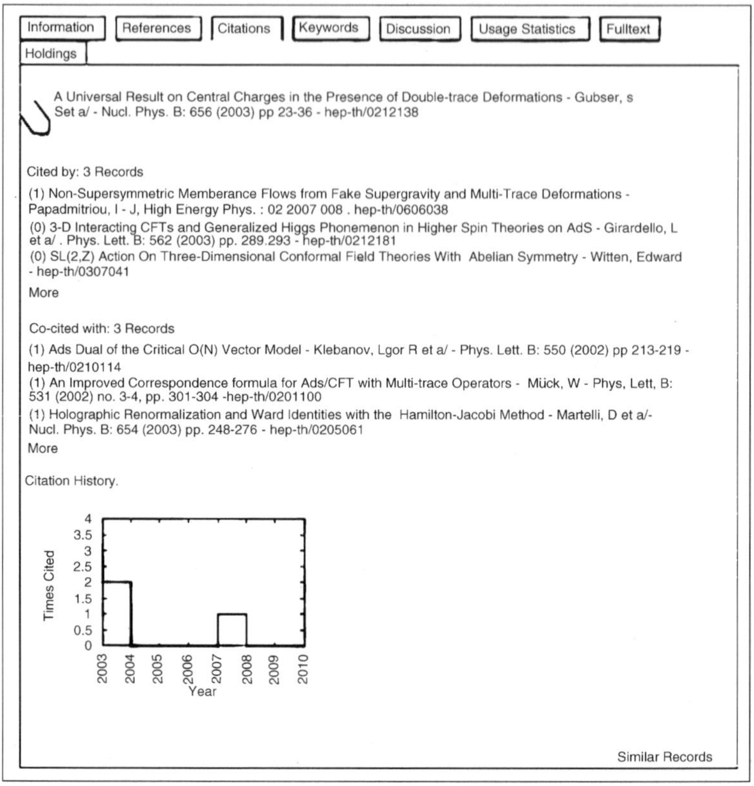

Thanks to integrated support for MODS and UnAPI standards, search results can be stored in Zotero, a powerful Firefox plug-in useful to organize a personal digital library. The system offers users powerful citation and author analyses.

COLLABORATIVE TOOLS

Invenio integrates several collaborative and typical web 2.0 tools such as baskets, to store and share records or external resources with other users, personal e-mail notification alerts, record commenting and reviewing, internal web-based messaging tools, approval/reviewing work-flows.

EXPORTING RECORDS

Data and meta-data can be exported in several ways, the most important being through OAI-PHM protocol and by means of a pluggable exporting module.

AUTHENTICATION AND AUTHORIZATION

While offering for free local accounts management, Invenio can be integrated with institutional user databases to delegate the authentication phase and to exploit externally available user details. Using the *role based access control*

(RBAC) model of Invenio one can define a list of roles, attach users to particular roles, and grant rights to perform actions such as view-restricted-collections based on user group membership, user IP address, and more.

CIRCULATION

Invenio supports the operation of a physical library by integrating a circulation module, as well as by supporting inter library loans. Users can submit loan requests, and follow the request status, the librarians have a web interface to accept/reject loan requests, to send overdue letters, to set up sub-libraries, etc.

CREATING JOURNALS

As an example of an application that has been built on top of the core Invenio, the web journal module lets repository administrators create online web journals with regular issues built from articles stored in the repository itself. A specific appearance can be set up in order to have a layout providing journal-like reading experience. This is currently used today for producing the official CERN Bulletin, which is issued every two weeks.

DEVELOPMENT OF MANAGEMENT INFORMATION SYSTEMS

There were several reasons why many of the libraries visited lacked management information systems.

The criteria of an ideal management information system are that:

- They must be inexpensive to operate.
- They must not interfere with existing services.
- They must provide reproducible results.

The fact that some libraries claimed to have only 'informal' or 'partial' management information systems or to have no management information systems does not mean that they had no collection of external and internal data. They do collect and use information for establishing library objectives and priorities or for resources allocation, but they have not formalised their management information systems, typically because their institutions had not required them to do so. Other factors which had inhibited development are mainly technical and concern the libraries' infrastructures. The limited capabilities of their computers had resulted in misinterpretation of the output data, and faulty analysis by senior library staff.

This was compounded by a lack of staff training in analysing data. The emphasis on purchasing microcomputers for library users was also a drain on scarce resources which might otherwise have been used to set up automated management information systems. Incompatibility of computer systems also caused problems; for example, in the workload involved in inputting common data such as the identity of students as compared with simply capturing it from a central database. Although they had enough potential to support formal management information systems, less use is made of existing automated library systems than might be possible given some development of their software. Even in the two libraries which had management information systems, there is one evident weakness; neither library has identified a comprehensive range of performance measures.

The contemporary approach casts academic librarians as managers within the higher education system. Planning and controlling development is clearly an important aspect of that role. Academic libraries' objectives have become clearer than in the past, but British academic libraries' attempts to achieve those objectives have been threatened by government financial policies which, in effect, require academic libraries to provide more and better services with less money.

Consequently, every aspect of academic libraries' operations has to be reviewed so that they can be managed more effectively and efficiently. It is not easy to achieve this because academic libraries are complex organisations. What academic librarians need, now much more than ever before, is the information which will allow them to plan properly, to know whether or not the library service is meeting the needs of the academic community and to be able to demonstrate that to the internal and external authorities responsible for funding.

Performance measures are also necessary in order to reveal libraries' strengths and weaknesses when compared with internal and external targets, norms and averages. From the survey, it is clear that most library managers are very concerned with the need for management information about their libraries. Libraries have generally established objectives and forward plans; there are still differences in how they allocate resources to fulfil those plans, and clear divergences of opinion on what information is required for library planning and resources allocation. Changing circumstances may call for any aspect of libraries' resources and services to be reviewed, or for them to be considered from a different perspective, often pro-actively or at fairly short notice, and the advantages of a comprehensive management information system should be self-evident.

Similarly, although at present there is much data collection, formal evaluation processes are not common. Performance measures which can compare internal and external information have not been widely utilised and have made little impact in decision making, perhaps because there is no agreement on what constitutes appropriate measures of achievement. Structured management information systems could help library managers in collecting and processing data into a useful form to assist in decision making. Most libraries appear to collect the same data, but only two of the eight selected libraries had established comprehensive management information systems for their librarians' purposes, in particular to support the planning process.

Although they had not fully automated data processing and reporting, and the information from their systems needs to be carefully interpreted, these librarians are making decisions based on outputs from their management information systems. The introduction of computers into academic libraries was largely a response to the problem of dealing with increased workloads with fewer staff, and they are now able easily to handle most of the routine and repetitive work of the library staff.

In addition, they have the capability to enhance the provision of management information, since automated data processing is able to present reports more accurately and much faster than manual systems. A limited range of data processing for management information is currently supported by the computer systems, including microcomputers, available in academic libraries, but there are still significant weaknesses in library automation systems in respect of the production of management information. For example, much remains to be done in monitoring high cost areas such as serials management and staff deployment in reader services.

Consequently, apart from the one library visited which has a decision support system, current library automation systems are not fully used for formal management information systems. It has to be said that most librarians still consider the continuous costs of automation as a worrying expense, and that the development of management information systems is not seen as a high priority compared with the introduction or upgrading of new automation systems for handling routine operations. Nonetheless, most librarians claim that they would now like to install decision support systems, even though they see the expense as a problem. The likelihood of increasing requirements for information to be provided at institutional level to meet government demands that institutions should be accountable may change priorities and foster developments.

While waiting for these developments, and for this new technology to be proved, attempts must be made to find out whether there will be support for the establishment of management information systems or decision support systems, and in particular, whether there will be support from the parent institutions and the library staff. The introduction of automated management information systems seems unlikely to pose a threat to staff in academic libraries, as most already have a 'flat' management structure, but a priority must be training programmes on the use of information in management. Support from parent institutions is also essential since the technology required for decision support systems could be expensive, particularly if they are seen as separate from the replacement of the libraries' existing automated systems.

It will, therefore, be important to convince the vendors who produce turnkey library automation systems to develop new systems which provide more of the management information that meets widely recognised needs in terms of both contents and format. There is a bewildering array of information available from a variety of external and internal sources, and, in addition to the costs of collection and collation, it generally needs tailoring to meet libraries' needs for comparable data. Cooperative groups such as SCONUL have a role to play here in developing guidelines on the information needed, and the format(s) in which it should be presented for comparative purposes. Present outputs from library automation systems are crude, but the work currently being undertaken to develop both performance measures which have wide applicability and credibility, and more effective management information modules as part of library automation systems should eventually resolve that problem.

WORKPLACE ENVIRONMENT IN THE DIGITAL ERA

What might we expect of the workplace environment in the new millennium academic library?

Libraries will take Over Campus Computer Centers

Academic libraries will pursue bolder organisational experimentation. This will include focusing on the information and services needs of users. There will be wider distribution of administrative responsibility and authority, as hierarchical structures are broken down and key activities and operations are integrated.

We can expect more fluid and flexible structures, enhancement of team and small group processes, and more collegial and collaborative working relationships. Continuing a trend that is already taking root, the academic library will assume administrative control of campus academic computing services. With the expanding mandate for accountability, there will be a greater focus on data collection and analysis. This will entail a rethinking of standards and benchmarks for assessment and more creative approaches to defining output measures and quality impact.

Academic Library Funding will Remain Stable

Responsibility-center budget models will expand across higher education, embracing the library. This relatively new system of distributed financial authority places libraries into a more rigourous fiscal relationship with academic programmes. Units will be taxed to support library operations, requiting intensified communication and accountability. Library funding will remain stable. The greatest growth will continue to be in collection and information access programmes.

The library budget as a percentage of total campus budget will not change substantially. Library development and fundraising activities will accelerate, as more colleges and universities pursue external funding from private, corporate, and foundation sources. This will involve a greater focus on endowments rather than on raisin funds for specified capital projects. Library budgets will increasingly fund research and development, infrastructure upgrade and replacement capabilities, and risk capital for innovation and advancement. The trend towards outsourcing of library operations and services will accelerate. We have already seen substantial success with serials jobbers, approval plans, binding, photocopy services, building maintenance, and security. This will lead to further experi-mentation in cataloging, collection maintenance, document delivery, and preservation.

Digital Acquisitions Budgets will Quadruple, and more, Eating up 40-50 Per cent of Acquisition Budgets

Print-based collections will remain dominant over the next decade. However, substantial resources will be allocated to the acquisition of electronic information, as reference sources and scholarly journals become computer-based and the economic feasibility of the scholarly monograph is increasingly questioned.

The percentage of investment in digital information will grow from the current 5-10 per cent of acquisitions budgets to 40-50 per cent. There will be an ongoing need for investment in local collection building, however, because what has not been acquired and preserved cannot be made available to users and other libraries. Even as collections continue to expand, the gap between what is being published and what we can afford to acquire will continue to grow. As a result, there will be a dramatic decline in ownership: new information accessible through libraries will plunge dramatically.

Nevertheless, the role of the academic library as a depository and gateway for government information will expand, as traditional print-based distribution models are eliminated.

The academic library will expand its role in scholarly publishing and communication. Project Muse at Johns Hopkins and High wire at Stanford, and the Journal Storage Project spawned by Mellon are examples of the library's central involvement in the management of current and retrospective electronic publications. More than 50 per cent of reference transactions will take place over campus networks

Patron-initiated and Controlled Services will Expand Rapidly

Libraries are already beginning to employ self-circulation, computer renewals and recalls, direct interlibrary loan, and document delivery. Full-text databases are becoming commonplace. The role of library staff as interpreters and mediators of user information transactions outside of local collections and services will decrease. Inside the university, the librarians' role as instructor will be formalised in a separate college department focusing on information and network literacy.

The technology of the World Wide Web that is evolving rapidly and unpredictable with the World Wide Web Consortium co-ordinates many activities in the areas of user interface, technology and society. The World Wide Web which was first announced by CERN in 1991, 2-3 years ago most people had not heard of it but by the end of 1996, there were 300,000 Web sites. Libraries are creating Web sites to help students to distinguish between relevant and irrelevant information. The Web is likely to have a profound impact on education, communication and research activities of the universities.

Examples:

- *The Web empowers individuals:* They can easily reach a worldwide audience. Anyone can publish material that would never have been published in the past, and it is instantly available to millions of people.
- *The Web offers us the best of both worlds. Anyone can publish:* Their views cannot easily be suppressed, for good or ill. And anyone can comment, validate and offer judgement or advice.

The E-mail for example is extremely valuable for communication between the library and its users. Users Borrowers are expected to return their books within about two weeks. Very many do without reminders, but for those who need reminding, for some reason e-mail is a more effective spur than other methods. Online catalogs will increasingly define accessibility and not just local ownership. Thus the links between the local collection, the bibliography of a discipline, and the text of the publications/sources will become blurred. Remote use of online catalogs and databases is increasing rapidly at most colleges and universities.

An example, at Carnegie Mellon, already 75 per cent of catalog use is remote. Remote access to information necessitates new instructional efforts. Levels of all traditional collection circulation activity - general and reserve borrowing and interlibrary loan - will decline significantly. They will fall prey to the rapid growth in options for electronic document delivery and the implementation of electronic reserve systems. The new electronic journals already offer facilities unavailable to users of paper.

These include:

- The ability to search for particular content within a paper or a complete journal;
- The ability to move easily between the table of contents of a journal and the abstract.
- Facilities to annotate articles to create a personal virtual filing cabinet and
- The ability to move quickly from the article you are reading to one which it cites in its references, and that includes forward citing, example the ability to go to articles that cited the one you have just been reading but which were published later.

An example, the American Astronomical Society has digitised into electronic form all the articles in the last 20 years of its journal which can now be accessed. Academic libraries will house and manage campus usability laboratories focusing on the needs of the user and will involve users as part of the design team.

Reference assistance to users will be electronic-based, with more than 50 per cent of transactions taking place over campus networks in batched or real-time communication, up from the current neglible levels. User profiles linked to SDI-type services will ensure delivery of relevant, cur-rent information to faculty and students on a scheduled basis. Academic librarians will increasingly pursue service goals as part of multiple consortia-based relationships. There will be joint investment in commercial services and acquisition of materials, in the purchase and use of technology, and in the hiring and development of staff.

Librarians will be Key Players in Developing Technological Innovations

Technology is currently poised to transform the fundamental nature of operations and services. From the early days of automation in the 1970s, academic libraries have moved to the cur-rent distribution and individualisation of technology and digital conversion and production. The challenge of the next decade will be the application of intelligence to the searching and retrieval capabilities of library systems.

The library will play a central role in the future development of the campus information environment. Rather than reacting to campus technology decisions, library staff will be integrally involved in determining what the next innovations will be. In the new world of the desktop workstation, academic libraries have a mandate to integrate high-speed access both to scholarly and institutional information. They need to provide tools for filtering, analysing, and manipulating information.

The predominant mainframe-based library management systems will be completely replaced by client-server technologies and applications that include robust full-text content and intelligent links to network-based sources. Automatic language translation software will be introduced, contributing to the development of a renewed global acquisitions programme for both based and digital sources. Campus network infrastructures will extend to all student, faculty, and staff work and living areas.

This will provide dependable connectivity for a growing array of applications, including distance learning. Wireless technology will be introduced and will receive its initial testing in library services. The retrospective digitising of library collections, particularly unique materials, will evolve as a central activity in academic libraries. Newly formed digital knowledge centers will manage the operations and partner with academic departments, publishers, and other libraries.

The Number of Librarians Working in Academic Libraries will Decrease

Libraries will increasingly view staff development as an integral and essential component of organisational success. With retooling of skills emerging as a three-to-five year cycle, participation in training courses will be mandated for all employee groups. As technology programmes advance and dominate library collection and service activities, technical staff as a percentage of total staff will increase significantly. This will produce a net reduction in the number of librarians employed in academic libraries.

It will also promote more effective working relationships between librarians and technologists, improving current conditions marred by distrust, inadequate communication, and lack of shared investment in planning. Academic libraries have not responded effectively to demographic cultural, racial, and ethnic shifts. They will collectively enter the next century still recognising the important trends producing a more pluralistic society but without well-developed and well-coordinated strategic directions for the role and contributions of the library. Telecommuting, which is increasingly commonplace in commercial settings, will become a viable and acceptable option for *academic* library employees.

An expanding array of library operations and services will be performed from home, enabling improved competitiveness for the recruitment and retention of talented staff. Academic libraries and library education programmes will collaborate on the development of internship and certification programmes for new professionals. This will be necessitated by the anticipated rapid increase in retirements in the next 15 years, as well as by the need to develop new approaches to the preparation and orientation of the next generation of academic librarians. An example of a university library, De Montfort University in the UK that has been developing a digital library environment for some years past.

The lessons they claim to have learnt might be summarised under the following headings:

- The digital library will develop more quickly than people think;
- The digital library is still a complex, unstable entity for which little theoretical structure exists.
- Because of this inherent instability, investment and implementation are still high risk.
- Digital libraries operate in a global environment: new products and services can become *de facto* standards very quickly.
- Co-operation is therefore a key factor for maintaining competitiveness.
- The content of the digital library will become the dominant factor.
- Copyright issues will be resolved or side-stepped because the market will demand it.
- The economics of the digital library are not yet well understood.
- Library jobs and roles will change very rapidly.

KNOWLEDGE AND INFORMATION IN LIBRARY SERVICES

The libraries have transformed drastically from store-houses for books and journals to the powerhouses of knowledge and information since the middle of the 20th century. The information and communication technology is responsible for this revolution. The very existences of libraries are dependable on users' satisfaction. Users are getting satisfied when the library is able to rise to his or her expectation or meet the actual needs. A quality service is said to be one, which satisfy the users' expectation resulting a good experience. Throughout the history, libraries were mainly concerned with collection development and processing.

The library profe-ssionals gave less concern to quality in product and services, never checked whether the users were satisfied or not. Gradually the social and economic changes have prompted the libraries to develop services. The staff has a vital role in the satisfaction of users. The library being a service organization, its prime objective is to provide the right documents, infor-mation and services to its users.

Only the users' satisfaction survey will facilitate the assessment of their satisfaction with products and services offered. There are various methods, tools and techniques to measure, control and improve the quality of library services. Quality measurement and evaluation assumes great importance in modern libraries, as it brings immense benefits to the library as well as user community. Different methods such as collection of data for measuring the performance and quality of libraries; The SERVQUAL method, a multiple item scale to measure service quality; The LibQUAL, a tool developed on SERVQUAL for measuring the quality of library products and services.

QUALITY CONCEPT IN LIBRARY SERVICES

The library is an organization to offer reference and information services to its users. Library service is the combination of the services-process and its delivery. In a library, the service offered from acquisition section, technical section, maintenance section etc. are the processes carried out there and thereafter delivered to the users. The quality should start from the acquisition section, which should be carried uniformly to circulation section. A user who had an unpleasant experience from the library will tell it to many people, but a good experience will be told to very few. Therefore it is very necessary for librarian to understand the users, what they want, how they want, and when they want the documents and information.

SEVERAL DEFINITIONS OF QUALITY

The word 'quality' has several definitions. The conven-tional definition is " One that wears well, is well constructed will last for long time" and the strategic definition is "meeting customers' requirements."

- According to Juuran 'The quality is fitness for purpose'.
- According to Robinson, "Quality is meeting the requirements of customer-now and in the future."
- According to Sarkar "Quality of a product or service is the ability of the product or service to meet the customers' requirements.

IMPACT OF RANGANATHAN'S FIVE LAWS IN QUALITY SERVICE

The five laws of Ranganathan help in quality improvement of service as those are concentrated to the users very seriously. The laws directly advocate towards libraries' collection development, speedy processing, maintenance and quick retrieval of information by users.

The First Law

"Books are for Use" is a direction for measuring the quality of a library; quality in terms of contents, accessibility and availability as and when needed.

The Second Law

"Every reader his/her books" implies needs of users. In order to meet this law the library has to index all micro and macro documents so that every reader can find out his or her requirements.

The Third Law

"Every Book/Information its reader" implies the importance of book/ information selection in a library. The law advocates scientific document selection, subject based organization, advanced and in depth indexing, efficient and effective searching and locating tools, Staff assistance, open access, extension services, publicity programmes etc.

The Fourth Law

"Save the time of Reader" indicates the importance of fast and efficient services to the users with the advanced technologies, method, techniques and tools. Open access, digital services, classified arrangement of documents in shelves, location and directing guides, excellent searching tools, and techniques *i.e.* Online public Access Catalogue (OPAC) in an automated library, Xerox facility, Online Information services, qualified and experienced staff will ensure fast service to the users.

The Fifth Law

"The Library is a growing organism" implies collection development, changing of all components of a library.

Everyday the world of documents and information is changing tremendously. Now the information is recorded not in papers alone, to many media, the latest being the electronic and digital form. So in today's world the library may called as information and knowledge house of world as a whole if it is supported by advanced information and communication technologies.

IMPROVE THE QUALITY IN LIBRARY SERVICES

In this information age it is very easy to make a quality based library if the parent body or concerned authority assist financially as well as collectively. It is very necessary for the librarian and its parent body to look forward for the present and future generation to cope up with international phenomena. A user must be educated with proper technology to use the library effectively.

He or she should have knowledge of what facilities and services are available in the library and information centre and how to access those efficiently and effectively. To improve the service quality the user satisfaction survey is a tool that provides both quantitative and qualitative data. It is an important part of libraries for process and performance measurement.

Main steps to measure users' satisfaction are:

- Conducting sample survey.
- Data collection.
- Process and analysis of data.
- Interpret and present the data.
- Finding out result.

With the help of the result the librarian can take new steps for development of library. The regular survey will enable the library to understand the changes in users satisfaction and to plan the services accordingly.

Steps for Staff to Meet the Users' Needs

- Being responsible for the total service quality to the users both the Technical staff and frontline staff in the library should serve the users.
- Services must be provided to the users in a most effective way.
- Providing maximum benefits to the users form collection and facilities.
- Stay close to users: Library can not understand users' needs, tastes, interests etc. without listening to them, and services without users' interest will be a mere wastage.
- Users must be treated well, informed well and acknowledged well about the services to the users.

The Users' Satisfaction is based on Many Factors Like

- A source of up-to-date information, knowledge, accessing facilities and assistance.
- The library should organize its facilities visible to the users; otherwise they may not have it and get dissatisfied.
- *Accessibility:* The library resources and services should be easily accessible. Books should be arranged in shelves in proper classified order, so that the users can locate books quickly. In case of electronic

library the electronic database like OPAC will help the users to find out the books in stacks.

- *Tangibles:* The tangibles of libraries, namely the building, furniture and other physical facilities, collection, staff, machines etc. should be sufficient and appropriate and useful for the users.
- *Courtesy/Friendliness:* The library staff should be very courteous and friendly with the users.
- *Physical Appearance/Atmosphere/Cleanliness/Comfort:* The appearance of library, its facilities, collection, staff and services should be attractive and pleasant. A Welcoming atmosphere should be must. Furniture, floor, racks, documents etc. should be neat and clean.
- *Process-Reliability/Communications:* The processing part of the library should be dependable and efficient that suffices the expectations of the users. The way of communication, assistance and guidance also greatly affect the satisfaction of the users.
- *Some Useful Criteria to Measure Users' Experience in a Library are:*
  - Speed of services delivery (Access time, location, processing, etc.);
  - Value added services such as Xerox service, CAS, SDI etc.; and
  - Technology used.

It is observed that if something goes wrong that can be very easily learned from the users, so the users' complaints can be taken as good measure of user satisfaction.

INFORMATION EXPLOSION AND THE DIRECT RELATION OF INFORMATION TO DEVELOPMENTS

The present information explosion and the direct relation of information to developments in all walks of life emphasizes the need to give greater priority to the planning of systems which give library and information services to the people. Such systems can only be planned at national levels, if the total information resources of the nation is to be pooled together in a federal country like India, and shared between the cons-tituent states to make it available to all the users who require it in an equally and unbiased way at optimal cost.

Such library and information systems are to be founded upon sound legislation, if they are to attain their objectives the Society's information need has become so imperative that, many of the national and international library organizations has started to stress the urgent need for national library systems working together and sharing their services and materials at international level to provide better services to the people. Better can be defined here in quantitative and qualitative terms. Such national level and international level networking and resource sharing between library systems make possible service at lower cost, convenience of access, access to more materials and more rapid availability of materials.

PREAMBLE OF STATE ACTS

The preamble of a Library Act should summarise and state the aims and objectives of that Library Act. Even though the preamble of KPLA went on to explain the existing situations and the intentions with which the Act was initiated in an elaborate and vague form, it has given what is to be in preamble just before the preamble in precise and clear words as a long title ofthe Act. This summary or long title of the Act which we have to consider as preamble contains the basic concept of modern public library service which the actual preamble failed to state and the KPLA in its totality failed to support.

Like the Model Act, this summary provides for the establishment and maintenance of a system of public libraries and for the comprehensive development and organisation of all kinds of library and information services required for the people. The long title that follows the title of the Act in KPLA states, it is: An Act to consolidate and unify the library laws in the State and to provide for the reorganisation of the entire library system in the State of Kerala with a view to the develop-ment and maintenance of a comprehensive rural and urban library service and for matters connected therewith or incidental thereto.

Ranganathan has laid clear emphasis on legislation for public library service and for the organisation of a comprehensive library system. But all other Acts except KPLA provides for establishment and maintenance of public libraries only. They all cling to the obsolete concept of treating public libraries as independent units in their collection and services. So in this statement of the purpose of the Act, KPLA has accepted the most modern concept of Public Library legislation and the statement is a distinct improvement over those in all other existing State Acts.

THE MODEL ACT OF S.R. RANGANATHAN

To attain these objectives Dr. S.R. Ranganathan had framed the first model public libraries Act in 1930 which he placed for discussion at the Educational Conference at Banaras. Before framing the Act, this internationally reputed library scientist had travelled through most countries of the world where library legislation existed and had evaluated them and in many countries his ideas helped them to improve the systems.

In his Library Development Plan which he submitted in 1947 to Government of India he had included a union library bill and a revised state library bill also which envisaged the national public library and information system according to the most modern principles. Another model library Act was drafted in 1963 by a committee under the chairmanship of D.M. Sen on behalf of the Ministry of Education, Government of India. In 1966 the Library Legislation Sub Committee of the Planning Commission also prepared a model bill. The library Acts that came into existence in Madras, Hyderabad, Andhra, Karnataka and Maharastra totally or partially accept the ideas of Rang ana than as reflected in his Model Acts and bills. These States became the laboratories where the ideas evolved by Ranganathan were experimented and observed.

In the light of these observations and suggestions contained in the other model bills and Acts, Ranganathan has improved his model Act by rectifying the clauses found to be defective in working and by adding new provisions that seemed essential. This model libraries Act was published in 1972. This is the latest and most advanced Model Act. Ten States out of the 25 States and 7 union territories have enacted library legislation. They are Madras 1948, Andhra 1960, Karnataka 1965, Maharastra 1967, West Bengal 1979, Manipur 1985, Kerala 1989 and Haryana 1989.

Others are Goa and Mizoram. But none of them are considered perfect or efficient. So in this comparative analysis of the essential aspects of State Public Library Acts, the Model Public Library Act, 1972 of Dr. S.R. Ranganathan is taken as the measuring rod or ideal situation with which the State Act is compared. Whenever some notable additional provisions or improvements are found in other existing Acts the same is discussed at the concerned contexts. The Kerala Act to which stress is given in this study and Ranganathan's Model Act of 1972 will be referred herein after as KPLA and Model Act respectively.

PURPOSE AND ADVISING OF STATE LIBRARY COMMITTEE

The Model Act provides for a *State Library Committee* (SLC) for the purpose of advising the SLA on all matters arising under the Act. All existing State Acts and Model Bills enacted or drafted in India provide for appointment of such a Committee or Council. KPLA names it as Kerala State Library Council. All Acts of the states except Kerala's have prescribed its membership on somewhat similar lines. All Acts provides that this body will be headed by Minister for Education. Despite differences in nomenclature and composition the function of this committee or council envisaged everywhere is basically the same *i.e.,* to advise the SLA or State Government in all matters arising out of the Act.

Kerala State Library Council (KSLC)

A careful analysis of the Kerala State Library Council (KSLC) in comparison with the SLC as provided in the Model Act or other State Acts will reveal that it is not a councilor committee of advisory nature as SLCs are. KSLC is an SLC and at the same time an SLA by itself. Naming it as a council is a difference in terminology only. Instead of appointing a Minister as SLA as in Mysore it appoints a body as SLA. But the Act fails to name it as SLA. The duties, powers and functions assigned to KSLC is inclusive of all those assigned to SLA and SLC in Model Act.

Sub-section 1 of the Section 3 of KPLA dealing with the constitution and composition of KSLC states9; KSLC shall be a body corporate having perpetual succession and a common seal with power, to acquire hold and dispose of property, both movable and immovable and to enter into contracts and shall by its name sue and be sued. This is an adaptation of the class related to Karnataka State Library Authority of Karnataka Act. No other Act including Model Act has so clearly defined the nature of this body and assigned so much powers as this like the Acts of Kerala and Karnataka. The powers and functions assigned to KSLC includes both the advisory functions of the committees and councils provided by Model Act and other Acts and the duties assigned to SLA by Model Act and Karnataka Act.

Sub-sections of section 8 of KPLA provides that the KSLC may:

- Advise the government of all matters connected with the administration of that Act and... the overall library policy of the State.
- Co-ordinate the working of the District Library Councils and Taluk Library Unions and...supervise and direct all matters relating to library service in the state.
- Establish one or more State Libraries . . . at such place or places in the State as may be considered necessary.
- Appoint and control such officers and servants as may be necessary for the efficient performance of its duties and functions under this Act and the rules made there under.
- Give to the District Library Councils and Taluk Library unions directions in the performance of their functions under this Act and . . . they shall not in-the discharge of their functions under this Act depart from directions given by the KSLC.

While we consider these classes and compare them with the parellel sections of the Model Act or other Acts it becomes clear that the classes which assigns the duties, powers and functions of KSLC is a distinct improvement from all others. KPLA has identified most of the functions and duties expected from such a body and very clearly assigned them to it without giving space for doubt and vagueness.

Composition of KSLC

If KSLC is to become able to fulfil such duties and functions expected from it, the composition of the body should be done accordingly. Membership of such a body should include persons who have contributed to the growth of knowledge, who has evolved or developed methods and techniques for collecting, organising and disseminating information and who have wide experience in related fields of activity. It is not the method of representation but the quality of representation that will make possible the efficient functioning of the system. The sections which prescribe the membership of SLA in Karnataka Act and SLC in Model Act and other State Acts prescribe their membership on somewhat similar lines. Prof. P.B. Mangla in his study of library legislation opines that it should be a body having representatives from various institutions, organisations, government etc. interested in and connected with the growth and development of library and information services in the State.

The Model Act, the opinion of experts and recommen-dations of committees set for studying library legislation agrees that such a body should include among its members; the Minister for Libraries if there is one, otherwise Minister for Education, then Minister in charge of Local-Self-Government, Director of Libraries, State Librarian, sufficient number of representatives from State Legislative Assembly by election from among themselves, Secretary to Government for Education, representatives elected from Local Library Authorities by rotation to limit size of the body, representatives of associations of library profession and experts with specialization in library and information services and represen-tatives of Universities of the State.

It would be essential that the Minister in charge of Libraries should act as *ex-officio* chairman and the Director of Public Libraries or State Librarian should act as ex-officio secretary of the committee.

The rationale behind such a composition of this body is that it is a body which is to advise the government and discuss continuously on a most important responsibility of the government, that is organisation and dissemination of information required by the society. But disregarding all these principles KPLA provides for constituting a body of members who were not suitable to undertake this work.

The section 3 sub-section (2) related to the composition of the KSLC in KPLA provides: The KSLC shall consist of one member each from Taluks, elected by the general body of the District Library councils, and five members of whom one shall be a librarian, another a person belonging to the scheduled caste or scheduled tribe and another a woman nominated by the government. Library and information service is an intellectual service. It goes without saying that this body as provided in KPLA will not be able to fulfil satisfactorily the purpose for which it is intended.

In these days of information explosion and flooding of vast and varied types of books and other printed materials that originates every minute without wide familiarity of all spheres of knowledge and expertise in handling their information in most effective way at minimum cost the body which heads such a system will be having a mere formal and useless existence. As we have seen in section 8 of KPLA the most important function of KSLC is to advise the government on all matters connected with the administration of this Act and overall library policy ofthe State. It is not clear how this committee will be competent to render such expert technical advise when it has only persons as members, who has come through election without expertise or knowledge about information work and without even any educational qualifications. Library and information service to the people if provided efficiently will be the continuously active service of government and will require expert advise everyday on many matters.

The KSLC's inability to provide such expert advise will make government's efforts futile and to overcome this, govern-ment will be forced to create a continuous chain of Advisory Committees which is also not very practicable. While no hard and fast rule can be laid down about the size of this body it is generally felt that it should not have more than twenty members. The KSLC may remain a supreme body in name only for real powers of the council have been passed over to a smaller body which is the executive committee. But it also becomes an unwieldy body with membership of 25 persons.

Thus KSLC has acquired all the defects existing in SLAs and SLCs into one body. This Executive Committee is a new addition in our library Acts. But the findings of Ashok Mehta Committee and various committees appointed by many State Governments to study Panchayat Raj Institutions advise us against such an elected body like KSLC for organising important service as library and information service to the people. Instead of adopting the constitution and composition of SLA and SLC provided by the Model Act or followed by the other State Acts KPLA gave legal sanction to the organi-zational set up of an association that was already existing there, that is Kerala Granthasala Sangham.

The constitution and composition of KSLC and its Executive Committee is the same followed by Sangham for its general body and Bharanasamithi. In all other provisions KPLA follows the same pattern of Sangham with some minor alterations. For more than half a century Sangham was pressurizing the Government to give legal sanction to Sangham to be the SLA and to accept its system as it is,as State's Library System.

But experts have continuously pointed out during this period the futility of such a system for library and information service. But Sangham objected government's all other attempts to enact a modern library system legislation and at last come out successful in legalizing its own system. But this in fact totally prevents the State from having an advanced library legislation and developing its library and information services in conformity with the requirements of the time.

CONCEPT OF THE STATE LIBRARY AUTHORITY

The concept of the *State Library Authority* (SLA) underwent an evolution from State Library Committee to Minister of Education or Libraries; everywhere in the world. The Model Act recommends that for the purpose of promoting and organising a library system in the State the Ministry for Education of the State shall be the SLA.

It shall be the duty of the SLA to provide; for an adequate library and information service in the State and, for the progressive development of the institutions devoted to the purpose and to secure the effective execution by *Local Library Authorities* (LLA) of the national policy for providing adequate library service to the people in every locality. In the existing' State Acts only Karnataka Public Library Act, 1965 provides and clearly names SLA.

The Act provides for the constitution and composition of the SLA.6 SLA shall be a body corporate having perpetual succession and a common seal with power, to acquire, hold and dispose of property and to contract and may by the same time sue and be sued. It consists of twenty members from the fields concerned with information creation, organisation and services, with Minister for Education who shall ex officio be the President and State Librarian who shall ex officio be the Secretary of SLA. But it is desirable to make only one person, instead of a corporate body to be the supreme authority for providing this very important service, for that gives a unified command from administrative points of view.

And this person should not be any person less than the Minister for Education, because he is directly responsible to the legislature and his term of office being limited to a period of five years he is ultimately responsible to the people. Hewit who made a study of the library legislation in India; it will be observed that two kinds of supreme authority are favoured in existing legislation and in the drafts of the model bills framed in India. One is a body of persons *i.e.,*

State Library Councilor Committee and second is a Minister of State. He suggests the second as the better of the two, mainly because a Minister is responsible to his legislature, and through it, to the electors and many be called to account therein. A body of persons even though a Minister may be President or Chairman thereof is not so easily questioned.

In any case; so important an activity as the provision for public library and information service to the people fully justifies direct representation in State Legislature. So all the studies on library legislations and the evaluation of existing legislations throughout the world and especially in third world counties, like that of Gardners's study comes to the conclusion that providing up of a body or a person as SLA and clearly naming and defining its powers and functions is certainly essential for the successful working of library Acts. But KPLA is very vague in this aspect and it fails to name a person or body as SLA.

DEPARTMENT OF PUBLIC LIBRARIES AND OFFICIALS

It is generally emphasized that in order to develop a system of public libraries in a State or country on proper lines, it is essential that a separate department of public libraries be created at par with the department of education and that the former should not be a part of the later or any other' department. The Acts of Andhra, Maharashtra, West Bengal and Karnataka prescribe for the creation of separate department of Public Libraries.

Director of Public Libraries

Most of the recommendations related to public library system legislation emphasizes that the department of Public Libraries should be headed by a Director of Public Libraries (DPL), whose rank must be equivalent to that of Director of Education. He must be a person with qualification and experience in Library and Information Science. Emphasis on his being a professional is laid because it is he to whom the whole public library system in the State would look for guidance and inspiration and his professional outlook would normally greatly help the development of the system on desired lines.

The first public library Act in this country; the Madras Public Library Act, 1948 provided for the appointment of DPL. Andhra, Maharastra and West Bengal also prescribes for the creation of DPL. In Madras and Andhra the Director of Public Instruction is made the ex-officio Director of Public Libraries also.

The disadvantages of such an administrative set-up are quite obvious. The Department of Public Libraries becomes an additional burden to the Director of Public Instruction. This new department will be looked upon as an uninvited guest. A. R. Hewit has rightly pointed out that many of the duties of Director of Public Libraries would require technical knowledge and skill in librarianship. So professional experts only can undertake this responsibility efficiently.

State Library

All the Acts except KPLA which is not providing for these offices, combines the responsibilities of developing and managing the State Central Library Superintending and directing all matters related to the State library system in a single person called State Librarian or DPL.

The Model Act also recommends this pattern. But the Sinha Committee report suggested the creation of two separate posts for this purpose when it said "The DPL may have the overall responsibility to organize develop and supervise the public library system as the Head of the Department of Public Libraries. The State Librarian should have the responsibility to manage supervise and develop State Central Library and should be the Chief Technical Advisor of the DPL, with no responsibility for the administration of the service in the State. This responsibility should be entirely that of DPL. But in KPLA there is no provision for appointing a Director of Libraries or State Librarian. While the class by class discussion of the Bill was going on in Assembly Mr. V.M. Sudheeran; member presented an amendment to add a new clause in the Act providing for appointment of a Director of Libraries. But was not considered.

Administration

For the administration of public libraries all the State Acts have created a department or directorate of public libraries. It is put under the charge of Director of Libraries or State Librarian who is to be the *ex-officio* Secretary of SLA. The functions of these posts as prescribed by all Acts including the Model Act are: to supervise and direct all matters relating to public libraries, to direct and control the working of LLAs, submit reports to Government and deal with schemes and plans relating to libraries. Many of the highly technical and specialized works of State Central Library also is to be supervised by them.

So it is clear that these posts which are carrying heavy responsibility concerning various matters-financial, advisory, administrative, technical, supervisory and so on-under the Act would require technical knowledge and skill in library and information service. So the Secretary or High Officer of this body should be a whole time officer having the prescribed qualifications to practice the library profession. Disregarding all the facts KPLA assigns all these duties and powers to a Secretary elected by members of the Executive Committee ofKSLC.

Section 3 sub-section (5) of KPLA provides that the elected members of the Executive Committee shall elect a President, Vice-President, Secretary and Joint Secretary from among themselves to be the President, Vice-President, Secretary and Joint Secretary respectively of the State Library Council and of the Executive Committee. Their term of office will be for three years.

KPLA assigns to the Secretary of KSLC the duties and powers which other State Acts assign to State Librarian or Director of Libraries. Section 9 Sub-section (1) States: the Secretary of the State Library Council shall be Chief Executive Authority of KSLC.

The nature of the office of Secretary of KSLC requires professional knowledge and experience as well as continuity of office for the successful operation of the Act, so it is inevitable that this provision will prevent KPLA from fulfilling the objectives for which a modern library legislation should exist. This serious defect of the Act has been pointed out by many members during the discussion of the bill.

Dr. M.Kuttappan has brought to the notice of the Assembly that such an important system like that for library and information service requires qualified government officials as their secretaries at State, District and Taluk levels. The period of an elected non-official member may be over by three years and if he misappropriates government fund allotted for library development it will not be possible for the government to take action on him. Sri Ishac Kurikkal suggested an amend-ment to the Bill to provide that the Secretary of the SLC shall be appointed by the Government on the advice of the Kerala Public Service Commission. Another member Sri Kodiyeri Balakrishnan opined that the Secretary of KSLC should be appointed by Government and the Act should specify the qualifications and method of appointment for this post. Sri Ramesh Chennitthala presented an amendment to add the following sub-clause in KPLA namely: The Secretary shall be a person not below the rank of a Joint Secretary to Government appointed by Government from among persons qualified and competent to hold such post. But all these suggestions were rejected and principles were disregarded to maintain a democratic system for constituting the SLA.

Library Co-operation

To make the best possible use of the document resources not only in the public library system but also in other types of libraries in the State such as universities, special libraries etc, a system of inter library co-operation needs to be developed in the state as a whole. It would also be useful and economical if centralization of different aspects such as acquisition programme, technical processing etc. of documents should be introduced at State level or at different levels of the system. The KPLA gives no such provision for co-operation or centralized processing and the institution which is to give leadership in such activities that is SCL is absent in KPLA.

State Central Library

The existing State legislations and the Model Act provide for a State Central Library (SCL) as an integral part of the Public Library Service. The SCL is normally the copy right collection. It should collect as far as its resources allow, expensive work and literature published abroad, material for which the local public library would have little need and could not afford. All the countries of the world possessing adequate library systems, have national library systems and all have national central library as distinct from the other libraries in the system, but is accessible to all through any library of the system.

The same role of National Central Library to the National system is done by SCL to the State system. Usually the library legislations designate the biggest collection available in the State as SCL and makes its resources and services available to the system. Even though various Acts and Model Act give different names to SCL like State Service Library, etc. in a public library system only one such library will be maintained and its resources will be shared by all participating units. Maintaining more than one SCL is unnecessary duplication of work and waste of resources.

Most of the State Acts and Model bills drafted, designate the biggest public library existing in the State as SCL and adopts it to the system and shares its resources among participating units. But instead of designating Trivandrum Public Library, the oldest and biggest collection in the State as SCL, the KPLA deems it to be one of the many State libraries it will establish.

The Act provides for no SCL in its system. Instead it provides that KSLC shall establish one or more state libraries at such place or places in the State as may be considered necessary. The relation of State libraries with other state libraries and different level service units and the purpose of more than one such institution is not defined in the Act.

State Library Service

State Library Service brings the manpower of the State in one pool and thus avoids the waste of time and money involved in filling up posts that would otherwise involve, if every Local Library Authority were to appoint the staff independently. A State Library Service further avoids the influence of members of the Local Library Authority in day-to-day management of libraries. Mysore Act has created a special state library service and it ensures proper administration and economy through State Library Service. But KPLA gives to KSLC and Local Library Authorities that is DLC and TLU the powers to appoint and control required officers and servants.

GROWTH AND DEVELOPMENT OF A PUBLIC LIBRARY SYSTEM

For the growth and development of a public library system in a State, there must be a specific provision in the Act for required financial support. Since education is an essential responsibility of a welfare State, public library system should obviously be established and maintained at the expense of the State.

The Model Act of Ranganathan, the suitable sources for this purpose are:

- Library cess,
- Grants from the State Governments, and
- Grants from Central Government.

In the provisions related to finance; KPLA accepts all the generally accepted principles. The Act provides that the KSLC shall levy a library cess in the form of surcharge on building tax or property tax collected by local bodies at the rate of five paise for whole rupee. The cess shall be paid to the KSLC by local bodies. The government may also make every year a grant to the KSLC of a sum which shall not exceed one per cent of the budget for education. This amount of grant is insufficient.

Ranganathan's Library Development Plan, the documents on National Policy on Library and Information Science and Indian Library Association suggests that six per cent of the Education budget of the State should be set apart for libraries. The Act also provides for a State Library Fund from which all expenses of KSLC, DLC and TLU shall be met. Grants of State and Central Governments to KSLC, contributions by persons, bodies or authorities etc. to KSLC and other funds transferred to it shall be credited to State Library Fund. KSLC shall distribute from State Library Fund such amounts as required for each DLC and TLD. Against creating such Library funds as suggested by Model Act and some State Acts at State and local levels; these provisions of KPLA related to finance providing a centralized fund are truly a notable improvement.

LIBRARY AND INFORMATION SERVICE AUTHORITY

Library and information service is to be rendered locally by thousands of service points spread throughout the state. The State as a whole in view of its large size is not suitable for being considered as a single unit for organizing these services. So it becomes essential to organize this service system on a decentralized pattern.

The units of responsibility at different levels, their nature, functions and relation with other levels should be clearly specified in the Act. In the Model Act Ranganathan recommended two types of Local Library Authorities; District Library Authority in a district and City Library Authority in a city. The KPLA improves the scope of decentralization of services; providing a three tier system that is after State level at District and Taluk levels parallel to Government's Administrative machanism.

The District Library Councils (DLC) and Taluk Library Unions (TLU) are miniature forms of KSLC. Their constitution, composition, powers and functions are all the same as KSLC; limited within the geographical area of its coverage. DLC and TLU shall elect their Executive Committee which will elect the office bearers very much like in KSLC. All the defects of KSLC are reflected in these bodies also. The Act does not provide for City Library Authorities. It is the duty of the Taluk union to organize and administer the library and information service to the people living in cities and villages.

MANAGING ACCESS TO THE WEB-BASED DIGITAL RESOURCES: ISSUES AND IMPLICATIONS

The invention of the printing press in the 15th century was a landmark in the history of scholarly communication. It was possible to produce large number of documents with the help of printing press. Moreover, the libraries, in the real sense of the term, came into existence only after the invention of the printing press. But now with the emergence of *information and communication technologies* (ICTs), the LI profession is finding itself into a paradoxical situation. The web, which has no head and tail, is both blessing and curse for the stakeholders. As there is no competition for space in the web, a lot of junk is being made available by the information elite. The non-elite members of the society are being left behind in the emerging information society. As such, the existing gap between the 'info-rich' and the 'info-poor' is widening further at a warp speed. Therefore, there is a strong need that we take cognizance of this phenomena and develop certain policies and strategies to separate web-based junk from the quality information, as well as to bridge the widening gap, between the 'haves' and the 'have nots'.

RESOURCE SHARING

We are surrounded by rapid economic, educational, political, cultural, and technological changes. Declining library budgets, growing user expectations, shifting priorities of governments, commercialization of education, consumerism, and digitization of documents are forcing the LI professionals to devise new ways and means to survive and thrive in the networked environments.

There is a shift from just- in-case to just-in-time approach for managing access to right information. It is not possible for a stand alone library to meet all the information needs of its end-users. Resource sharing via networking is the only alternative. There is a trend towards library and information networks. LANs, MANs, WANs, Intranets, and Extranets are manifestations of this trend. The Internet is a striking development of our times. It is a vast storehouse of information and a perpetual discourse of human minds is going on it. Moreover it has dramatically changed the whole process of scholarly communication. Conceptual access to tacit knowledge has been improved significantly.

The traditional pattern of authorship is also changing. Validation and creditation of intellectual property is becoming more difficult as there is no stability on the Internet. Moreover many people contribute to discussions via virtual conferences, seminars, discussion lists, newsgroups, and bulletin boards. As such the traditional competencies are falling short to manage access to the web-based digital resources.

It is very important for the professionals to know:

- What information is available;
- Where it is located; and
- How to access it.

All this can not be done in a piece meal manner. We must develop systems thinking and follow a holistic approach. Following are a few ways and means to do this.

STRATEGIES FOR ACCESS MANAGEMENT

As has already been pointed out that there is a trend towards managing access rather than ownership of information. The first and foremost requirement is to enhance awareness of the authorities, professionals and end-users of the web-based resources. Electronic journals, virtual reference desks, opacs, digital databases, scholarly discussion lists, mailing lists, electronic newsletters, bulletin boards, community telecentres, etc are the new resources and services on the web which must be managed to satisfy the info-literate end-users. It is essential now to get commitment from the higher authorities for providing the Internet connectivity. This is the basic requirement to get benefits of the web.

REDESIGNING THE LIS COURSES

The Library and Information Science courses must be redesigned to incorporate the IT components. Only this way we can provide competent manpower to the LI profession. There should also be a provision for continuing education and training programmes. ILA, IASLIC, IATLIS, SIS, INFLIBNET, NISSAT, UGC, universities and other organizations such as INSDOC, NASSDOC, and DRTC can contribute a lot in this regard. These bodies are already very active, but still there is a strong need for regularizing and coordinating their efforts.

EMPOWERMENT OF THE STAKEHOLDERS

The LI professionals and the end-users are the main stakeholders who are going to be directly affected by the widening gap between the stand alone and networked libraries. As such there is a strong need to empower the LI professionals and the end-users. LI professionals must be provided with opportunities to update their knowledge base and develop their skills. Efforts must be made to change their mind-set to overcome their resistance to integration of web-based resources in libraries. Critical thinking, and thorough understanding of the networked environment must be cultivated among them. Similarly, it is now possible to empower the end-users also. With the emergence of user friendly 'drag and drop' and 'point and click' systems it is possible for the end-users to find pertinent information in many cases. Information literacy is a way to empower the end-users.

INFORMATION LITERACY

It includes basic computer and network literacy. Besides, the end-user must be enabled to search right information as well as make its judicious use in a timely manner. LI professionals have a pivotal role to play in this regard. They should not only act as facilitators and tutors but also as motivators.

QUALITY INFORMATION MANAGEMENT

As there is no competition for space in the web, it has become very difficult to retrieve relevant information in time. In case of general information web returns thousands of entries, and in case of esoteric information sometimes not even a single relevant reference is available. The end result of this phenomenon is a frustrated end-user.

We must make efforts to help the end-users to come out of such a demoralizing and demotivating situation. LI professionals must search the web on regular basis and customise the retrieved information according to the interests of the end-users. Only this way we can manage access to the web based resources. LI professionals have an ethical commitment to serve as gatekeepers. Quality information must be sifted from the information deluge which is engulfing the emerging information society.

WRAPPING UP

There are certain issues which must be addressed immediately. These relate to implementation of the National Policy on Library and Information System, enhancing end-users' awareness of the web-based resources and services, empowering the LI professionals, getting commitment from the purse holders for the Internet connectivity, managing access to digital documents, customizing digital resources to the needs of the end-users, and developing and mounting indigenous databases on the web. Inflibnet and Delnet are doing a good job in this regard. Library associations, universities, R&D organizations, the UGC, Nissat, Insdoc, Nassdoc, DRTC, etc should provide leadership to the LI professionals for bridging the existing gap between the 'haves' and 'have nots' at least in India.

This is not an easy task. It has wide implications for the LI professionals. As suggested, have to develop suitable policies and strategies, adequate infrastructure, and competent LI professionals. Besides, there must be a provision for continuous maintenance of the LI infrastructure as the ICTs will never be stable. We are living in an era, where uncertainty is the only certainty, instability is the only stability, and change is the only constant.

We must learn to create and manage change. Only this way we can survive and thrive in the networked environment, and provide delight to the end-users.

We must automate our library and information systems, but not our thinking. Our biggest challenge is to provide access to multimedia information. Biggest challenge it is because information today has become fluid and transcendental. Managing access to digital information is just like hunting a moving object. Only competent LI professionals with thorough understanding of the web-based environment will be in a position to manage access to web-based digital resources.

METAMORPHISM OF LIBRARIES

During the movement of library system, developmental changes such as, closed access to open access, the role of library from a store-house to active information service organization and reading place to center of recreation have been seen. Now digital media is being used to store, process and retrieve information that causes Metamorphosis in the very form and function of library, though the philosophy of librarianship is still the same.

METAPHORISM OF LIBRARY TO DIGITAL LIBRARY

Metamorphism of library means that, the library has passed through certain amount of pressure and environmental change to be addressed, in today's electronic age, as digital library. Basically the term Metamorphism is borrowed from geology and according to Webster's Dictionary it is "a pronounced change effected by pressure, heat, and water that results in a more compact and more highly crystalline condition."

Technology

Technology has influenced libraries in many aspects:

Media

Electronic storage forms have changed through magnetic tapes, floppies, CDROM and now DVDs. The very storage capacity of CD-ROM made 20 volumes of The Oxford English Dictionary available only on one CD. The newly developed DVD technology stores 4.7 GB-17GB data, depending upon the specifications. These powerful storage devices have compressed the size of Library in Digitized form.

Cost

Cheaper and reliable technologies have reduced the cost of products resulting in increased storage capacity of libraries in less cost. The cost of CDs has come down very fast in last two years. But new technology like that of DVD is still costly, but may come down after wider use. Compared to traditional books or other materials, the digitized products are cheaper from the library point of view. The 20 volumes of normal OED cost £ 1800 and in leather jacket cost £ 3750, while in CDROM cost £ 175 and updation is £ 51.06. Duplication through computer is cheap. Practically one can copy any amount of data within short time. Besides, documents lose fidelity in traditional environment and offset printing is too costly. Digitized duplication does not lose single per cent fidelity. But copyright issue is not to be overlooked.

Access

In online digital environment information can be accessed at any time. Such facility can be extended to user's home or office. Besides, there is no danger of non-availability of document due to circulation.

Publication

Technology has no doubt changed the trend of publication. Lots of products are available on Internet and in electronic form. Though most of the products are of low quality, content or presentation wise, but the advantage with these products is, ease of accessibility. So, such products force standard products to go online in order to keep them-self in market. For example, Encyclopaedia Britannica couldn't cope the challenge posed by inexpensive, CD-ROM encyclopaedia and thus it had to be published electronically. In case of e-publishing, there is scope for improvement in performance, because such publications can be well reviewed by many persons. Better version of the work can come very fast compared to paper form. This particular characteristic is making digital or electronic publishing common and more feasible than the traditional one.

Barrier for use

Studies show that as the distance to library increases, users become more unwilling to go to library.

A study by Andrew Odlyzko shows that in Penn State, USA, the idea of offsite repository was disliked by users for all journals published before 1973, which where less used, though it takes only one day to retrieve an article from the off-site collection.

The frequency of use of off- site collection was only 4 items per person per year among the total users in institute numbering 1050.

Usage of Electronic Information:

It is hard to measure online activities but studies show that usage of electronic information is increasing almost at the rate of 100 per cent. For example, take the data of Library of Congress:

Table. Library of Congress Statistics

Month	GB	Request (million)
Feb 1995	14.0	1.1
Feb 1996	31.2	3.9
Feb 1997	109.4	15.1
Feb 1998	282.0	36.0
Feb 1999	535.0	48.6
Feb 2000	741.1	61.3

Usage of theses and dissertations is not restricted to institute. Now there are Internet based digital libraries, which provide full text access to theses and dissertations.

The Brazilian SciELO (Scientific electronic Library Online) project started out in early 1958. The number of pages transmitted from Brazilian SciELO project grew from 4943 in January 1999 to 63,695 an year after.

Similarly, data from Firstmonday shows that in early 1999, full paper download growth ranged from 50,000 to 60,000 per month, which went to 110,000 - 120,000 per month in early 2000. That shows how fast electronic form is picking up.

WHAT IS IT?

In digital libraries information is stored in digital form *i.e.* on computer or CD-ROM or magnetic tapes and is retrieved through digital information access tools.

MODELLING THE DIGITAL LIBRARY

Development of digital library involves several issues. It may extend from administrative level to accessibility of information. The development of digital library can be taken as a project in the traditional library.

Digitisation

This is the heart of the project. Following questions must be answered before digitization:

- What element of the original to be captureed?
- How to capture?
- Copyright permission

The exposition of recorded knowledge takes place in four forms:

- Image
- Text
- Audio
- Video

Cataloguing

Library catalogue, as we know, gives the information about the holdings of library. In Digital library, there are two ways of doing the work:

Creation of Catalogue

Catalogue pages can easily be created in HTML format, having the information about title, author, publisher, place and so on. Or even library automation packages, having OPAC module, can be used for the same, provided they have facility of web interface.

Metadata

The term metadata stands for data about the data. There are many popular metadata approaches and the most popular, particularly for the Internet resources, is Dublin Core. It contains the following 15 elements:

Content	Intellectual Property	Instantiation
Title	Creator (Author)	Date
Subject	Publisher	Type
Description	Contributor (Other agent)	Format (Form)
Source	Rights	Identifier
Relation		
Language		
Coverage		

There are two different approaches of using metadata.

Approach 1

- Metatags can be embedded in the HTML documents. For example,
- <meta name = "DC.Author" content = "S.R. Ranganathan">
- <meta name = "DC.Title" content = "Prolegomena to Library Classification">
- <meta name = "DC.OtherAgent" role = "Assisted by" content = "M.A. Gopinath">

- This tag resides in the <head> and before <title>.
- *Disadvantages:*
  - <meta> tags is being used for many things like reloading a page or directing a page to some other URL.
  - It doesn't give flexibility. For example, there are well defined set of tags, which gives robustness to document structure.

Approach 2

Warwick framework: Resource Description Framework:

- Warwick framework supports the existing metadata. Basically it uses the "Container Package model". That means, there is a Container, inside which there are packages of different nature. Packages can be of different types:
  - *Primitive Package:* Contains one or more elements of metadata. Each of them has a type. Ex: MARC package, Dublin Core package, etc.
  - Indirect package: Basically these are links, giving direction to the other information resource.
  - *Containers Package:* A package itself can be a container.

Resource Description Framework (RDF):

- This was instantiated by W3C. A project called *Platform for Internet Content Selection* (PICS), to rate the webpages was started by W3C.. Later on, the scope of this project increased and one can set its own parameters to rate the webpages. The second approach leads to description of resource and thus *Resource Description Framework* (RDF) was born.

RDF Model:

- Resource is an object that is uniquely identified by a *Universal Resource Identifier* (URI). Resource has Properties. Properties have Property types. And these Property types have Values.

If we generate an RDF model, resources are at nodes, property types are links and values are in quotes.

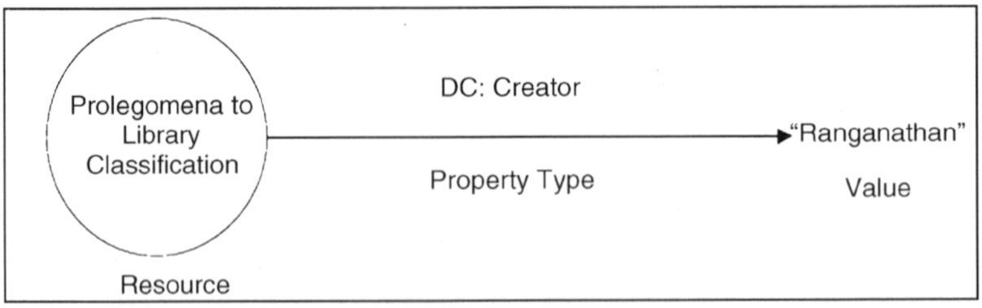

Fig. RDF Model Representation

Basically RDF uses XML, where one can define its own tags unlike to HTML.

Databases

The current approach is to store information in databases. These databases are made accessible through web-browsers or any other interface depending on the library. Any user can search these information using search techniques and a search engine. In such databases search can be done on a specific field and it removes the need of catalogue.

Disadvantage:

- The major disadvantage of this system is that the reader has to browse the whole document to find its relevancy.
- It makes mandatory to use bibliographic database system, because commercially available popular database systems do not give sub-field level description of document.

AN EXPERIMENT

A catalogue-based approach has been adopted for developing Digital Library model. The library gives access to all sorts of documents including text, audio, video and image in different formats. Browser is used as front end for search and delivery of documents. For searching the document, search engine, provided within MS-Frontpage, is used. The formulated query uses catalogue for search and displays the hit records in a list format. Each item in list is hyper- linked to the catalogue entry page. Each catalogue page in-turn is hyper- linked to the original document. Establishing a digital library is definitely a Herculean task. It involves so many decisions and problem solving. There are certain issues, which hinder the development of digital library.

Advantages:

- This type of cataloguing is very much helpful for the audio, image or video collections where it is difficult to index the collection. So such catalogue can be used as document surrogate and can be searched easily using any search engine.
- An abstract gives a clear view to reader about the usefulness of document for his/her study.
- It is a simple approach and can be built using common softwares like, Frontpage.
- It does not use any database.

Disadvantages:

- This approach is only feasible in the small libraries and specialized libraries, which have collection that can't be indexed.
- For large size library, powerful search engine is required, because search engine indexes the content of whole catalogue pages and searches through them, which takes time.
- The results are only based on pattern matching so there are no semantics associated to search.

CHALLENGES FOR DIGITAL LIBRARY

Intellectual Property Rights (IPR)

No doubt the primary aim of life is to earn. Due to this approach of life the concept of IPR came in picture, which suggests the benefit of creator if his/her work is used for the monetary gain or so. This monetary gain became the chief concept in publishing industry. This particular concept really hurts the library philosophy, because it stops copying of documents or its any part for use, without the prior permission of copyright holder. In digital library, actually the media of document is changed which is even more serious problem than the earlier.

At this particular juncture many of the digital library projects die. In such an environment, even if library somehow gets the permission to change the document form or accepts the publication in digital form, it is difficult to save the document from unauthorized distribution and copying. Watermarking is a sort of a solution of it. There is wide variety of softwares, which can be used for watermarking like Digimarc, SysCoP etc. But side-by-side there are softwares, which can change watermarks, for example, StirMark. IPR and security are the two major issues, which dampen digital library projects.

Economic Issues

Development of digital library involves lot of resources and in terms of money it is not a small amount, which has to be dealt with.

Operating Cost

It is true that to set up a digital library, big money is required. Once it is set up the operating cost for maintenance has to be considered. No doubt duplication and printing cost is negligible, but it really doesn't cut some of the costs, which are there in traditional library. Readers are still very comfortable in reading through printed form and on demand it is library's duty to give in print. So paper stationeries and printing may still be required. Side by side money is required to have backups, buying electronic stationeries, system maintenance, electric charges etc. Besides, library has to consider payment to ISP and telephone line and any other communication mode.

Revenue

Copying can be done in digital environment with 100 per cent fidelity without cost. But to distribute a non-digital product in a digital form, library must have to pay to copyright holder, and if all agree that library should generate its own funds, the question of HOW comes. Charging to user is big problem, because as it is known that publishing industry works on non-linear pricing, which influences libraries to have non-linear prices. For example, for two different products if library is paying different amount then it is required to charge differently to users. Thus publishing industry plays havoc for digital libraries.

Monitoring

If digital library, working on Internet, gives links to other Internet resources, due to volatile nature of web documents, it is a must to keep track of presence of web documents. There are few softwares, which do this work like MoMSpider and Web: lookout, which can trace any changes on the linked webpages. But the real issue is that if the link is entirely changed how to trace that which is quite common on Internet.

Communication

If library delivers its service through the Internet or Intranet it has to have a user interface. Now it should be taken care that how fast the interface get loaded to reader's machine and how fast the results of searches are displayed. For that, librarians should have sound knowledge of technology and changing web environment.

WRAPPING UP

In library development movement, digital library is a milestone. Though developing a digital library seems to be easy from the point of view of technology but the real challenge lies in the culture of society. To propagate the knowledge it is required to have a sharing of knowledge and in which the publication industry poses biggest challenge. That is why, many of the digital library projects went up to putting the home publication on digitized form not the collection of library. It seems that such problems can be solved if learned bodies or libraries start publishing themselves. But this revolutionary concept may rouse many moral and ethical issues in the librarian's lobby. It is a matter of debate or deep discussion which librarians have to go through and finally again we have a Yaksha Prashana- Are we really ready for this change?

3

Digital Geolibraries and Digital Collections

One approach used by librarians in making digital geospatial data available to their users is to incorporate Web-based mapping functions with their library geospatial information holdings. Such efforts combine the locational aspects of the metadata descriptions of the geospatial data in the catalog with the mapping capabilities of GIS software. In building Web-based functions into their geospatial collections, some libraries have termed their collection a 'digital geolibrary.'

Different perspectives about geolibraries have been discussed in the scholarly geography and information science literature such as from Boxall and Goodchild. Goodchild refers to a geolibrary as being comprised of georeferenced information that can be accessed by a geographic footprint. Likewise, in his discussion of geolibraries, Boxall notes that their scope extends beyond the traditional map library if the construct of a geolibrary is based upon the idea that information has a geographic footprint. His discussion references earlier research that explains georeferenced information as including such things as photographs, videos, music, and literature that can be given a locational variable that defines a footprint.

The collection areas of geolibraries extend beyond the traditional scope of map libraries and archives to include almost all information contained within libraries.

He later mentions that it can include information outside of libraries as well. This is the theoretical basis for what we now view as geolibraries. Boxall discusses that a significant focus of geolibraries is on digital information and metadata, as well as the distributed nature of the libraries and 'collections.' He adds that '...Distributed geolibraries provide a useful framework for discussion of the issues of dissemination associated with the National Spatial Data Infrastructure (NSDI)". The vision is readily extendible to a global context. Boxall feels any discussion of "Digital Earth' (DE), the 'Global Spatial Data Infrastructure' (GSDI), and 'Distributed Geolibraries' should be framed around the broadest definitions of information and infrastructures; namely to include and focus upon the people, technology and organisations which give rise to and sustain such infrastructures'.

An early significant effort at establishing a digital spatial library was the Alexandria Digital Library at the University of California Santa Barbara. The Alexandria Digital Library was one of six federally funded library projects. The U.S. National Science Foundation founded it in early 1994. The Library's collection and services focus on georeferenced information: maps, images, data sets, and other information sources with links to geographic locations. Much of the information in the collection was primarily of the University's service area, or Southern California.

A key aspect of the collection is the ability to perform data queries and retrieve results by geography location. The basic means of describing and finding information is with a geographic footprint. A footprint depicts the location on the surface of the earth associated with either an object in the collection such as a map, remote sensed image, or aerial photograph, or with a user's query. The footprint may be represented as a point or polygon, with latitude and longitude coordinates. As a user queries the collection through a user interface, the user creates a footprint or an interactive map to indicate the area of interest.

The query area is matched with the object footprints in the metadata to retrieve relevant objects about the query area. This approach to query structure allows the user to choose arbitrary query areas and is not limited to geographic areas with place names. The objects in the collection that fall within a particular query area do not have to have the names associated with them that the user enters for a text based query. By translating a user's textbased query into a footprint query for a certain geographic area, the user can retrieve all types of information about a location such as remote sensed images, data sets, aerial photographs, and textual information. The catalog for the Alexandria Digital Library is configured for searches that will retrieve objects that are either in an online format or physical location as a map.

Using the Alexandria Digital Library as a model, the Idaho Geospatial Data Center was started in 1996 by a team of geographers, geologists, and librarians. The aim of the team was the establishment of digital library of public domain geographic data for the state of Idaho. As a theoretical and practical foundation for their digital spatial collection, which they termed a 'geolibrary,' the team used a set of parameters as defined by Goodchild. Goodchild defined a geolibrary's components as including a browser or specialised software application running on the user's computer and providing access to the geolibrary through a computer network. A geolibrary also includes a 'basemap' or geographic frame of reference for the browser's queries.

A basemap would provide an image of an area corresponding to the geographical extent of geolibrary collection. The basemap would depend on the scale of the search being performed from a large geographic area, such as a state, or a smaller location, as a city block. A gazetteer or index that would link place names to a map would also be included. A large collection of collection catalogs would be maintained on distributed computer servers. The servers would be accessed over a network with the browser, using basic server-client architecture.

A geolibrary would ideally provide open access to many types of information with geographic referenced queries regardless of the storage media Using a grant from the Idaho Board of Education's Technology Incentive Programme, the team built a geographic digital data repository or the Idaho GeoSpatial Data Center (IGDC). The library contained a number of digital geospatial datasets that was searchable through a flexible browsing tool. The collection contained a number of public domain information such as Digital Line Graphs and Digital Raster Graphics from the United States Geological Survey and U.S. Bureau of the Census TIGER boundary files for the state of Idaho. The site provided an interactive visual analysis of selected demographic/economic data for Idaho counties.

The site also contained interactive links to other Idaho and national spatial data repositories. A key aspect of the IGDC's collection was the development of the GeoLibrary's browser, which was implemented using MicroSoft Visual Basic 5.0 and ESRI MapObjects technology. The interface of the browser consisted of three panels resembling the Microsoft Outlook user interface. A first panel, a map panel, would be used to explore the geographic coverage of the geolibrary and to select an area of interest.

A second panel in the interface was where the query would be performed. The final panel is where the query results would be displayed for analysis and to download spatial data. In many ways, librarians are well aware of the ideas outlined in the discussion on the concepts and components for digital data infrastructure. Library collections and services in electronic form, such as a digital library, integrate many aspects of the client-server architecture in providing access to materials in an online distributed environment. Digital libraries have in them collections of digital information objects of various formats in an ordered database defined by descriptive data standards.

Organised in a regular manner, the database is searchable using query applications via a user interface, usually through an online catalog. Information is compartmentalised in short descriptions using metadata tags to ease search and retrieval applications. The overall structure is guided by administrative oversight that takes into account the needs of the various users involved in the community. Researchers, such as Goodchild, envision an intersection of the concepts of the digital library and that of the spatial data infrastructure in a sort of 'geolibrary'.

Researcher envisions a geolibrary as a library filled with "georeferenced information that can have a geographic footprint.' Including multimedia, images, and music that could be assigned a location attribute, geolibraries would thus extend beyond the scope of a traditional map library and provide new services and resources for users to discover. The survey of the characteristics of spatial data databases and related infrastructure indicate the involvement of many different factors in assembling a data infrastructure. However, in addition to data providers, databases, metadata, data networks, technology, and institutional arrangements, there is also a significant in organisational and human resource factors.

Researchers offer six talking points that are essential to consider in building a spatial data infrastructure. These include technology, policies and standards, human resources, institutional arrangements, spatial data and metadata, and data networks. They suggest that spatial data infrastructure should not recreate the wheel in its technology development. It would be prudent to look at what information technology has accomplished to date, and then integrate that knowledge with GIS expertise, regardless of the difficulties involved. Integration of existing technology also applies to standards and policies. Standards enhance communication and development with a common language and concepts, leading to guidelines that affect architecture, processes, methods, or policies.

There should be a common consensus of minimal guidelines that can accommodate those working with geospatial data, retrieval, and discovery. User-guided development is also critical when examining the human resources side of GIS information and technology. Further, the use of qualified researchers and developers is essential. To create institutional frameworks, agreements have to be certified to establish national, regional, and global spatial data infrastructure. These spatial data infrastructures should be created over the geographic data, stored in the spatial databases, and their description in rich, descriptive metadata. Finally, open systems and ease of access is of strategic importance to ensure quality and accuracy from remote systems.

The need for data description standards for digital geospatial data is especially apparent in the proliferation of WebGis applications in the wake of spatial data distribution enabling initiatives, such as the NSDI. WebGIS (also known as Internet GIS) describes a type of geographic information system. WebGIS basically consists of client, server, and network model, wherein the client is integrated in a Web browser. While creating many opportunities for librarians in making available unique geospatial datasets, the tremendous growth in WebGIS has created many challenges for libraries in trying to incorporate digital geospatial data in their services and legal considerations in the use of distributed data.

LINKING DIGITAL LIBRARY RESOURCES TO RELATED RESOURCES

This part emphasizes the ability of knowledge organization systems to link digital library resources to other related resources. The basis for this linking is the identification of information within a digital resource that can be extracted and used to search and locate information within a KOS. The KOS may then be used to expand codes to more explanatory full text, to provide more descriptive records, or to link entity names to resources of physical specimens.

EXPANDING CODES TO FULL TEXT

Practitioners of a discipline use coding schemes to facilitate communication within that discipline. It is often helpful to connect these coding schemes to the full names for which the code stands. The examples provided here include links between databank registration codes and the biological sequence data, and between industrial codes and the full name that the code represents.

Linking Sequence Numbers to Biosequence Databanks

The lengthy biochemical and genetic sequences that molecular biologists, biotechnologists, and geneticists identify each day are kept in databanks. Several databanks have been developed, for example, to cover protein sequences, nucleotides, and cell lines.

One of the largest databanks contains information on the mapping of the human genome. As molecular biologists began to discover these sequences, they reported them in scientific journals. Difficulties in composing, proofreading, and printing the text soon arose. Through an ad hoc standards process, major biomedical publishers agreed to require the inclusion of codes or databank numbers for these sequences in objects when they are published. In addition, the sequence itself must be registered in a databank before the paper can be published. Some of the most frequently referenced databanks are listed on the Web site of the National Center for Biotechnology Information. They include GenBank and the Research Collaboratory for Structural Bioinformatics Protein Data Bank. Each sequence number is different, but all begin with a persistent code identifying the databank.

How can the link be made between the literature and the databank? Through a search profile, a text analysis programme, or keyword indexing, the text can be analysed and the sequence databank numbers identified. An active link can be embedded. The active link consists of a search strategy to locate that sequence number in the databank where the actual sequence is stored. When the user clicks on the active link, the script is generated and launched from the user's browser. The Web-enabled database is searched, and the sequence record is returned to the user. Depending on the services provided by the databank site, the user can analyse the sequence using a number of tools provided by the databank or download the sequence for local manipulation. This type of connection exists between the *National Library of Medicine's* (NLM) search service, PubMed, and GenBank at the National Center for Biotechnology Information. If a search in PubMed yields records that have GenBank numbers, the user can automatically search and display the sequence records from GenBank.

Linking Individual Industrial Codes to the Full Scheme

In business, classification schemes serve to communicate important facts about a company or product. These codes are generally controlled by a government, professional, trade, or international standards organization. They often serve as shorthand for users interested in material in a particular area of industry or a specific business sector. Perhaps the most familiar scheme is the SIC code, which was last updated in 1987. The SIC codes have been used by the U.S. government, economists, financial markets, regulators, and procurement offices to identify manufacturing, agriculture, and service sectors of the economy. In 1997, a new scheme was approved for use within the United States. The North American Industrial Classification System was developed with Canada and Mexico as a means of providing an agreed-upon scheme for the collection, reporting, and analysis of information about the economy by sector, both within and across borders. Information about NAICS is available from the Web-site of the U.S. Census Bureau.

The digital library can provide related information by using the authority files for the coding schemes as a linked authority file. If a company or economic sector mentioned in the digital library's collection can be linked to an SIC or NAICS code, the code can be searched against the official tables of definitions maintained by the U.S. Census Bureau. These files provide definitions of the codes and place each code in the classification scheme with other economic sectors.

The digital library's content can be further enhanced by making a link between the SIC and NAICS codes. If the digital library resource has the SIC code, it can be extracted and searched against the Census Bureau's *1997 NAICS and 1987 SIC Correspondence Tables.* The table returns the corresponding code from the alternate scheme.

LINKING TO DESCRIPTIVE RECORDS

Linking the name of an entity, such as a personal name, organization, or location, to additional information about that entity was one of the first uses of hyperlinking. Knowledge organization systems such as dictionaries, glossaries, and classification schemes can be used to link the entities in one resource to richer descriptions of that entity in another resource.

This is particularly helpful for users who are new to a topic and in cases where the additional information can make the user's task more efficient. The examples that follow are from three disciplines. The first example links organism names to records that not only describe the species more fully but also put it in the context of the overall classification scheme for living organisms. The second example links chemical names to descriptive records and molecular structures. In the third example, proper names are linked to the biographies for the person.

Linking Organism Names to Taxonomic Records

Genus-species names are the Latin names for organisms, *e.g.*, plants, animals, and microorganisms. Taxonomists, who study and classify living organisms, create records for each of these organisms. Generally, these records are linked relationally to the other organisms in a hierarchy. Beyond the organism name and the information that it and its placement in the hierarchy convey, taxonomic records use other elements to describe the organism. These may include distribution patterns, the authority for naming and classification, and the date the organism was identified. Scientists base the information on specimens that are retained because they serve as the physical evidence of the description. Natural history museums, private collections, and individual scientists number, or code, the specimens in their collections. Sometimes specimens are supported by photographs or line drawings, which may be digitized.

By using a taxonomic authority file as an intermediate authority file, one can link a text or an image file containing a name or picture of an organism to additional related information. By automatically processing the text or embedding a link from the organism name in the text or from the image to the taxonomic authority record, one can extend the knowledge conveyed by the text. The text can include the descriptive and historical information in the taxonomic record and, ultimately, link to a photograph, a drawing, or appropriate video or audio segments. Because of the ambiguity in organism names, many examples of this type are now created manually.

However, depending on the extent of the files involved, the ambiguity of the Latin and common names for organisms can be overcome. An example of a taxonomic intermediate file is the *Integrated Taxonomic Information System* (ITIS). ITIS is a partnership of U.S., Canadian, and Mexican government agencies, private organizations, and taxonomic specialists cooperating to develop an online, scientifically credible list of biological names of North American plants and animals.

It is used by many U.S. government agencies for consistent naming of plants and animals for regulatory and monitoring purposes. To link textual material in a digital library to the ITIS record, the organism name can be identified manually or automatically in the text and submitted as a query to the ITIS database. When a match is found, ITIS presents the ITIS record, which provides essential information about the organism. The information includes synonymous names, including some common names, and an indication of the placement of the organism in the larger taxonomic classification scheme.

Linking Chemical Names to Molecular Structures

The unique identification for a chemical substance is not its name but its molecular structure. However, chemical names are commonly used in research documents, project plans, catalogs, and directories, all of which may be resources in a digital library. There are competing systems of nomenclature as well as common and commercial synonyms. The ambiguity is resolved by providing links between the chemical names in the text and the molecular structure. This is done through a chemical registry number or code that is connected to a particular chemical name and an authority record that provides additional information about the chemical. This information includes the chemical's synonyms and some of its chemical and physical properties.

Most important in today's research environment is the link from this authority file to a chemical structure file. Structure files, used with the appropriate software, graphically depict the molecular structure. This sophisticated software allows for three-dimensional visualization, rotation, and substitution of the chemical bonds. An example of the use of the chemical registry number to link chemical names with molecular structures can be seen in the work of BIOSIS, the world's largest not-for-profit producer of biological and biomedical databases. In 1993, BIOSIS began processing its bibliographic citations to automatically identify chemical names. BIOSIS assigns CAS Registry Numbers (RNs) to the chemical names identified in this process. In the STN International online system, hosted in the United States by CAS, a user of BIOSIS can select one or more of the records resulting from a search and extract the RN.

The extracted RN can be applied against the CAS Registry File, which contains more than 21 million substances, including organics, inorganics, biosequences, metals, and alloys. The registry file record for the chemical name, including the link to the synonyms for the chemical name and the structure file itself, can then be accessed. With special tools developed by CAS, the structure can be viewed and manipulated. It can be imported into modeling tools that allow the chemist to manipulate the structure and thereby envision new chemicals. Alternatively, the user can start with any database that contains CAS RNs and extract the resulting RNs to perform a search for complementary bibliographic records in the BIOSIS database. Linking chemical names to structures using RNs on a large scale is neither inexpensive nor easy.

There are two approaches to identifying chemical names in text. Some journal objects include the CAS RN for the major chemicals discussed. In this case, an analysis of the text for the terms "RN", "CAS RN", and variations preceding numerics can identify RNs that can be used as a link. Alternatively, a programme to identify chemical names in text, similar to that developed by BIOSIS, could be devised. Developing the identification programme, as well as searching chemical databases, is costly; however, if the digital library has license agreements for chemistry databases, this type of linkage may be possible. In addition, many organizations have small chemical files of their own that may include RNs and other information of particular relevance to the organization's research. It may be possible to link to these local databases using methods that are more direct.

Linking Personal Names to Biographical Information

A common type of authority file is the personal name authority, which controls variants of personal names. For example, the *Library of Congress Name Authority File* (LCNAF) is used to control variant personal names for authors, editors, artists, and others. The *Union List of Artist Names* (ULAN), developed by the Getty Vocabulary Programme, is another example. Name authorities serve as tools for catalogers and indexers. They ensure that the proper form of the name, rather than an unapproved variant, is used and bring together all works by or about the person. A name authority file can also be used to link a bibliographic record or document containing the person's name to a variety of other related materials. If the digital library's resource has a standardized form of the name, it can be identified and searched against the authority file to locate variants. The standardized and variant forms can be joined in a search against a variety of other resources that can provide related information. For example, in the case of a digital library of images of artists' works or biographical or critical text, a name authority file such as the ULAN or the LCNAF can act as an intermediate file to provide additional information.

The file, which contains integrated variant names, can be searched by the name appearing in the digital library collection. When the record is found, the information about the artist can be displayed, providing a wide range of contextual material for the user. Citations to significant biographical or critical works about the artist, some of which may also be available on the Web, may also be provided in the name authority file. The variant names from a name authority can also be used to locate and provide automatic links from the personal name in the text to a biography, without requiring that the name be presented in the same fashion in the two resources. One such resource that could be linked to for biographical information is Gale's Biography Resource, which contains more than 142,000 biographies and related citations from more than 1000 periodicals.

However, to produce this kind of link, there must be a mechanism for locating personal names in text. Several programmes can do this type of text analysis; among those that have been developed commercially are NameFinder from the Carnegie Group and the Intelligent Agent from IBM. In addition, variant names can be extracted from the name authority itself, grouped, and run as a search against the text to locate name occurrences.

LINKING ENTITY NAMES TO PHYSICAL SPECIMENS

In some cases, it is possible to go another step and connect entity names in the digital library resources to physical specimens. The curation of physical specimens or artifacts is critical to the advancement of many disciplines. Exhibition catalogs describe the art objects in a particular exhibition. Museum catalogs provide inventories of the art, natural history, or cultural objects held by a particular museum. These catalogs, increasingly available as computerized databases, are knowledge organization systems that not only provide descriptive records but also point to the location of the object in a museum, an archive, or another collection. For example, in biology, a physical specimen is particularly important when it is the result of the discovery and description of a new organism or of the reclassification of a known organism. A type specimen is the example collected from the field by a taxonomist to serve as the prime example for the description of the organism and the validation of its taxonomic classification and naming.

These specimens are held by natural history collections, and their deposit is required by the rules of various taxonomic societies. As part of the curatorial activity, the collections assign identification codes. While the primary use of identification codes has been to organize the physical collections, numerous projects are under way in the natural history community to digitize photographs of specimens and create database records for the specimens, including their identifiers, and thereby make them more readily accessible. The degree of digitization varies from specialty to specialty.

For example, in botany, virtually all significant research herbaria are digitally cataloging their type collections instead of maintaining paper records. Many are also making digital photographs of the type specimens available over the Web. The publication of identification codes in the journal literature is also changing. Historically, identification codes have been presented in the "Materials Used" parts of journal objects. The level of specificity of the identification code has varied, depending on the biological discipline. For example, botanical journals tend to list only the institution and the catalog, while vertebrate journals provide the code to the specimen level.

The current trend is to require lists of specimens that are more detailed. As the lists become longer and the printing costs increase, journal publishers are beginning to request links to independent Web sites maintained by the researchers or their organizations that carry all the specimens used in the study and provide some level of identification.

If the digital library collection contains resources that include the identification codes, these codes can be extracted and matched against the Web-based catalogs or databases. This link can provide users with location and contact information to allow them to access the physical object mentioned in the digital library resource. Curators or registrars of artistic, archaeological, and cultural history collections also assign inventory or accession numbers to items in their collections. Identification numbers may also be found in scholarly catalogues raisonnés. Links similar to those described for natural history can be made between text related to works of art and the physical work in a particular collection

An object about a work of art can be linked to additional information about the physical specimen by linking the identification number in the text with an online catalog containing the number and additional information about the work. As museums digitize their collections to establish a presence on the Web or to reduce the handling of the physical objects, KOSs that can link the digital library resources to the physical object are being developed. If there is a museum with a collection that complements that of the digital library, it is worthwhile to discuss ways in which the digital library and digital museum collections may "co-evolve."

NATIONAL DATA INFRASTRUCTURE

In 1994 the Federal Geographic Data Committee (FGDC) recommended that a National Spatial Data Infrastructure (NSDI) be organised. The NSDI would be an "umbrella of policies, standards, and procedures under which organisations and technologies interact to foster more efficient use, management, and production of geospatial data". The NSDI was conceptualised as fostering more cooperation and interaction between different organisations from the public and private sector.

The recommendation was a response to alterations in the traditional flows of data across the government based on new convergences of information, computer technology, and communication. A significant component of the data being used in government transactions and commercial transactions was digital geospatial data. The FGDC considered digital geospatial data as being critical to solving many "environmental, economic, and social problems." The FGDC had also recognised that "the use of GIS technologies for the digital analysis of spatial problems had become pervasive". With the integration of GIS and increased use of geospatial data into problem-solving operations, a major goal of the NSDI was to make "an environment to respond to the current need of digital geospatial data."

The FGDC envisioned building the framework around the procedures, technology, and guidelines that enhance integration, sharing, and use of these data, and the institutional relationships and business practices that encourage the maintenance and use of data. The framework would represent the best available data for an area, and be certified, standardised, and described according to a common standard. Today, the FGDC standards provide a foundation on which organisations can build by adding their own detail and compiling other data sets.

MEETING DIGITAL GEOSPATIAL DATA NEEDS

The FGDC reported that many billions of dollars are spent by organisations on an annual basis in both the public and private sector in attempts to manage digital geospatial data. With digital geospatial data becoming a valuable asset within the business practices of many public and private sector organisations, most organisations can only afford to collect or purchase only a small portion of information they require. Often only the most basic digital geospatial data is acquired by organisations, usually a dataset that pertains to a specific geographic area or that has some unique attribute characteristics.

The datasets are often incompatible with other datasets, due to differences in software platforms. Researchers at the FGDC found that data collected by differing organisations may be similar in geographic extent use different geographic bases and standards. Hence, many of the resources organisations spend on geographic information systems (GIS) go towards duplicating other organisations' data collection efforts. The same geographic data themes for an area are collected again and again, at great expense.

A data framework would improve the ability for organisations to share data. The framework would provide a basic geographic data in a common format and an accessible environment that anyone can use and to which anyone can contribute. In this environment, users can perform cross-jurisdictional and cross-organisational analyses and operations, and organisations can funnel their resources into applications, rather than duplicating data production efforts. Researchers at the FGDC further noted in their findings that geographic data users from many disciplines have a recurring need for a few themes of basic data: geodetic control, orthoimagery, elevation, transportation, hydrography, governmental units, and cadastral information. Many organisations produce and use such data every day.

The framework provides basic information for these data themes. By attaching their own geographic data, which can cover innumerable subjects and themes, to the common data in the framework, users can build their applications more easily and at less cost. The seven data themes provide basic data that can be used in applications, a base to which users can add or attach geographic details and attributes, a reference source for accurately registering and compiling participants' own data sets, and a reference map for displaying the locations and the results of an analysis of other data. Researchers at the FGDC envision the information framework to be an evolving data resource to which geographic data producers can contribute.

Integral components of the information network incorporate procedures, guidelines, and technology to enable participants to build, integrate, maintain, distribute, and use framework data. These elements ensure that users can depend on accurate, detailed data that can be certified and integrated into the framework to create a trustworthy data source; users can update their data holdings from the framework data; and users can attach additional information to the framework. These procedures would ensure the standardisation of datasets and enable the efficient transfer of digital geospatial data across the

Internet. The FGDC envisions the information framework integrating data from all types of organisations in both the public and private sector. The framework environment is designed to be responsive to the needs of the geographic data community in terms of data creation and maintenance, and provides unrestricted access to data.

DATABASES, WEB SERVICES, AND INTERNET GIS

There are a number of advantages to a GIS that is available from the Internet including world wide accessibility, use of a standard interface, and cost-effective maintenance. The traditional model of GIS is a system that consists of a single software package, and accompanying data on a single machine. With the advent of distributed producers and consumers of digital geospatial data, this model is no longer valid.

As Green and Bossomaier note "many GIS projects are often multi-agency, multi-disciplinary, multi-platform, and multi-software. Large numbers of contributors may be involved, and there may be a large pool of potential users". Further, "a central practical issue is how to provide widespread, device-independent access to GIS for large numbers of contributors and users". The essential differences between a traditional GIS and an online GIS are the "separation of user interface, data storage, and processing". In stand-alone GIS, all of the elements are within a single machine; in an online environment, the elements are distributed across many computers.

During the 1980s, GIS was conceptualised strictly as a software application: "a computer based system that provides the following four sets of capabilities to handle georeferenced data:

1. Input;
2. Data management;
3. Manipulation and analysis; and
4. Output".

This definition is accurate when conceptualising GIS as an application; however, it does not address GIS as an interactive system where hardware, software, data, methods, and people come to create geographic knowledge for distribution. In the early 1990s, the concept of a GIS system evolved. ESRI, a privately held consulting firm, defined GIS as an "organised collection of computer hardware, software, geographic data, and personnel designed to efficiently capture, store, update, manipulate, analyse, and display all forms of geographically referenced information". The exploitation of geospatial data within diverse policy environments, allied with the increasing attention being afforded to cross-discipline social and environmental issues, has led to the demand for infrastructures to assist in the discovery, dissemination, and exploitation of geospatial data.

The authors also note that the structures are often referred to as spatial data infrastructures (SDIs). Most SDIs will integrate geospatial data and metadata, which can provide the means to access the data and also establishes the needed licensing agreements between users to make use of the data. The diverse information services of SDIs mirror information services of digital libraries, the latter defined as a collection of services and the collection of information objects that support users in dealing with the information objects and the organisation and presentation of those objects through electronic means. Three significant factors of SDIs are the provision, organisation, and presentation of information and services to a specific group of users.

By integrating with the digital library environment, the process of mining through digital geospatial data becomes more varied with additional data added to the original projection datum. In delivering digital geospatial data over the Internet, the identification, retrieval, and delivery of information in a virtual environment is described as a "URL-addressable resource that performs functions and provides answers". Web services are described as an "encapsulation of existing software functionality in a common form that allows the services it performs to be visible and accessible to other software applications". The single Web services-based application can request services from other Web services, and can expect to receive the results or responses from those requests in an expected form.

One advantage of Web services technology is its ability to interoperate in a loosely coupled manner, an 'ask and wait' approach. The user can request a certain type of service across the network, and wait for responses. Web services can also be found and used by other applications, agents, and clients on the Internet. In a digital geospatial data retrieval system, a Web service can be published inside or outside the host's firewall by providing a document describing its operation and function.

Using the Web services definition language (WSDL) markup language, the core of the document may illustrate a service when interpreted on a national grid reference responds with relevant coordinates on the host's mapping system. The document then described how the service is prompted and what the executables are. The document can also be published to a node, a clearinghouse, or other Internet site using the Universal Discovery, Description, and Integration (UDDI) registry.

Parson also notes that communication between Web services pass "XML messages wrapped in an interoperable framework to allow the messages to cross different networks, use different application architectures and systems". The widespread use of digital geospatial data by a number of different individuals and agencies in both the public and private sectors will continue to create large amounts of archived data. To make such data sets searchable across the environment of the Internet, librarians must be willing to take a varied approach in determining the appropriate metadata scheme to enable effective mining across the World Wide Web. A significant factor in the development of Web

GIS services and in online services in digital libraries has been the National Spatial Data Infrastructure initiative by the Federal Geographic Data Committee.

CO-USAGE OF DOCUMENTS IN A LARGE DIGITAL LIBRARY

Creating relationships between similar documents is an activity that has a long distinguished history in Information Retrieval. In his textbook on the subject Korfhage (1997) writes "Probably the single key concept behind information storage and retrieval is document similarity". A practical motivation for the search for similarity is to improve information retrieval. When users have found one document they can be directed to similar documents that may be worth their attention.

A more theoretical motivation is the discovery of patterns of thought within a body of knowledge that is dispersed across a collection of documents. There are, of course, many ways in which similarity between documents can be assessed. One way is to use the judgement of an expert.

This is typically done by classifying documents according to a subject classification. This is a tried and trusted method. However, it requires human expertise and labour. These do not come cheap these days.

Therefore many collections have no classification data. Within the collection of documents that we study in this paper, three in four documents do not have a subject classification. Other classic measures of relationship between academic papers are the strengths of co-citation and bibliographic coupling. Such an analysis presumes that a citation index for the papers is available. Producing one manually is even more expensive than subject classification.

It is possible to use recently available software for autonomous citation indexing. Barrueco Cruz and Krichel report on on recent effort s using the same digital library that we study here. In this paper, we introduce a completely new concept of similarity that is user-centered.

We start with the idea that two documents are similar if they respond to the same information need. Thus roughly speaking we can think of two document as similar, if many users will withdraw the papers together while they are working on the system. Provided that we have a digital library with a long log of usage, we can find which papers have frequently been used together. This is what we will refer to as "co-usage" in the following. We are not aware of a study that has developed and tested this concept within a digital library context.

We are, of course, aware that commercial systems use a related concept. Amazon.com, for example, suggests to a customer who is considering to purchase an item x that other people who bought x also bought item y. But since users are anonymous in our digital library, within the scope of our collection, the evidence on common usage is more difficult to gather.

MEASURING CO-USAGE

Our dataset comes from logs of the usage of the RePEc digital library. We have built this library over many years. RePEc is the largest free distributed academic digital library in the world. It is a pioneering effort in three respects.

First, RePEc pioneered the business model of the Open Archives Initiative distinction between data providers and service providers. RePEc has grown over 200 archives that are used in 10 different user services.

Second, RePEc is more than a collection of data about documents. RePEc offers a comprehensive picture of academic output by describing collection of documents, persons that are involved as authors of documents or editors of collections, and the institutions to which they belong in a relational database scheme.

Third, RePEc is essentially volunteer driven and has no owner. It is a public good much like the Internet. The data that we examine comes from the WoPEc user service. This service, founded in 1993 is available on the web at three locations since 1994.

These are Hitotsubashi University in Tokyo, Japan, Manchester Computing in the UK, and Washington University in St. Louis in the USA. The web site has static pages for each paper. In addition, there are a number of pages that link different papers together.

There are pages that list papers that have been issued within same series, and there are pages that group papers with the same subject classification. The log data also contains indication about what searches users have been making. However, as far as we are concerned, only the access to the description of the individual papers is relevant.

To begin with, recall that WoPEc is a non-commercial service. WoPEc does not enter into a contractual arrangement with a customer, with or without an exchange of money. Contractual arrangements with customers are expensive to arrange because they involve complicated negotiations, privacy issues etc. On the other hand contractual arrangement—even without exchange of money—generate customer data. The customer data itself has considerable value, see Shapiro and Varian for an illuminating discussion.

In the period that we examine, cookies have not been used. Therefore we need to wade through the log to find traces of usage by the same persons. All that the log offers is a trace to the Internet address (*i.e.* IP number) of the client machine, a file or action performed, and a time when this happened. Over recent years, the Internet is more and more accessed through personal computers rather than through multi-user systems.

However, we can not be completely sure that an IP number corresponds to the machine of an individual user, because there are caching sites. Therefore we must be watchful of IP addresses that appear particularly frequently. Let us for the moment make the assumption that the usage data from one single machine comes from one single user. We are then in the happy situation that we have identified the user.

However, to be able to claim that papers that are appearing together are joined together because they correspond to the same user need, we still have to assume that the information need of the user remains the same throughout the period of observation. This is problematic. Typically users will regard WoPEc as a reference source, and therefore naturally turn to it with different information needs. Therefore it is likely that the log contains material that corresponds to different information needs, even if they are expressed by the same user.

Therefore, we have chosen to think of users using the system within sessions. We typically think of a session as an academic, using a web browser on a desktop machine, going to the WoPEc site, make a few searches and look at a few results. Or we can think of it as a student, walking into a computer lab, uses a search engine, finds a page on the WoPEc service and navigates it for further data.

Technically, we define a session as a subset of the total log that comes from the same IP address within a certain time frame. In fact we assume that there must not be more than one hour between two consecutive log entries for them to qualify to be within the same session. In addition, we do not consider repeat access to the same paper as two different accesses to that paper. Such access is likely to occur mainly for technical reasons, such as that the user did not have time to read the article at the first discovery.

Under these restrictions it appears to be convenient to model sessions as sets of papers. We can now proceed to a formal definition of co-usage. Let D be the set documents in the library and S be the set of sessions. Each session s contains a subset of the set of documents, *i.e.* s Ì D. Introduce | · | as as notation for the number of elements in a set. Let there be two documents di and dj. Let u(di, dj) be the set of all sessions that contain both di and dj. For convenience of notation, write u(di) = u(di, di). Then we propose to call the co-usage coefficient c(di, dj) as follows,

$$c\left(d_1,d_j\right)=\frac{\left|u\left(d_i,d_j\right)\right|}{\left|u\left(d_i\right)\right|\left|u\left(d_j\right)\right|}.$$

The motivation for introducing the product in the denominator is to ensure that we do not have situations where one paper appears frequently with another by the sheer size of its own usage. It also leads c(di, dj) to gain the attractive properties that 0 <= c(di, dj) <= 1 and that c(di, di) = 1. It is clear that the measure that we propose here is an intuitive one. It is not a scientifically developed metric of the likelihood that, whatever size the session is, we will see the two papers appearing together in the session.

It is possible to evaluate that probability. However that calculation is not attempted here. It is left for future work. Even if we can theoretically ascertain how to calculate the probability, we can not in practice calculate it for all possible document couples, because of the amount of calculations that would have to be made within a large digital library as ours.

Results

We ran a programme to search for co-usage on a log for three years 1999–2001. There are 102551867 lines in the log. We discarded 24836221 requests for images, 401614 requests for CSS files, and 9315 contained another error. 3164598 requests contained a 404 error and were omitted. Most of them went to robots.txt. 3966837 distinct hosts accessed the system.

We exclude all accesses from hosts that accessed robots.txt. In addition, there are cache and proxy sites that we would like to remove as well. This is a more difficult terrain. The rule that we chose was to look at each day's log, and detect all hosts that issued more than 100 requests. In total, we detected 23068 such hosts, and discarded 17484961 lines because they were made by these hosts. This left us with 23413849 to analyzed. We detected 5251337 sessions.

We limited ourselves to sessions that had more than 3 accesses and less than 100, and that included at least one search. There were 69179 sessions that remained for analysis. We can not make the results available here, for obvious reasons of space. Therefore we have placed them at http://openlib.org/home/krichel/kumegawa/report.htm. We print the top couples that have the highest co-usage, up to a rounded coefficient of 50 per cent. The following results appear when we look through the data.

First, papers in the same series seem to be much more prone to co-usage than papers from different series. It is often papers by the same authors, over different periods of time, available in the same working paper series or journal that appeared to be co-used a lot. This observation suggests that the original split of the data in different series does not only provide an organizational layer to the data, but also a semantic one. Second, from reading through the related couples, it appears that a key concept that appears in the title immediately explains the co-usage. Thus, it should be possible to gain insights into key concepts that are of user interest by looking at the title data of papers that are co-used, and find the common words. This would be an interesting subject for further research.

This paper has introduced co-usage as a means to make document to document relationships. The concept of co-usage has been found to lead to excellent empirical results. Our results suggests that the concept of co-usage is a valid and interesting one.

Any remaining problems that we are experiencing to make it work in practice are consequences of poor measurement of usage, rather than flaws in the underlying theoretical reasoning. Just in the case of co-citation and bibliographic coupling, there will be a debate on how useful co-usage analysis really is. We have opened that debate with this paper.

There are two further consequences from this paper. In the short run, we intend to incorporate co-usage similarity into future developments of WoPEc, to build links from the description of one paper to the description of another as suggested by co-usage analysis.

In the longer run, we believe that our work can be seen as simple, but pioneering step towards information retrieval systems that are learning. Instead of having a system that has a fixed procedure that is applicable whatever the query an the collection, we can imagine that future information systems will learn from past user behaviour to better serve the present user. Co-usage appears as a key concept to move things forward in that direction.

COLLECTION OF A LIBRARY FOR PROVIDING WEB BASED SERVICES

COLLECTION OF A LIBRARY FOR PROVIDING WEB BASED SERVICES

Electronic journals form a large part of the collection of a library for providing web based services. Today many journals are available electronically - some are full text and some contain only bibliographic information with abstract. Major advantage of electronic journals is that they are constantly updated and easy to access but disadvantage is that breaching of copyright law is very easy. They are available as bitmaps, PostScript, PDF, ASCII, SGML and HTML. Library services may be delivering to users on CDRom, through e-mail or through web. Some international societies and associations have developed their own digital libraries through which users can get access to all their publications. Services are available to the members of society or associations through subscription.

DATABASES OF WEB PAGE

Search Engines are huge databases of web page files that have been assembled automatically by machines where as the subject directories are human-compiled and maintained. Search engine indexes every page of a Web site and subject directories linked only homepages. Search Engine is the popular term for an information retrieval (IR) system.

A search engine is computer software that searches a collection of electronic materials to retrieve citations, documents, or information that matches or answers a user's query. The retrieved materials may be text documents, facts that have been extracted from text, images, or sounds. A query is a question phrased so that it can be interpreted properly by search engine. Depending on the type of software, it may be a collection of commands, a statement in either full or partial sentences, one or more keywords, or in the case of Non-text searching, an image or sequence of sounds to be matched.

SEARCH ENGINES IN SUBJECT DIRECTORIES

Subject directories differ from search engines in that search engines are populated by robots that finds and index sites whereas humans making editorial decisions that populate subject directories. Subject directories are basically index home pages of sites and can be classified as general, academic, commercial or portal. Among the well known subject directories are the Argus Clearinghouse and Yahoo. Strengths include relevance, effectiveness and relative high quality of content. Weaknesses are that they lack depth in their coverage of the subjects.

WEB-BASED USER EDUCATION

Web guides and teaching tools are found everywhere on the Web because they are easily updated, accessed, and printed on demand. The web-based user education provides a high degree of interactivity and flexibility to the users. The library web sites can use web-based user education for imparting training to users in teaching the basic library skills along with glossary of library terms, using Library OPAC, locating books, magazines, biographical data and other library materials, understanding how to navigate the libraries Web site and how to select the most relevant database, instructions for searching CD ROM and guidance in locating web-based databases and other electronic resources and instructions on subject searching training, using Boolean operators and searching internet resources through search engines.

WEB FORMS

Library web sites have some web forms for suggestions and comments on the Library Services. Different types of Web Forms are available on web that may be an Indent form for acquiring some publications, interlibrary loan request form for document delivery, Ask-a-Librarian forms, on line reservation form or user survey form, etc.

VIRTUAL LIBRARY TOURS

Web sites of libraries provides virtual library guide to the physical facilities including collections, services and infrastructure available in the library. The combination of library maps and floor plans, library departments and photographic views are used for the tour. Virtual library tours are also using new technologies such as QuickTime movies etc and are beginning to replace image maps on main campus Web sites.

ASK-A-LIBRARIAN

Ask-A-Librarian services are Internet-based question and answer service that connects users with individuals who possess specialised subject knowledge and skill in conducting precision searches. Most 'Ask-a-Librarians' services have a web-based question submission form or an e-mail address or both. Users are invited to submit their queries by using web forms or through e-mail. Once a query is read by a service, it is assigned to an individual expert for answering. An expert responds to the query with factual information and or a list of information resources.

The response is either sent to the user's e-mail account or is posted on the web so that the user can access it after a certain period of time. Many services have informative web sites that include archives of questions and answers and a set of FAQs. Users are usually encouraged to browse archives and FAQs before submitting a question in case sufficient information already exists.

REAL TIME SERVICES

A new and exciting method of digital reference service that libraries are attempting to provide more and more now is live reference. These are real-time, interactive reference services in which the users can talk to a real, live reference librarian at any time, from anywhere in the world.

User and librarian can interact using chat technologies, and unlike with e-mail reference the librarian can perform a reference interview of sorts by asking the users to elaborate or clarify if needed before proceeding to answer the question. The librarian can perform Internet searches and push Web sites onto the user's browser, and can receive immediate feedback from the users as to whether their question have been answered to satisfaction.

BULLETIN BOARDS

A bulletin board is an electronic communications forum that hosts posted messages and articles connected to a common subject or theme or interest. It allows users to call in and either leaves or retrieves messages. The messages may be directed to all users of the bulletin board or only to particular users. But all messages can be read by all users. Several libraries are using bulletin boards for their web-based library services. The bulletin board system is also used as an interactive interface to invite suggestions on activities and services of a library. It can also be used as an interface to distribute library services.

WEB SITE FOR A LIBRARY

The roles of libraries and the Internet in providing information in the 21st century are firmly intertwined. It behooves any librarian working today to understand not only how to find things on the World Wide Web, but to have a basic understanding of how it works. Librarians will be called on to become information architects, to be able to create Web sites with clearly stated goals, that are aesthetically pleasing and filled with relevent content and functionality.

As more and more libraries set up comprehensive Web sites, there becomes an increasing demand for librarians who have an understanding of HTML, as well as other types of Internet programming skills such as javascript, SQL, CGI, ASP, and Cold Fusion.

Librarians should know the principles of setting up an efficient information resource. As the Internet becomes more interactive, there is a push Towards making databases accessible online; the best example of this is the library card catalog. Other interactive options include e-mail and bulletin board service, and moving from CD-ROMs to online subscriptions. A library Web site is not merely establishing a presence on the Internet.

It can be a virtual addition to the existing library structure, reaching out to patrons around the clock and providing valuable information resources. Additionally, a library's Web site is an important source of information about the library. The library's Internet policies, special programming, and new materials can all be made viewable at any time from the Web site. Libraries, too, should be designing their own Web sites that serve as portals to interesting sites that have been reviewed and annotated by professional librarians. Librarians will continue to play an important role as information professionals in the Information Age, well into the 21st century.

COMMUNITY INTERNET INITIATIVES

The combination of municipal and commercial computer networks in some large metropolitan areas has led to the creation of community information networks. Community information networks are often built around existing social networks involved in Neighbourhood activities like employment and economic opportunity centers, youth and family centers, health, education, and affordable housing initiatives.

One such project in Chicago, the Chicago Area Northside Neighbourhood Online Network, is an organisation that offers training and Internet access to community based entities throughout the city. Building on existing human networks in the communities, the project has successfully trained residents and staff of over 60 community organisations, creating a unique multiracial, mixed-economic, and mixed-gender pool of community users.

The NeighbourTech Programme works with Chicago's inner city Neighbourhoods. NeighbourTech uses a variety of methods to draw in Neighbourhood residents, small businesses, and Non-profit organisations located in disadvantaged Neighbourhoods. The Erie Neighbourhood House, a Non-profit, multiservice agency in Erie, New York, operates the Erie Technology Center. The mission of the Technology Center is to provide computer and information literacy to West Town residents with limited English proficiency and low educational attainment. By working with other educational Programmes in the area, the Technology Center integrates traditional teaching/learning methods with current technology applications for students ranging from prekindergarten to senior citisens. Grants from federal agencies, such as the U.S., Department of Commerce, are also used to build community information networks outside of urban areas in rural locations.

The ItascaNet network, established in the town of Grand Rapids in north central Minnesota, is mostly rural, with a shrinking population base. Local community leaders used the grant funds to build an online network to increase the community's access to, and use of, the national information infrastructure, reduce disparities in access levels among community residents, increase information available to community members, and facilitate the sharing of data and information among partner organisations. The ItaskaNet network involved five partner agencies that oversaw the purchasing of a server and cable for connections between the agencies.

A significant member agency of the partnership was the public library. Internet-linked computers were made available to students in the public schools and to citisens in the public library, and free computer training classes were offered to the community. Researchers have identified libraries as an important cultural resource in contemporary American society. They can be an important node in the contemporary computer network and provide computer access and information service to the user community.

ROLE OF LIBRARIES IN THE INFORMATION ECONOMY

The emergence of the new information economy comprised of computer networks that link users to one another or to larger organisations is creating a class of singular information users. To aid users in participating in the information economy, libraries designed a virtual presence to deliver information services, usually in the form of a 'digital library.' Digital libraries can offer a more varied informational experience to the community of online users. Libraries, with their traditional strengths of information collection, description, organisation, and dissemination, can provide a more holistic learning experience for these new user communities.

In commenting on the structure and environment of digital libraries, the DLF (Digital Library Federation) has offered the following definition: "Digital libraries are organisations that provide the resources, including specialised staff, to select, structure, offer intellectual access to, distribute, interpret, preserve the integrity of, and ensure the persistence over time of collections of digital works".

In elaborating on the concept, researchers define six major characteristics that should be integral to digital libraries:

- *Collection of data objects*: A library holds together a collection of data objects, items and resources. The items can be books, journals and documents, multimedia objects. The library objects can be available locally, or indirectly, by using a network to access them.

- *Collection of metadata structures*: A library contains a collection of metadata structures, such as catalogs, guides, dictionaries, thesauri, indices, summaries, annotations, glossaries, and so forth.
- *Collection of services*: A library provides a collection of services, such as various access methods for as well as consultation for. different users; management of the library (purchase, shelf arranging, computerisation, communication); logging/statistics and performance measurement evaluation (PME); selective dissemination of information (SDI) or push mode, as it is called on the Internet.
- *Domain focus*: A library has a domain focus and its collection has a domain focus; purpose. For example, art, science, or literature. Also, it is usually created to serve a community of users and therefore, is finely grained.
- *Quality control*: A library uses quality control in the sense that all its material is verified and consistent with the profile of the library. The material is filtered and its metadata is usually enriched.
- *Preservation*: The purpose of preservation is to ensure protection of information of enduring value for access by present and future generations. Preservation includes the allocation of resources for preservation, preventive measures, and remedial measures to restore the usability of selected materials.

As librarians compile digital collections of materials, the networked environment of which they are a part offers access to many more information resources. In describing libraries and the new online environment in which they operate, libraries are placing lesser emphasis on the materials they collect and house, and more emphasis on the kind of material they are able to obtain in response to user requests. The trend includes libraries forming partnerships to deliver material from elsewhere in time to answer a user's information needs. The shift to on-demand delivery of material from elsewhere is an effect of recent growth in digital networking in an environment where standards for description were established and refined over the past 35 years. Librarians are also moving primarily away from being caretakers of physical collections to people who identify resources that exist. The earlier survey of the information economy has illustrated a variety of information sector industries and organisations that utilise information, such as geographic data, in their varied production and distribution functions.

The flexibility of spatially referenced information, and its applicability to a variety of research techniques and spatially referenced applications, create a powerful tool in which librarians can raise the profile of their institution's involvement in the information sector.

THE LIBRARY VERSUS THE WEB

Net Gen students clearly perceive the open space of the World Wide Web as their information universe. This is in opposition to the worldview of librarians and many faculty, who perceive the library as the locus of information relevant to academic work. Students usually approach their research without regard to the library's structure or the way that the library segments different resources into different areas of its Web site. Library Web sites often reflect an organisational view of the library (for example, how to access the reference department or online catalog); they do not do a particularly good job of aggregating content on a particular subject area. Students usually prefer the global searching of Google to more sophisticated but more time-consuming searching provided by the library, where students must make separate searches of the online catalog and every database of potential interest, after first identifying which databases might be relevant. In addition, not all searches of library catalogs or databases yield full-text materials, and Net Gen students want not just speedy answers, but full gratification of their information requests on the spot, if possible.

Recent surveys exploring college student use of the Web versus the library confirm the commonly held perception of faculty and librarians that students' pri-mary sources of information for coursework are resources found on the Web and that most students use a search engine such as Google as their first point of entry to information rather than searching the library Web site or catalog. Several campus studies also examined where students gather information for a paper or an assignment. One study at Colorado State University yielded information that 58 per cent of freshmen used Google or a comparable search engine first, while only 23 per cent started with a database or index. The world of information is large and complex.

There are no easy answers to providing simplified searching to the wealth of electronic information resources produced by a wide range of publishers using different structures and vocabu-laries. Students may perceive that librarians have developed systems that are complex and make sense to information professionals but are too difficult to use without being an expert. However, as new generations of information products are developed, producers and system developers should try to address the information seeking habits of Net Gen students.

Libraries and the global service provider OCLC are working with Google so that information from peer-reviewed journals, books, theses, and other academic resources can be accessed through the Google Scholar search service. This is a step in the right direction, taking library resources to where students want to find them.

Libraries also need to integrate more multimedia resources into their searchable content; this type of digital content is becoming increasingly important to Net Gen students, who may wish to study an audio recording of political speeches and incorporate segments into a term project as well as access books and journals on the topic. However, libraries typically incorporate information objects into their catalogs only when those resources are owned or licensed by the library. Is this still a relevant strategy in a world of global access to information via the Internet?

LOCATING QUALITY DIGITAL INFORMATION

Providing mechanisms for information seekers from academe to locate quality information resources in a particular subject area is also a challenge for libraries—a very important one. Many academic libraries provide "library guides" or pathfinders to quality information resources, available through the library Web site, but typically they are not heavily used. A limited number of subject disciplines have developed coordinated Web guides to information resources; a notable example is AgNIC, serving the field of agriculture. Some libraries are developing mechanisms to link subject pathfinders into course management systems for every course at the institution.

This useful strategy brings the information to the place where students will be actively engaged in academic work. Librarians at the University of Rochester looked for new ways to bring quality subject resources to the attention of students. They recognised that "undergraduate students' mental model is one focused on courses and coursework, rather than disciplines." Therefore, they developed a mechanism to incorporate pathfinders into every course at the institution using the course management system. Both students and faculty believe that the library is doing a poor job with helping them discern which Web resources are suitable for academic work. Libraries are addressing this concern by developing portals to catalogs, licensed databases, and Web sites that would meet the kinds of criteria used in building academic library collections and by working with such projects as Google Scholar.

LIBRARIES AND INFORMATION SERVICE

Librarians often take great pride in the personalised information services they offer to their constituencies and the classes they teach to incorporate information literacy into the academic curriculum. While many of today's Net Gen students have grown up with technology, they do not necessarily have the requisite knowledge or skills to use technology and digital information in ways appropriate to the academy. Librarians should persist in their efforts to find ways to help students learn about digital information, including important policy issues in this arena, such as privacy and intellectual property. They should consider updating some of their methods for teaching students, incorporating gaming technology, or developing more visually oriented instruction aids, for example. One-on-one services offered electronically should be tailored to students' characteristics, such as their propensity to work late hours and use a variety of technologies, including laptops and cell phones.

Designing Web pages that are responsive to Net Gen students' style would also help guide students to appropriate content or help them when they have problems with searches. A study of high school students' Web searching revealed that students relied heavily on information displayed in graphic form on Web pages and often relied on graphics and visual cues to interpret the relevance of such pages. Libraries and information service providers generally do not design their resources with such criteria in mind. Incorporating students on design teams and giving them the go-ahead to re-envision the way the library displays its resources would be a useful method of developing information that resonates better with Net Gen students.

To summarise, Net Gen access services will:

- Continue to integrate library information into Google or other popular access mechanisms
- Offer simplified and graphic ways for students to approach subject searches
- Integrate subject guides or pathfinders into CMS or other locations conducive to use
- Integrate searching of "open" Web resources and materials owned or licensed by the library

FLUENCY WITH TECHNOLOGY AND INFORMATION LITERACY

Are Net Gen students already so technology literate and information savvy that they have no need for instruction or personal assistance in using technology and library and information resources? We know that Net Gen students come to campus having played hours of video games, having spent much of their spare time surfing the Net and instant messaging their friends, and having used multiple electronic devices simultaneously. On the other hand, we hear complaints from faculty that students use inappropriate sources from the Web to support their ideas in term papers instead of peer-reviewed academic resources; that they submit multimedia projects that are superficial and full of glitz, not substance —and that they no longer read, period.

When students graduate, their faculty in graduate degree programmes and their employers expect that they will have a facility with technology and with digital information that the older generations do not have. New office recruits are often hired because of their Internet skill and are given projects that exploit their technology and information skills, developed during their college years.

In addition, today's college graduates live in a world where it is important to understand key information policy issues. Intellectual property, privacy, and First Amendment issues are fundamental to operating as an informed citisen in today's information society and directly affect the work of individuals who create, as well as use, networked information. While Net Gen students generally can multitask, learn systems without consulting manuals, and surf the Web, they lack technology and information skills appropriate for academic work. Higher education institutions do not integrate or package technology and digital information skills instruction into the mainstream curriculum. A National Academies report described a model set of skills for "fluency in information technology," which incorporates both information technology and literacy skills. The report's authors divided skills into three categories: foundational concepts, contemporary skills, and intellectual capabilities. They recommended that each university's subject area curriculum develop ways to incorporate instruction in these topics; however, they lamented that this is not currently the case.

The Association of College and Research Libraries (ACRL), a division of the American Library Association, has also developed guidelines for information literacy, but they have not been widely implemented by universities. Technology and information literacy are generally perceived to be "library" or "IT" problems, not overall curricular issues.

At Southwestern University, a team of IT professionals, librarians, and faculty developed a student survey based on both the National Academies' fluency with information technology principles and the ACRL Information Literacy Competency Standards. Their findings revealed that while students rated themselves highly in their ability to find information on the Internet, they recognised that they floundered when they attempted to find materials appropriate for their research and wasted much time in the process.

The students also expressed a desire for more technology applications to be integrated into their courses. This model is being explored through a Mellon Foundation–sponsored project at the University of California, Berkeley, where selected faculty and librarians are working in partnership to incorporate information literacy skills and undergraduate research into large-enrollment courses with the goal of assisting students in developing skills that will serve them throughout their coursework at the institution.

DELIVERING SERVICE WITH STYLE IN INFORMATION AND TECHNOLOGY LITERACY

Information and technology literacy represents a content area in Net Gen students' education that has not been fully addressed. Separate but related is the "style" issue of how best to deliver this educational content and provide information and technology services to Net Gen students. Net Gen students work in information environments, and a very important one in college is the course management system.

Libraries should develop tutorials, exercises, and guides that can readily be embedded in course materials within course management systems, and some are already doing this. They can develop games to teach these skills; TILT, the Texas Information Literacy Tutorial developed by The University of Texas at Austin libraries, is an early example. Simulations such as Environmental Detectives can incorporate information-seeking skills into the game, reinforcing Net Gen students' interest in figuring things out and working in groups.

Libraries should explore blogs as a mechanism for students to exchange information on valuable information resources they find for particular course assignments.

Blogs sponsored by the library might be particularly effective for graduate students beginning their dissertations and needing advice from peers and information professionals on locating materials for their literature reviews. An emerging area of literacy is the need for students to increase their fluency with representing their knowledge in the digital, multimedia world. George Lucas stated that students need to learn a "language of screens" in order to be effective communicators today.

The Visible Knowledge Project, in which university faculty are working with multimedia content and developing assessment mechanisms to measure the effectiveness of their instruction, is also working on guidelines to assist faculty in evaluating student multimedia projects.

While Net Gen students often prefer creating a multimedia project rather than a term paper that is entirely text, they need assistance in understanding how to represent their knowledge in a form that is appropriate for academic work, just as they need to learn to write in a way that meets the standards of the academy.

LIBRARY PROFESSION TO SUCH A GREAT EXTENT AS INTERNET

Perhaps no other recent innovation has impacted the library profession to such a great extent as Internet. Not only is our world becoming an interconnected global community, but this early use of the Internet has changed the fundamental roles, paradigms, and organisational culture of libraries and librarians as well, which created profound impact on LandIS by offering new modes of information delivery and a vast information source. There is a continuing evolution of the roles and functions of libraries and librarians, which appears to parallel the growth of acceptance and use of the Internet by library professionals.

The innovative use of Internet technologies enable us to reach both local and distant users much more easily and effectively than hither to possible. Technologies such as e-mail and Web provides tremendous opportunities for library and Inf. Scientists to deliver the information to the desktops of our users. Web offers significant advantage by integrating different library and information services with a common user interface offered by Web browsers. Realising the potentials, many libraries are rushing to getting the connectivity. The following listing will give an idea of which various functions of libraries may take advantage from Internet and Web technologies.

Acquisition:

- Correspondance with Book seller and Publisher.
- Reminders, Price verification

- Biblographic details and downloading of bib. records etc
- Ordering, billing
- Bookshops are on-line, *e.g.*, amazon.com

Classification:

- Network resources
  - Available on the net
  - Subscribed or free or trial basis
- Dewey Online
- Maths. Classification System
- Engineering Electronics Lib. Classification
- Search engines – such as yahoo use DDC.

Cataloguing:

- Cataloguing of network resources
- Online Catalogues
- WorldCat (OCLC)
- WebOPAC – web sites
- MARC adds 856 field
- OCLC Scorpian project- MARC and AACR2
- Metadata standards - Dublin core

Collection Development:

- Ownership vs Access
- Subscribe in print or e-form
- Subscribe in print as well as in e-form
- Pay-per-use
- Consortial approach

Circulation:

- Remote login
- Status check
- OPAC access
- Reminder to users
- User requests
- Direct borrowing
- ILL

Resource Sharing:

- Union Catalogue
  - Access, adding, downloading
- Access to databases over networks
  - Ohionet, ILLINET, WLN, OCLC, BID (UK)
  - Full text journals access, etc.

Services:

- ILL
- Document Delivery Service, *e.g.*, Ariel

- Reference/ Inf. Services
- CAS
  - Recent additions,
  - Contents pages
- SDI
  - From library collection
  - Databases
  - Internet Sources
- OPAC
- Database access
  - Bibliographical
  - Full text
  - Many vendors and organisations are moving to Internet (web) access

Subject Lists/ Gateways:

- Internet Public Library
- *EEVL* – Engineering
- *SOSIG* – Social Science
- *OMNI*- Medical
- *ADAM* – Arts, Design, etc.

User Education:

- Through E-mail
- Through Web
- Setting Intranet.

Preservation and Storage:

- The Internet is also a medium for the preservation and storage of information. In past, libraries were seen as the main storage facility of information. As society becomes increasingly more digital and more information resides on the Internet, the focus on storage and preservation is shifting. For example, some academic libraries are now faced with the problem of whether or not to purchase serials that can be just as easily accessed on-line. Preservation of these same media also becomes an issue of economics, not the 'just in case' preservation ideology of the past paradigm. Co joined to the function preservation is the destruction of information. Because the Internet can be seen as a medium for preserving information, the process of destruction of information also is affected. As more and more information is created and stored on the Internet, the capacity to store this information is also decreasing.

RESOURCES AVAILABLE ON THE INTERNET

The advent of IT and other communication technologies changed all means of information services and sources. The Internet has given the world numerous easy-to-use and inexpensive research tools. Internet is changing the way we view information sources.

Information bundled in World Wide Web in the form of structured and Non-structured sources create huge problem for professionals who are dealing with information. The shift in publication process takes place as individuals, institutions, publishers, professional associations, business houses and many others are publishing information on Internet.

Electronic publishing is considered as the speedy, accurate and effective way of communication among academia and research community, and becoming a favorite idea among information professionals to experiment with. The library and information professionals have a vital role to play in organising the information and bridging the *information gap*. Internet has become a part of library environment today. Internet for reference work in the library is gaining popularity. It can be successfully utilised for providing short-range and long-range reference service because various primary and secondary sources of information are available online from many sites. As information professionals, we can arrange the sources on net as we come across, in a structured manner.

These can be;

- E-journals
- E-books
- Standards
- E-TDs
- Preprints
- Library catalogue
- Bibliographical Tools
- Share wares
- Old books
- News papers
- Dictionaries
- Magazines
- Encyclopaedias
- Databases
- Directories
- Films
- Maps
- Technical reports
- Audio/Video
- Proceedings
- Patents
- Web sites of Companies, Institutions, Organisations, Associations, etc.

EVALUATION OF INFORMATION SOURCES

When we access or retrieve something on the Web, we need to decide whether the information is useful, reliable, and appropriate for our purposes. The resources identified can also occasionally contain inaccurate and misleading information. The nature of the Internet and WWW makes it easy for almost anyone to create and disperse information.

People also have considerable freedom and variety in the formats with which they publish information on the Web. We have to double -check the facts before giving it to users. Here we need to use some general guidelines or criteria when evaluating information sources. We should ask the following questions about whatever information we found:

- Who is the author or Institution?
- How current is the information?
- Who is the audience?
- Is the content accurate and objective?
- What is the purpose of the information?
- How easy to use it?

More than that, we can consider coverage, presentation and arrangement of information in the sources to find out its value. The tremendous increase in online information sources made the searching difficult, where organising skill is required for library and information professionals. Libraries role is also enhanced where they will have to adapt to changing environment. The scope is only limited to the imagination of information professionals, where they have to acquire thorough understanding of changes in their profession. Willingness to take up the challenges in information resource management is the need of the hour for us.

RETRIEVAL OF INFORMATION

Directories, Search Engines, Meta Search Engines and Information Gateways/Virtual Libraries etc are widely used to retrieve relevant information from Internet.

Search Engines:

- They are also called Meta crawlers or multi search engines
- Do not crawl the web compiling their own searchable databases
- Search the databases of multiple sets of individual search engines simultaneously from a single site and using the same interface.
- They function as intermediary
- Present the results of their searches in two ways
  - Single lists
  - Multiple Lists.
- There are three types of meta search engines,

  - Listing
  - Options
  - Automatic
- While you query, options less
- Cover all major search engines
- Do not return all results retrieved, they take only top ones from the list.
- They are very fast.
- Use them when you are in a hurry
- Helpful when you want to have quick overview on a subject and/or unique term.
- Use them when you are,
  - Conducting a relatively simple search
  - Not having any luck pulling up documents in your search.

MARKETING OF LIBRARY SERVICES

In recent years, libraries of all types from all countries have found it necessary to compete for both money and clients as major changes have occurred. The Internet brings a whole new dimension of competition that public, academic, and special libraries are facing daily. Whereas budget problems have been around for some time, the recent competition from the Internet can translate into fewer users, despite the fact that the Internet is also a crucial tool used by librarians for research and marketing. Because of all of these existing challenges and intensifying changes at least a handful of libraries have turned to 'tried and true' business models for improved planning and development, and that they are employing marketing plans as one method for moving forward. As time goes on, libraries must think about marketing of their services and resources to achieve goals. It is important to clarify what marketing means in a library environment.

Marketing is not so much about 'selling' information products to researchers, as it is more about spreading the word about potentially useful new tools. It is also about keeping users informed about library activities and involving them in collection development. It is more about integrating new research tools into existing, effective research processes, and in some way enhancing researchers' work, rather than selling the tool to users as an end in itself. As librarians market new tools, they should know how the tools may offer clarity, and not simply contribute to noise for the users. Effective marketing can only occur when librarians understand, at least in a broad sense, what the scientists, professors, and graduate students are already doing to keep informed, and what their research projects are about.

AUTOMATING THE MAINTENANCE OF GREENSTONE COLLECTIONS

Many applications generate multimedia documents, such as images and video, on a daily basis. For example, many municipalities have a photo-radar system to catch vehicles that violate traffic laws such as speeding or ignoring red lights.

Many pictures of vehicle licence plates are created every day. If these images are organised into a digital library, the collection would need to be updated regularly to incorporate new images. Another example is a traveller who wants to update a digital library of trip photos with new pictures of her travels while travelling around the world. When documents and metadata are added to a digital library collection on a regular basis, such as hourly, daily or weekly, an automated and scheduled approach to collection maintenance is preferred over having to manually update the collection. In addition, an automated approach should be simple to use, therefore making time available for other important tasks. Digital library software such as Greenstone, DSpace and Fedora require that items be added manually to the collection.

In Fedora, data is retrieved at the time of viewing. However, a location needs to be manually configured. Further, although Fedora and DSpace do provide Application Programming Interfaces (APIs) to extend functionality, programming knowledge is required for using an API and for setting up tools based on it. We present a solution for automating and scheduling updates that occur on a regular basis. Our solution is implemented in the Greenstone digital library software system and comes in two parts. The first part of our approach is a command-line scheduling module. The Scheduler both automates the construction and modification of a collection, and schedules the construction to occur at specific intervals, such as hourly, daily or weekly.

In addition, the owner of a collection can update the collection manually, without affecting the scheduled collection builds. Further, the Scheduler interacts with the existing task scheduling mechanism on the host system, which keeps the Scheduler minimal, yet powerful. The second part of our approach involves incorporating the Scheduler into the Greenstone Librarian Interface (GLI). This will allow users who are more comfortable with managing collections through a graphical user interface to take advantage of the functionality of the Scheduler. In addition, this allows us to handle certain tasks associated with scheduling in a uniform and flexible manner.

GREENSTONE

Greenstone is a suite of software for creating digital library collections and making them available locally or via the Internet. A collection can contain documents of different formats, including images, PostScript and PDF files, audio, formatted and unformatted text, and many others. A collection built using Greenstone can be customised in many ways. For example, a collection owner can customise the types of documents that can appear in the collection, the appearance of the interface to the collection, and how the collection will be accessed by other users. In addition, Greenstone is extensible.

For example, functionality to support other data formats that are not provided with Greenstone can easily be added to a collection. There are two types of accessors in Greenstone. The first is an index that provides support for searching. The second is a classifier that provides support for browsing. A collection can be configured for browsing by any metadata that is specified by the collection owner or extracted by Greenstone. Furthermore, a collection can be configured for searching on the same metadata fields, as well as full text.

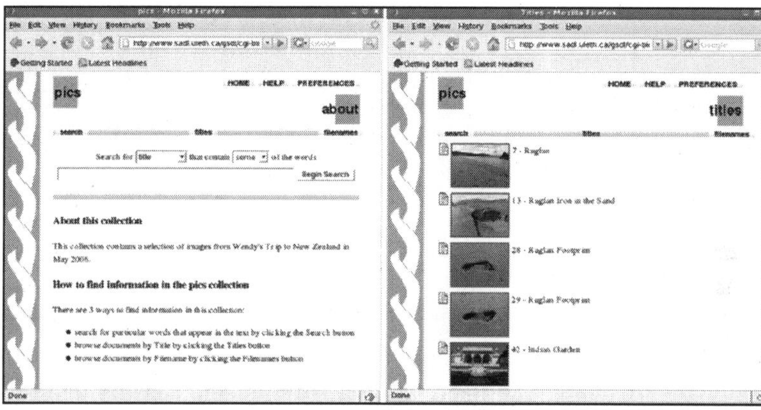

Fig. Pics Collection in Greenstone *(a)* Front Page of Pics Collection *(b)* Viewing Pics Collection

Figures *(a)* and *(b)* depict a Greenstone collection called pics. The pics collection is configured to accept images only. Figure *(a)* shows the front page of the collection, which provides general information on the collection. In addition, the collection is configured for both browsing and searching by either Title or Filename. Figure *(b)* shows a display of some images from the pics collection. In this view, the collection is being browsed by Title. The user can click on any image to obtain a larger image for viewing.

Figure depicts the internal representation of a Greenstone collection. Here, the four main directories of a collection—import, archives, building, and index—are displayed.

The purpose of each is described below:

- *Import:* The import directory contains all documents that are to be added to the collection. If desired, the documents can be organised in a hierarchical directory structure within the import directory.
- *Archives:* The archives directory stores all documents that have been processed from the import folder and added to the collection. All documents in the archives directory are represented in a canonical XML format.
- *Building:* The building directory is a working directory for creating all indices and classifiers that are specified for the collection.

- *Index:* The index directory contains the indices and classifiers after they are created.

A Greenstone collection is created or modified by the following four steps: document addition, document importation, accessor creation, and collection activation.

Each step is described in detail below:

- *Document Addition:* New documents that will be added to a collection are placed into the import directory for the collection.
- *Document Importation:* Each document in the import directory is processed for inclusion by creating a canonical XML representation for it. This is accomplished by specifying an import command. Different importing options can be specified by the user. For example, documents in the import directory can be added to an existing collection by using a–keepold option. Alternatively, all documents in the import directory—new and existing—can be used to create a new instance of the collection by using a-removeold option. All imported documents are placed in the archives directory.
- *Accessor Creation:* After the documents in the import directory are added to the collection, indices and classifiers are set up by processing the canonical XML representations of all documents. This is accomplished by specifying a build command. New indices and classifiers can be built by specifying a–removeold option. Alternatively, existing indices and classifiers can be modified by specifying a-keepold or-incremental option. The resulting indices and classifiers are located in the building directory.
- *Collection Activation:* Finally, the collection is activated by moving the indices and classifiers from the building directory to the index directory. The collection is now viewable online.

The command for each step can be executed in a terminal or command window, or via the Greenstone Librarian Interface.

GREENSTONE LIBRARIAN INTERFACE

The Greenstone Librarian Interface (GLI) is a graphical user interface that provides a user-friendly method to build and configure Greenstone collections. It incorporates the steps above. The only steps that are required by the user are to place documents to the import directory via the Gather panel, and to add the documents to the collection via the Create panel. In addition, the Librarian Interface allows a user to create new collections, select metadata sets, configure which document types to allow, and select import and build command options. Figure shows the Librarian Interface.

CRON

Cron is a programme for users to schedule tasks that will run automatically at a specified time. A task can be one command, or a script containing several commands that are executed in sequence. Initially, Cron was implemented for Unix and Linux platforms, with most systems running Vixie Cron. Mac OS X also runs Vixie Cron. In addition, versions of Cron now exist for Windows platforms, such as Pycron. We summarise the general ideas behind all implementations of Cron that are applicable to our work. Cron runs continuously in the background of the operating system. Every minute, Cron reads several task configuration files. Each such file is called a crontab file.

A crontab file contains a record for every task that is scheduled for execution. Cron locates and runs all tasks that are scheduled at the current time. The format of a crontab record is, where min, hr, dom, moy, and dow are the minute, hour, day of month, month of year and day of week, respectively, user is the username that the command will run under, and task is the command or script that is executed at the specified time.

A task can be scheduled to run hourly, daily, weekly, monthly, or yearly:

- *Hourly:* An hourly scheduled task executes every hour at a specified minute.
- *Daily:* A task that is scheduled daily executes at a specific hour, which is required, and a specific minute. If no minute is specified, execution will occur every minute during the specified hour.
- *Weekly:* A weekly scheduled task runs on a specified day, which is required, and at a specified hour and minute. If no hour is specified, execution will occur every hour during the specified day.
- *Monthly:* A monthly scheduled task runs on a specified day.
- *Yearly:* A yearly scheduled task runs on a specified month.

Any unspecified values are replaced with an asterisk in the crontab record. Systems that use Vixie Cron support two types of crontab files-system crontab and user crontab. The system crontab files are primarily for system administration and maintenance tasks. Also, even if all tasks have a specified low-level username, root privileges are required for modifying a system crontab file.

User crontab files, on the other hand, can be set up by any user on the system to execute tasks under their own username. Assuming the user has permission to execute the task, no root permissions are required. In addition, Pycron only supports user crontab files. Therefore, the Scheduler will employ a user crontab file.

```
30 * * * */ collect/pics/gsdl.pl
59 23 * * */usr/bin/cleanup.bash
00 6 * * 7/home/someuser/alarm
00 0 1 1 * echo 'Happy New Year!'
```

It contains 4 tasks that are scheduled for specific times. The first task,/ collect/pics/gsdl.pl, is scheduled to be run at 30 minutes past every hour.

The second task,/usr/bin/cleanup.bash, is scheduled for execution daily at 11:59pm. The third task, home/someuser/alarm, is scheduled every Sunday at 6:00am. Finally, the fourth task, which echoes 'Happy New Year!', is schedule for execution every January first at 12:00 AM.

THE SCHEDULER

We first present our design for the Scheduler command-line module in Greenstone. The Scheduler is written in Perl and runs on Linux, Windows and Mac OS X. It also utilises the Cron scheduling service for scheduling collection re-building.

We chose Perl because a Perl script can be executed across different platforms without the need to recompile. Similarly, we chose Cron because it is available for Linux and Mac OS X. Therefore, we can maintain the the crossplatform requirement of Greenstone.

The Scheduler requires the following parameters from the user as input:

- The collection to be rebuilt;
- The full import command that is required to import documents into the collection;
- The full build command required to construct the indices and classifiers for the collection; and
- A specification of either an hourly, daily, or weekly build.

For example, if the user wants the collection pics to be scheduled for construction on a daily basis, the parameters would look something like this:

- Schedule.pl pics 'import.pl–removeold pics'.
- 'Buildcol.pl–removeold pics' daily.

Where pics is the name of the collection, 'import.pl–removeold pics' is the Greenstone command for importing documents into the collection pics, 'buildcol.pl–removeold pics' is the Greenstone command for creating the required indices and classifiers for pics, and daily indicates that the collection will be scheduled for construction on a daily basis.

Using the arguments provided by the user, the Scheduler performs two main tasks:

- Create a script that automates the building of the collection; and
- Create a crontab record that schedules the execution of the build script at specified intervals.

Automation Script Generation

The Scheduler generates a build script for any import and build command, and for the Linux, Windows or Mac OS X platforms. The build script contains all instructions that are required for building the specified collection. The commands include those for setting the Greenstone environment variables required for the collection building process, the import command and the build command.

```
#!/usr/bin/perl
SENV{'GSDLHOME'}='/gsdl';
SENV {'GSDLOS'}=' linux';
SENV {'GSDLLANG'}='EN';
SENV {' PATH'}='/usr/local/gsdl/bin/script:/usr/local/gsdl/bin/
linux';
system('import.pl-removeold pics');
system('buildcol.pl-removeold pics');
system('\\rm-r/gsdl/collect/pics/index/*');
system('mv/gsdl/collect/pics/building/*
/gsdl/collect/pics/index/');
system('chmod-R 755/gsdl/collect/pics/index/*');
```

Fig. Sample Automation Script for Linux

Figure shows a sample build script for Linux that contains the instructions for building the collection pics, as specified in the schedule.pl command above. The first four instructions set the environment variable that are required for the import.pl and buildcol.pl commands.

The next two instructions are the specified import and build commands. The remaining instructions handle cleanup in order to activate the collection.

```
#!/usr/bin/perl
SENV{'GSDLHOME'} ='C:\\gsdl';
SENV{'GSDLOS'}='windows';
SENV{'GSDLLANG'} ='en';
S E N V { ' P A T H ' } = C : / /
gsdl\\bin\\windows\\perl\\bin;C:\\gsdl\\bin\\windows;
C:\\gsdl\\bin\\script;C:\\Perl\\bin\\;
C:WINDOWS\\system32;C:\\WINDOWS;
system('import.pl pics');
system('buildcol. pl pics');
system('rd\/s\/Q \'C:\\gsdl\\collect\\pics\\index\'');
system('md \'C:\\gsdl\\collect\\pies\\index\'');
system('xcopy \/E \/Y \'C:\\gsdl\\collect\\pics\\building\\*\'
\'C:\\gsdl\\collect\\pics\\index\\\'');
```

Fig. Sample Automation Script of Windows

Similarly, Figure shows a sample build script for Windows that is generated for the same schedule.

Crontab Generation

A crontab record is created to execute the automation script at a specified interval. The user has the option of specifying an hourly, daily or weekly build. An hourly build is scheduled for the beginning of the hour, a daily build is scheduled for midnight, and a weekly build is scheduled for Sunday morning at midnight. After creating the crontab record, it is added to the crontab file or replaces an existing crontab record.

```
0 0 0 * * */gsd;/collect/pics/gsdl.pl
```

Fig. Crontab Record for Linux

Figure depicts the daily crontab record for the automation script in figure, while Figure depicts the crontab record corresponding to the automation script in figure.

```
0 0 0 * * * C:\gsdl\collect\pisc\gsdl. pl
```

Fig. Crontab Record for Windows

EVALUATION

The focus of our experiments is to evaluate the Scheduler for correct execution in specific situations.

For correct execution, we looked at the following:

- *Crontab:* Does the Scheduler generate a correct crontab record? A crontab record is correct if: 1) it is accepted by the crontab programme, and it causes Cron to execute the automation script at the proper time.
- *Automation Script:* In addition, does the scheduler generate the correct automation script to build a collection. An automation script is generated correctly if the collection it is created for is rebuilt correctly given the parameters that are specified when the script is created.

We conducted three experiments. The first is an hourly build of one collection. The second is an hourly build of two collections. The third is a daily build of one collection. All three experiments were performed on both Linux and Windows. These tests were not performed extensively on Mac OS X. However, the scheduler was executed many times on this platform to ensure that it does work.

Hourly Build of One Collection

The focus of this experiment is to ensure that the Scheduler produced a correct crontab record and automation script to re-build a collection of images every hour for 24 hours. To determine that each execution of the automation script was successful, we looked at the following. For Linux, Cron was configured to send an e-mail message containing the output of the automation script.

The e-mail message for each of the 24 builds contains an output for a successful Greenstone build. For Windows, Pycron maintains a log that contains two records for each automation script execution–one record indicating the start of execution, and one record indicating the end of execution and a return code. The terminating records for all 24 builds have a return code of zero, which indicates a successful execution of the automation script. In both cases, a visual inspection of the collection was also performed periodically to verify the success of the Scheduler.

Hourly Build of Two Collections

The focus of this experiment is to ensure that if multiple collections are scheduled to be rebuilt at the same time, they are successfully rebuilt. We scheduled the building of two collections on hourly intervals for 24 hours. A perusal of e-mail messages (for Linux) and the log (for Windows) verify that both collections were rebuilt successfully.

Daily Build of One Collection

The focus of this experiment is twofold. The first is to ensure correct daily execution of an automation script generated by the Scheduler. The second is to simulate a situation of a collection that has images added to it on a daily basis. We schedule one collection to be built daily for seven days. The collection starts with 10 images, and 10 images are added daily. In addition to the successful daily build, the collection did reflect the addition of the new images that arrived daily.

SCHEDULING IN THE LIBRARIAN INTERFACE

The Scheduler is a minimal, yet powerful tool for maintaining Greenstone collections. It hides the details concerning the collection building process, and also the details for scheduling a Cron task. However, the Scheduler has two main limitations.

The first is that the user is still required to know the syntax and command-line parameters for both the import and build commands in order to perform scheduling. The second is that, currently, notification of collection building success—or failure—is still dependent on the version of Cron (and indirectly, the operating system it is running on) that is used. The Librarian Interface provides a user-friendly tool for building collections, including configuring the import and build commands. Therefore, it is ideal to extend the Librarian Interface to allow the configuration of the Scheduler as well.

Currently, the Create panel is displaying most of the parameters (*i.e.*, Schedule Options) for the Scheduler. Notice that no explicit options exist for the import and build commands. This is because the import and build commands are created based on the arguments selected from the Import Options and Build Options panels. Therefore, the user no longer needs to know the exact syntax of the import and build commands.

User Modes

The Librarian Interface has four modes of use—Library Assistant, Librarian, Library Systems Specialist, and Expert—stepwise increasing the functionality available to the user. It was important to determine which modes would have access to the Scheduling Options, and for those modes that were granted access, how much access each would be granted. It was decided that Library Systems Specialists and Experts would be provided access to the Scheduling Options. In addition to determining which options to make available to each user mode, it is also necessary to determine how the Scheduler would interact with the existing import and build functionality in the Librarian Interface.

Mode Level for Options

The Scheduler was first modified so that the passing of command-line arguments conformed with that of other Greenstone commands, such as import and build. This also allowed us to easily specify which user mode could have access to each argument when it is added as a Schedule Option in the Librarian Interface. The Expert user mode is granted full access to all Schedule Options, while Librarian Systems Specialist is only granted limited access to options. This user mode can only specify whether or not to schedule a collection build with the default values—a frequency of hourly, and no sending of e-mail.

Scheduling and Building

Another important decision was how the Scheduler would interact with the collection building functionality of the Librarian Interface. The question asked was, should scheduling be done at the same time as collection building, or be a completely separate task? For Expert mode, the functionality for Scheduling is separate from that of collection building. This is because an expert user may want to configure and manually re-build their collection before scheduling an automatic re-build of it. For Library System Specialist mode, the Scheduling functionality is done at the same time as collection building. If the specialist chooses to schedule, a new scheduled build is created. If the specialist chooses not to schedule, any existing scheduled builds are deleted.

Cron Event Logs

It is important to maintain logs that keep track of the outcome of a scheduled collection build. Both Vixie Cron and Pycron maintain a log that keeps track of the attempted execution of all scheduled tasks. Neither scheduling service keeps track of the success or failure of a scheduled task, nor do they keep track of the output of a task. In addition, to view logs created by Vixie Cron, the user must have root access. Another desirable feature of maintaining logs is the ability to be able to only record output that is considered important, and to disregard all other task output.

For example, if the output from the input and build commands of Greenstone is required, but the output from moving indices and classifiers is not considered important, the log should reflect this. Therefore, the Scheduler is modified in two ways to handle the logging of building script output. The first is to create a custom log for each execution of the automation script. The automation script creates a unique filename every time it is executed by using a timestamp. The second is to specify in the automation script which actions will have its output redirected to the logfile. The actions whose output is to be ignored will have its output redirected to the 'bit bucket'.

E-mail Notification

It is also important than an e-mail notification service be provided, which will inform users of the outcome of their scheduled collection build.

We handle e-mail notification from the Scheduler and Librarian Interface for the following reasons:

- *User Notification:* Whether Cron notifies users about the outcome of a scheduled task depends on the its implementation. For Vixie Cron, the outcome of a task is e-mailed to the owner of the task. Pycron does not send e-mail notification.
- *Flexibility of Notification:* In Vixie Cron it is possible to suppress e-mail notification, either by setting an environment variable to null, or by redirecting all output to a file or the 'bit bucket'. However, this is normally an all-or-nothing event—either all output, or none, is sent by e-mail. Similar to logging, a desirable feature would be to send e-mail that contains only the most important parts of the building process, and ignores other parts of the building process.
- *Greenstone E-mail Support:* Greenstone comes with a Perl e-mail script, that is a wrapper for the Perl sendmail command. The e-mail script is platform-independent. Therefore, it is ideal to use it to provide a uniform way to send e-mail concerning the execution of a scheduled task. In addition, the script does not require the piping of build output directly to it, but instead can send the contents of a file.

Therefore, both the Librarian Interface and the Scheduler are modified so that e-mail notification is handled in a uniform and user-friendly manner across all operating systems. First, options have been added to the Scheduler that are required for the Perl e-mail script—specifically, a flag to specify that e-mail will be sent (–e-mail), the sender (–fromaddr), receiver (–toaddr) and the e-mail server that will be used to send the e-mail (–smtp). Also, the corresponding fields exist in the Schedule Options pane of the Librarian Interface. In order to assist users in using the e-mail features of scheduling, the Librarian Interface attempts to populate the fields-toaddr,-fromaddr, and-smtp in the Schedule Options pane by consulting the configurations for the Librarian Interface and Greenstone.

If suitable values are available from these sources, they are assigned to the appropriate fields. Second, the output from the building script must be captured and re-directed to the Perl e-mail script. The capturing of output already takes place, in the event log. This serves as the file that the e-mail script will send to the user. Also, since, it contains only the output that is considered important, this will be reflected in the e-mail message as well. Finally, the Scheduler is modified so that, if specified, the automation script will send an e-mail message containing the contents of the log to the specified recipient. An added bonus is that if e-mail is not specified, the log can still be consulted by the user if required.

Scheduled Building in Isolation

An important modification to the Scheduler is to ensure that a scheduled build is completed in its entirety without interference from another scheduled build. A build may take a significant amount of time depending on the size of the collection—from seconds for a small one to 33 hours for a collection containing 20 GB of raw text and 50 GB of metadata. To handle this, the automation script for the collection checks for a lock file, which indicates that a collection build is underway.

If the file exists, the collection owner is notified via e-mail and information is placed in the event log. Otherwise, a lock file is created before the scheduled build begins, and is removed when the build finishes. This ensures that multiples builds do not occur concurrently.

EXAMPLE: COLLECTING PICTURES WHILE TRAVELLING

We present a simple application of scheduling from the Librarian Interface. In this scenario, we have a traveller who wants to post pictures of their trip in a Greenstone collection for her friends to view. Instead of waiting until the end of the trip, the traveller wants to post her pictures from each day, incrementally adding to the collection on a daily basis. The traveller does not want to worry about obtaining the Librarian Interface to rebuild the collection while traveling. Instead, she simply wants to upload the pictures to the import directory of her collection, and have her collection rebuilt automatically and on a daily basis.

This can be accomplished by setting up a scheduled, automatic rebuild of the collection of travel photos from the Librarian Interface. First, before departing, the traveller runs the Librarian Interface and creates a new collection. Then, the user selects the Create tab to display the collection creation pane. From here, clicking on Schedule Options will display the available options for setting up a scheduled, automatic collection build of the collection of travel pictures.

Here, the traveller selects schedule, which indicates that she wants to set up a scheduled, automatic build. Also, she selects a frequency of hourly and an action of add. Next, the traveller clicks on Schedule Build. This will set up the building script for the collection of travel pics, as well as the crontab record that will indicate to Cron that the collection is to be rebuilt daily. The collection is now ready to be re-built while the traveller is away. At the end of the first day of travel, she uploads three pictures, which are added to the collection when the collection is re-built automatically overnight.

The updated collection is depicted in Figure. The next day, the traveller uploads three more pictures. When the collection is re-built overnight, these pictures are added to the existing collection. Figure depicts the updated collection with the new pictures. Although not shown here, the user can switch to the Import Options and Build Options and select any options that are required for collection importing and building. These options are incorporated into the automatic building script that is created for the collection. In addition, the user can manually build and configure their collection as many times as necessary to confirm the right sequence is being performed, before setting up a scheduled, automatic build.

4

Information Communication Technology and Digital Storage in Libraries

INTRODUCTION

The relatively recent change from the term *Information Technology* (IT) to *Information and Communication Technology* (ICT) due to the convergence of IT and ICT has open up new challenges for libraries. Information Technology is the collective name for a group of technologies that are concerned with the storage, retrieval, manipulation, analysis, and transmission of information. Since the fabrication of the first modern computer in the mid 1940's, computer technology has developed at a tremendous pace to the point where it has penetrated almost all occupations and has spread to the far concerns of the world.

Similarly, communication technology has made rapid progress in the post World War II period. But it is the development of this technology in the last 15 years that has made IT so important. The development in this area have been brining about a revolutionary change in the way humans work, and in the way they interact with each others. The spread of telecommunications has brought into limelight the Internet, the global intercommunication of computer networks. This has made available a large store information to all concerns of the world. Information Technology provides the following services for information:

- Storage of large amounts of information in a cost effective manner.
- Structuring of information to enable quick retrieval of what is required.
- Analysis of stored information to help in decision making.
- Sharing of information among people geographically dispersed.
- Quick transmission of information over large distances.

IT consists of five components, *i.e.*, electronic science, computer science, tele-communication science, artificial language and human interface.

INFORMATION COMMUNICATIONS TECHNOLOGY – CREATING NETWORKS WITH GROWING REACH

It involves rapid advances in two technologies – digital storage and processing of information and satellite and optical fibre transmission of information– are creating new and faster ways of storing, handling, distributing and accessing information. These innovations enable the processing and storage of enormous amount of information, along with rapid distribution information through communication networks. For example in 2001 more information can be sent over a single cable in a second than in 1997 was sent over the entire internet in a month. Linking computing devices and allowing them to communicate with each other creates networked information systems based on a common protocol. Individuals, households and institutions are linked in processing and executing a huge number of instructions in imperceptible time spans. This radically alters access to information and the structure of communication extending the networked reach to all corners of the world.

TECHNOLOGICAL TRANSFORMATIONS

Today's technological transformations are intertwined with another transformation, globalization and together they are creating a new paradigm – the network age. These transformations expand opportunities and increase the social and economic rewards of creating and using technology. They are also altering how and by whom technology is created and owned, and how it is made accessible and used. Technology is not inherently good or bad the outcome depends on how it is used.

SOME INITIATIVES IN IT SECTOR

The Department of Information Technology has setup Community Centre (CICs) at 487 blocks in the seven North Eastern States 9 Arunachal Pradesh, Assam, manipur, Meghalaya, Mizoram, Nagaland, Tripura) and Sikkim to provide connectivity at the block level and thus promote application of Information Technology for accelerating socio economic development of the region.

INFORMATION TECHNOLOGY ACT

The Government of India has created the necessary legal and administrative framework through the enactment of the Information Technology Act, 2000. While on the one hand it seeks to create the public key infrastructure for electronic authentication through digital signatures.

DIGITAL LIBRARY

Digital Libraries are a form of information Technology in which social impact matters as much as technological advancements. Future knowledge networks will rely on scalable semantics, to automatically indexing the community collections so that users can effectively search of billion repositories.

NATIONAL INFORMATION CENTRE (NIC)

It provides informatics services for decision support to government offices/

bodies at national, state, district and block levels. It offers network services. NIC also provides video conferencing facilities.

INFORMATION TECHNOLOGY USE IN LIBRARY MANAGEMENT SYSTEM

The IT revolution has also embraud the library system. A massive and rapid computerization process throughout the levels of the library system has made IT an integral part of the library management scene in many countries all over the world. The incorporation of IT into the day-to-day activity of libraries has a strong impact on virtually every aspect of their management processes. Although there is no agreed definition of IT, the term "IT" includes three main components – *management information system* (MIS) or *decision support system* (DSS), hardware, and human factors. A management information system is the set of structure and procedures that govern the collection, processing, analysis, presentation and use of information within an organization.

IMPACT OF ICTS IN LIBRARIES

Technology is changing the nature of libraries and librarians, and it continues to exert a major influence on the strategic direction of libraries in society. Today the library services are transitioning from local traditional collections to global resources provided on demand via the most advanced networking technologies.

DIGITAL DATA STORAGE IN LIBRARIES

Digital data storage media for storing digital data are constantly being developed, improved or superseded, and any discussion of them here can only be taken as description of the current situation i. e., optical discs, magnetic media, other media for digital data storage. The concept of the "digital library" evolved out of potential for digitization of all forms of media: print, image, sound, complex data sets, and computer simulations of non-time-bound sequences, otherwise not demonstrable events, etc., and retrieving them in context of multiple networked information systems.

The digital library often serves as a multidimensional catalogue or index to bring together the resource discovery information of every resource that was topically, creatively, or by reason of other connections generatively related. A digital library does not only consist of digitized and digitally born information resources, but also of electronic metadata on non-digital objects. Digital Data: Considerable attention is now being paid to the possibility of converting the intellectual content of items in library collection into digital data by electronic means and storing it on magnetic tapes or discs.

Both textual and pictorial information can be converted. For example by using optical character recognition devices which convert texts into their digital code equivalent, or by using scanners to convert text or, more usually, pictures into an analogue form.

Text can also be input by keyboarding. In addition to information already in another format being converted to digital format, much information is now originated in digital form and may appear only in that form in the library. Digital data have considerable advantages. They can be rapidly duplicated and speedily transmitted without deterioration through electronic communications networks to whatever the user is working. Storage: It is a mainly technical requirement, although new media may complicate storage decisions and costing. Today's large digital repositories use multiple level of mass storage media and mechanical robots to locate and mount the media.

Phases of Digitization: Undoubtedly, digital media will have to co-exit with print media. Different kinds of collection could be digitized at different times depending on the priorities of the library. To start with, any one type of collection, for example, important out of print publications could be made available in digital form. Feedback of its usage can be sengut and analyzed. In the next phase, another type of data could be converted into digital form. Digitization Process: Digitization is a process of converting paper documents to electronic format. Scanning process does the conversion.

Digital information can be transmitted and received anywhere in the world where the infrastructure to send and received is in place. Due to the implementation of the IT, the librarian need to be well aware of the technical issues, potential problems involved, trained manpower available, the hardware required, document management systems, *optical character recognization* (OCR) technology for implementing digitization of the collection and services. As been know the concept of digital library is growing very fast globally. It is a welcome trained that various institutions and professional societies are involved to provide opportunities for the library and librarians to upgrade and enhance the professional knowledge about digital library. Various important aspects like digital libraries issues, architecture, electronic publishing, collection building, storage, organization, transmission of digital information, creation and use of hypertext and hypermedia system, networks and their implications, manpower development etc. We are in the early stage of a transmition from a print-based to a digital society.

The latest technologies offer cheap computer processing power, cheap mass storage, inexpensive and ubiquitous access to high speed networks and retrieval devices give us the ability to create, to manipulate, to storage and especially to transfer large quantities of information in digital form at low costs. Digital information can be stored on any medium that is able to represent binary digits 0 and 1.

Conversion from the conventional storage to digitized format required discrete analysis as the primary function, based on user electronic storage and retrieval system. Some of the common digitized storage media that are presently used world over are the Hyper books, CD-ROM, Multimedia. New media are constantly being developed. Some that are still in experimental stages or have been only very recently introduced are digital videotape, digital audiotape and digital paper.

IMPACT OF INFORMATION TECHNOLOGY ON INFORMATION PROFESSIONALS

As quoted by Matson, new technology is, of course, very powerful and brings in 'an imperialistic thrust' not only into librarianship, but into everyday life. Not surprisingly, the new roles created by the changing technology have commanded attention and have made up a large part of recent literature about librarians. He added the resulting proliferation of online catalogs, librarian have been spurred by technological developments to become more efficient organisers and planners. They have, in short, brought their traditional skills to the service of the new technologies. As claimed by Hyams, the role of the New Information Professionals (NIP) in the learning environments is likely to be much more global. It is a call for librarians to rethink their job functions and the future of the academic library as center of technology. The change that's happening isn't at all like the automation change the librarian went through. It is a fundamental kind of change: 'To Who We Are and What We Do."

NEW ROLES, NEW SKILLS AND NEW PEOPLE

Researcher argue that library jobs and jobs for information professionals are changing at the same—or even greater as experienced in other parts of our economy and society. Are librarians, new and old, keeping pace with these changes? Are they stuck in a traditional mind-set about their jobs and the settings for those jobs? What are some of the new horizons available to librarians willing to 'think outside the box" as far as their careers are concerned? What prepares the librarian for these emerging jobs? The struggle of librarians in academic libraries to cope with the dynamic changes brought by technology is real. The new roles and skills include:

As Library Webmaster

The single most significant factor in the changing information jobs has been the Internet. It has changed everyone's job, some people's job descriptions', and the job market itself, example as Webmaster.

Definition of Webmaster

The essential assignment of the Webmaster as defined by Richmond is:

- "... a person who manages a Web; a mediator between Web authors and system administrator—ensures that applicable standards such as HTML validity and link liveliness are met; optimises the Web architecture for navigability; takes editorial responsibility for the content, quality and styles of the site; finds, creates and installs tools to create Web content and check consistency; develops and enforces the house style; liaises with graphic artist; provides first level user support..."

From this definition, it is clear that Webmasters must be responsible for several roles in their day to day activities.

Task Analysis of the Webmaster

Van der Walt strongly believe that Webmasters were originally depicted as members of an organisation who were early adopters of Internet and Web technologies and who saw the need to educate the rest of the library users in using those technologies. His statement is strongly supported by the researchers who claimed that an area where early Web expertise could be found was the *academic,* and specifically *university,* environment.

Vander Walt listed several responsibilities of the Webmaster such as:

- Administration and daily management of a Web site such as home page design, Web-based online searching, searching Web sites, Intranets and Internal database publishing
- Understand the broad purpose and potential of a Web site—that is, what the site can accomplish and what it may be able to do in future
- Possess a thorough understanding of the organisation and have a background in marketing, familiarity with the Internet
- A solid understanding of programming languages and technology
- Keep up with and also recognise the significance of emerging technologies and business models, and be able to inform and educate the rest of the organisation
- Experiment with unproven technology to develop WWW sites and the Webmaster is a solo space explorer, often looking at way-out-in-front technology'
- A person with the necessary technical talent in user interfaces and a good knowledge of operating systems, as well as creative skills in graphic design, marketing, advertising, copy writing and event planning

The Growing Importance of the Webmaster

These basic responsibilities are slowly being enhanced. Today the Webmaster has become an integral part of an education venture vital to the entire strategic planning of the library.

As a newcomer in the information retrieval field, the Webmaster forms an essential part of the online presence of any organisation, as it is he or she who leads the Web site development team in managing an effective and efficient Web site.

The value of librarians as webmasters in the university as claimed by Stover is for a number of reasons:

- First, to support the scholarly communication process because disseminating information is a function that traditionally been associated with librarians
- Second, librarians have a certain measure of expertise in the area of organising and providing access to information. What better way to share their skills with the academic community than by turning Web documents into one-stop-shopping malls that offer the end user subject access to a document along with the full-text of the document itself?
- Third, Web publishing gives us a higher profile on campus, which is an important asset these days because of the changing nature of higher education and changing role of librarians
- Fourth, the Web provides unique access to scholarly information because of its serendipitous nature, its immediacy, its hypertext structure, and its universal appeal. Why wouldn't librarians want to be involved with this exciting technology at the publishing level?
- Fifth, it provides our parent institutions a positive reputation in the national and international academic communities. This is more important ever given the current climate of declining enrollments that many colleges and universities face today.
- Sixth, Web publishing allows us to bypass the profit-based system of print publishing that has tormented librarians for years by gouging out huge chunks of money from their budget.

As claimed by Van der Walt, many Web sites are now becoming mission critical in the sense that they are seen as a marketing tool for the university and also as a support tool for the end-user or library customers. The Internet and World Wide Web are both essential elements in the IT infrastructure of any organisation. Thus the Webmaster can play an important role in managing the library assets according to the information center's strategic planning.

As Systems Librarian

Shearer describes the term Systems librarians as:

- "Individuals who are responsible of designing, supporting and developing systems to enhance access to and management of the library's collection. Ensuring that the computer-based systems are essential to the library's work at all times."

Responsibilities

- Evaluation, planning, implementation and maintenance of library automation and Internet access, network maintenance as well as web page design and maintenance.

- Evaluation and selection of databases and software and staff training.
- Maintains computer security and hardware.

Skills

- Knowledge of networking, Internet and software applications.
- Ability to master new computer hardware and software.
- Ability to diagnose and solve hardware, software and networking problems.
- Ability to communicate technology to the uninitiated.
- Ability to work in a dynamic and changing environment.

Electronic Access to What and by Whom

Selecting academic information resources requires a broader view. For any library, the determination of which databases to provide and who will access them has become an ever more complex due to the number of databases that are now available has grown by leaps and bounds over the past few years. Today's systems librarian is often involved in the decision of which database service to supply to end-user desktops. There are myriad choices of general topic and specialty products available online, on the Intranet, on CD-ROM, and via the Web, at all price points. In today's academic setting, the librarian not only has to take into account the resource for the library's own collection but has to weigh offering the database to a wider user base against what end users within the university are already accessing by way of their own desktops.

Thus the systems librarian must weigh the type of access to provide against questions of:

- Timeliness,
- System capabilities, and
- Client expectations of good service.

Access Policies

Schuhnan quote that once the library decides which databases to select, it must determine how to deploy them and who will have access to them. As electronic access to external databases becomes more prevalent throughout all academic areas, the systems librarian's budget and equipment come under greater pressure. Whenever contemplating the addition of a new database resource it's also a good opportunity to review internal corporate access policies. As quickly as events dictate change in resource selections, policy revisions will naturally be carefully thought about more frequently. Decisions such as supplying access to information for those with a 'need to know' are undergoing modification.

Increasingly, those with a 'need to know' occupy expanding outward circles within organisations. Schulman added, smart organisations are extending information resources access to more employees as competitors become more aggressive and move more quickly. They are finding that providing more employees with timely access to competitive information allows an organisation to respond to competitive threats more quickly.

As the system librarian continuously evaluate databases and the provision of access to them, here is a series of questions to ask each time considering a new source:

- Is this source unique or does it duplicate an existing resource.
- If it's a close duplicate, is it less expensive, easier to use, or unique in another beneficial way.
- How does this database fit in with the corporate mission.
- Who within the university will benefit from this database—all users, faculty members and university community.
- What is the cost-benefit ratio.
- What critical element does this database supply that overcomes a poor cost-benefit ratio.
- Does this resource fit within our existing budget.
- Does another resource have to be eliminated to bring on this resource, and, if so, what impact will that have to the budget and to those who depend on the resource under consideration for elimination.
- Will this resource improve service to our clients/customers? How?
- In what format will we purchase the database.
- How will this database be integrated into our other resources.
- What changes have to be made to the hardware/software configuration to accept this new database and how will this impact our budget? How will it impact access to other resources?
- How will we provide access to this resource?
- Who in which departments and at which levels within the university will have access to this resource? Directly? Indirectly.
- Will end-user training have to be provided?
- Will additional staff be required?
- What other departments should be involved in this decision?
- How much time and effort is involved in implementing access to this resource?
- When will the corporation see a return on investment?

Thus by using this list as a guideline and foundation for decision making should help the system librarian to revise the questions as the mission, budget, environmental influences changes and stay ahead of the game.

As In-House Content Providers

The meaning of In-house Content Provider refers to:

- "one who was interested in exploring the balance between making its content freely available on the Internet while protecting its print-based revenue stream."

Funke provide a comprehensive comment on the new role of the Information Professionals as an In-House Content Providers. He claimed that along with the new technologies comes interacting with different groups within an organisation such as the MIS people, an information professional must have the ability to effectively 'bring content to the table" and work effectively with MIS as a team to make this content readily available. In order for information professionals to effectively do this, they must keep up with the latest technologies related to text retrieval, content organisation, search technologies, and knowledge management.

Bringing Content to the Table

Making MIS people understand the importance and expertise of people who know content and how clients will use it can be a constant uphill battle. Many programmers in this situation view another 'player' either as a threat or someone who doesn't have their background. Unfortunately, the onus lies on the information professional to make programmers understand what we can contribute, the value we can provide.

For starters, before you can integrate content into a Web site, you must understand:

- The overall requirements of the current Web site, including servers,
- Their ability to handle various indexes; search engine capability; and
- How the parser is set up to integrate content.

The Information Professional can provide expertise on how to organise content on a site; how users might search for the content; and the search requirements needed to access the content.

Metadata

Many information professionals have taken courses such as cataloging and indexing. These courses can serve as a foundation for the resource-organising activities on the Internet involving metadata. Metadata provides document information on and from Web sites, producing an index or directory to the resource.

With the tremendous growth of content on the Web, there is a need to standardise the organisation of the information.

As metadata standards are further defined and organisations embrace these new standards, many questions will need answering such as:

- What will be worth cataloging?
- How detailed should the descriptions of various resources be?

Information Professionals can play a major role in helping answer these questions.

Search Engines

Researcher added, the evaluation and use of search engines is a 'product' that Information Professionals should manage within their organisations because they:

- Understand and know how to use Boolean logic.
- Can evaluate search engines from the user perspective?
- Know how to implement effective user searching of content.

Some of the major Intranet search engines available these days include Fulcrum Surfboard, Verity, Microsoft Index Server, and Excalibur. Thus, when implementing the Boolean logic features of these search engines, most programmers, will say that users cannot grasp Boolean logic or that such control is unnecessary as long as the search engines do relevancy rankings of documents retrieved. Users can go beyond basic Boolean operators such as AND, OR, NOT, which programmers usually dictate for them, and take advantage of proximity operators such as NEAR and NEARIN.

From experience, when one explains the differences in search results to users, *e.g.*, the effect of using the Boolean operators and NEAR, end-user searchers understand and respond positively right away. Programmers may support their positions by doing a query to see how many searches were performed using each Boolean operator. Information Professionals should try search queries for this type of data, too. Request the tools to perform this kind of query. What some programmers find difficult to understand is that you just can't implement a feature without some user education. Information Professionals can play an important role by providing this guidance within their organisations.

Information Retrieval Agents

Making sense of the overwhelming amount of indexed information constitutes one of the biggest challenges of the Web. To help, we see a rising use of Web robots, called information retrieval agents. These agents know where to look for relevant information based on user direction, advanced search algorithms, and learned behaviour. Major players in this area include NewsBot, Agent ware, and Wise Wire. As organisations move towards managing knowledge, intelligent information retrieval agent software tools will playa major role and will require people with the ability to manage and evaluate these tools. Search agents work when a user sets up search queries to 'train the documents,' whereby the agents learn from human behaviour and use pattern recognition to find relevant information to automate the retrieval process.

Information Professionals with expertise in searching and content analysis can help manage and evaluate these tools. Note that several of the traditional electronic publishers have already begun exploring this technology, *e.g.*, LEXIS-NEXIS and UMI with WiseWire Professional, an agent technology that evaluates user's viewing habits. Like it or not, new technologies are changing the information professional's role and the opportunities to enhance one's role have become boundless. To take advantage of the opportunities, Information Professionals must keep up with the emerging technologies, recognise the opportunities to utilise our skill sets, and work with MIS to effectively implement change. At times it can be frustrating and overwhelming, but the opportunities to grow and learn outweigh any negatives.

AS KNOWLEDGE MANAGER

Peter Drucker has predicted that the most important profession in the next century will be knowledge worker, and knowledge workers are not the same as computer systems specialists. He claimed that the most competent ones are likely to be reference librarians using sophisticated hardware and software, tools which the end user does not know how to use. Certainly, those who have exploited the almost unlimited opportunity to provide more information have taken advantage of this development.

Still, Drucker assumed that this deluge of knowledge would drown us and force us to seek people to manage that knowledge. Knowledge workers would assess knowledge on behalf of those who had neither the time nor the inclination to do so. The concept of knowledge management embraces the need to organise large data files, and to link and integrate different but related files and databases to one another so that users can move between and among related resources efficiently.

Thus, Church believe the transformation from librarian to knowledge manager is clearly underway; however, a deeper look at the direction that the Internet is taking business reveals the possibility of more far-reaching changes. As many library services processes move to the Internet, the use of information will become integrated with these processes. In this environment, information as a distinct function or resource may no longer exist.

Changing Roles and Responsibilities

The information transfer cycle is directly affected by Internet use. They should "embrace the entire new information transfer cycle, from the creation, restructuring and representation of information to its dissemination and use." They have an important and valuable role to tell users what users ought to see and read. It is to protect library clients from drowning in the information overflow and help them work smarter.

How their role as knowledge managers would evolve within the next few years, Church outline five key functions:

1. *Consultant:* Their role would involve less 'doing' and more consultation. This role would require remote support to endusers within the organisation. In effect, 'foot traffic' would be replaced by remote consultation for complex search strategies.

2. *Analyst:* Some information professional felt that their role would require increased value-added in the form of analysing and interpreting information that is presented to end-users.
3. *Intranet content manager:* With the integration of external data into corporate Intranets, a key function of the information services professional will be to source and manage the content which is accessible through the system.
4. *Product planner and marketer:* Data integration also forces information professionals to become product developers and planners, with responsibility for packaging information and marketing products, services and delivery strategies to internal audiences.
5. *Corporate knowledge manager:* Increased recognition of knowledge as a valuable strategic resource could heighten the importance of the information professional. It foresee a merger of all information functions into a single department or function. Being the Knowledge Manager just means that they create value to my organisation by facilitating access to high quality information and by networking people and their ideas together using the technological infrastructure.

These new responsibilities imply a totally different skill set. The emphasis will shift from:

- Technical skills in the library to communication,
- Facilitation, training and management skills.
- Interact with IT staff and managers beyond Knowledge Management (KM).

To adjust to these more far-reaching changes, information professionals must search beyond current bounds and think in terms of benefits to their organisations. Right now, information can be used to enhance competitiveness and productivity. These same benefits will remain in the future, no matter what the role involves.

If information is to be seamlessly integrated with transaction processes, then someone must scope out work-related behaviours to ensure that it is done in the most efficient and effective manner. And, if equal information and technology is available to everyone, then competition rests on the ability to interpret and apply these tools. Clearly the impending shift to knowledge management represents an exciting change for academic librarians. However, it's an opportunity that requires a great deal of preparation, and a new way of thinking.

AS COLLABORATORS/PARTNERSHIPS

All organisations are in the period of transformation including academic libraries and librarians should use this period of change to establish, refocus and strengthen partnerships with other professionals groups within their institutions. There are two significant groups with which library professionals should establish strong collaborative relationships:

1. Faculty and
2. Technologists.

Creth suggest in order for a real partnership to succeed, librarians need to see themselves as part of the teaching and research endeavor, and participate as an active and integral member of the education team. He added, for some librarians this idea of a partnership with faculty may require incorporating a different concept of their importance in relation to the faculty and developing new expectations and different behaviour. In the most general sense, librarians need to be certain that their commitment to service does not display itself through behaviour that is like of a servant.

Library professionals also need to reshape and strengthen their relationships with the computer specialists in the university with reasons such as:

- To eliminate much of the waste that occurs in most organisations where computer and information technology remains untapped or barely utilised because the learning curve is too steep for so many people and because the design of the equipment and software is so often far from intuitive.
- The New Information Professionals can provide constant feedback to designers and programmers about what works, what does not work, what new functions are needed.
- They can become the voice of the inexpert user, the typical person who is not technically inclined but strongly needs the service that the technology promises to deliver.
- They are both dealing with changing and chaotic times, and their activities are centered around information technology, so they should naturally consider themselves partners in addressing the many challenges that exist.
- They need to be willing, to share the act of discovery, to be able to identify shared goals, and to work together as peers.

If, librarians are to be prepared to absorb and even help shape the magnitude of predicted change into this 21st century, then it will be important for librarians to realign their relationships within the university so that strong partnerships exist to provide us with necessary support as well as knowledge for meeting the challenges ahead.

AS EDUCATOR

Anderson emphasised that librarians have always played a key role in education. They have formed relationships with subject specialists to build library collections to support instruction in the classroom and provided instruction in the form of classes on library skills and have conducted library instructional orientations sessions to assist students doing research in their classes. Today, in the digital age, librarians can no longer be simply information providers or the 'keepers of knowledge'.

The changes in technology using electronically stored and retrieved information has changed the way patrons and students are able to access, retrieve and use information. The instantaneous access of information through the Internet has made vast amounts of information and data available to anyone with a computer, a modem and a provider. Digital information is changing the role of librarians from "a person who students ask for assistance in finding information to someone who needs to provide services and instruction regardless of place, time or format." But how do we make important and valid information available to our faculty and students that may appear on the Web tomorrow?

Big Six Information Skills

As educators, Eisenberg have suggested that librarians must acquire these skills; the ability to:

- Define the task,
- Information seeking strategies,
- Location and access,
- Use of information,
- Synthesis,
- Evaluation.

The librarian's role too has:

- Expanded with a much broader instructional and participatory role in the instructional process. This role can be one of actively participating in the building of on-line courses by providing assistance in finding current and valid information for instructors delivering instruction on the Internet.
- Extend into the area of providing instruction and librarians must be involved in creating independent thinkers.
- Enhanced their roles to knowledge navigators and instructors teaching the discipline called information literacy.
- Be one of teaching critical thinking and resource-based learning.

New vocabulary in education such as: living curriculum, critical literacy, information power, information literacy, and information problem solving mandate that we re-examine our roles as professional information providers and educators. Students need to acquire the skills of evaluating information. This new vocabulary is bringing new challenges in library instruction. Changes in education such as the infusion of instructional technology and the use the Internet to deliver instruction has also changed how libraries and librarians can provide and assist instructors in teaching in the digital age.

New Trends in Instruction—Web Based Course Delivery

The trend in education towards distance learning and web-based courses is providing new challenges for information professionals as service providers as well as instructors. We are required to provide access to quality and valid information to support on-line instruction as well as provide on-line instruction both indirectly in the form of guides and on-line tutorials as well as directly in the form on courses to teach information literacy. Universities are recognising the necessity of requiring an information literacy course as part of the curriculum in the digital age.

As educators, the librarians are using a variety of tools and teaching techniques to assist students such as:

- *Provide instruction through learning guides and on-line tutorials:* Finding quality information is the biggest challenge our faculty and students are faced in the research and instructional process. With the advent of distance delivery of instruction and web-based pages for libraries using the vast amounts of information available on the Internet, it is essential that independent learners are skilled in locating information. Students can access these tutorials and guides from home or from the computers in the library and walk through self-paced instruction on any topic from "What is the Internet? To How do I do research?"
- *Provide access to guides to recommended search engines for the Internet:* Using search engines effectively and choosing the best search engines for your specific needs may be the most challenging skill that learners need to master. Guides to recommend search engines that introduce and compare search engines in a standard format are an invaluable tool for independent learners. Students can readily compare the different features of several search engines and access the search engines directly from your library's page.
- *Provide instruction in the area of Information Literacy:* Teaching Information Literacy in the electronic environment is a new and exciting role for librarians. Creating courses and formal instruction in the discipline of information literacy with the purpose of encouraging independent learners and critical thinkers to meet the challenges of the new information age is the role of the future for librarians. In today's workplace, employees are not only expected to work well with others, communicate well, find creative solutions to problems; they will also be expected to use the Internet and electronic information effectively to solve problems and conduct business. More and more businesses are moving towards conducting business on the Web for advertising, delivering services and products as well as using the Internet as a communication tool. Librarians must be involved in

creating valuable employees with the current skills required to be successful on the job.

Librarians are the most appropriate professionals to lead the team of people in finding the answers to the challenges we are facing in the digital environments of electronic information and the Internet. They have always been the experts at teaching people how to use the tools to locate that information regardless of format. They are the most effective searchers and researchers and their basic role of teaching those skills has not changed. Thus, in this fast and ever-changing information environment, librarians need to make full use of information and multimedia technology to support a greatly expanded teaching venture. The technology and varied format of information is changing and making new demands on their profession. In this fast-paced world it is important that they change with the changing roles and challenges.

AS MANAGERS

Researcher address how change has affect everyone in the organisations from leaders to employees and clients—the needs to shift his or her mind-sets, seeing the organisation and their established and new roles sometimes highly threatening and unfamiliar activities. Thus he added, employees need emotional support to adapt to change; support in learning new ways of working and relating. Linda claimed that information technology has changed a librarian's jobs; they have to readjust to new situation and develop new skills of managing the investments of an organisation—in people, technologies, and collections. As managers, they need to look for outcomes rather than just thinking about managing a resource at the resource level. The human resource in any organisation is the key to its success or failure.

Changes in Library Management

We have seen that the major external force that is technology had affected libraries; that means the library managers must use new structures in their management. *Strategic planning—strategic thinking*—should be a fundamental concept that librarians incorporate into their daily activities. Overall they need to give greater attention to strategic planning at the organisation and departmental level, and then integrating these strategic plans into the goals and activities of individual professionals. With a shifting organisational environment and culture, managers should shift their responsibilities and approach to one that is more consultative and supportive rather than one of authority and control.

The role of the manager should focus on:

- Coaching and mentoring staff.
- Development of staff.
- Developing shared values and vision among staff.

- Providing resources within framework of cost-benefit assessment.
- Taking pride in the accomplishments of others,
- Providing incentives to team work.

Library staff who are struggling to keep up with the demands in today's work environment require, indeed deserve, new ways for accomplishing their work. The redesign of the library organisation is imperative if we are to move rapidly and with an entrepreneurial spirit in the delivery of services in the current interactive high- speed communication environment.

Thus to be successful, libraries must reshape the prevailing corporate culture and build into their organisational structures and their approaches to work.

As managers, researcher stress that they must possess:

- The ability to identify, anticipate, and quickly respond to constantly changing customer needs.
- Capable of leaps forward and breakthrough performance.
- Must be ready to abandon formerly successful approaches to work, strategies, processing systems and services.
- Good communication at all levels, staff participation and training.

The librarians in transition that want to consciously manage their change efforts need to help their staff understand the change process and how they can positively participate. Creating an overall framework that shows the considered changes are a natural evolution from current practices, assessing that the organisation has the expertise and climate to implement the proposed changes.

Instead of organising personnel around how librarians do their work, librarians must:

- Organise around customers and how they do their work.
- Reduce hierarchy, flatten the organisation, and eliminate redundancy in order to be more responsive to changing needs and new opportunities and developments.
- Give up their need for control and their desire to create stability.

We Live in a Time of Change

The information has change our profession and library managers today have to pick up new skills to adjust to changes and to be able to survive in the future.

AS INFORMATION RESOURCE MANAGER

The term Information Resource Manager refers to:

- "Individuals who are responsible for the provision of information resources—be they print or electronic or technical infrastructure—and the power of digital technology, which grows everyday. To provide the leadership to conceptualise and manage the broad array of information resources that are necessary to support its mission".

As an Information Resource Manager, the librarian would continually go through a ten-step process:

- *Step 1. Define the Customers:* Who are the library's primary customers?
- *Step 2. Understand the Customers Needs:* One of the best ways to help you analyse the needs of the workforce and effectiveness of your current information strategy, is to arrange an information audit examples:
  - Implementation of custom survey designed to take an inventory of products, services and personnel related to information activities
  - Interviews with key personnel
  - Understand the users needs
  - Analysis of surveys and interviews
  - Creation of 'information strategy' designed to help maximize investment in users and services
  - Recommendations
- *Step 3. Map Needs against Decisions and Sources:* This will list information originators and users; sources required and decision supported. It will also identify high pay-off opportunities, for example where certain information has multiple uses.
- *Step 4. Implement a Sourcing Strategy:* The source/needs map from step 3 will point to clusters of information needs that can give economies in purchasing. For example, purchasing a networked CD-ROM may be more cost-effective than doing multiple ad-hoc online searches.
- *Step 5. Define Information Policies and Standards:* Steps 1-4 will reveal, often to many people for the first time, the sheer wealth of information that is available. This step therefore involves:
  - Classification standards,
  - Ownership,
  - Life-cycle management standards
  - Agreed 'protocols and procedures' between owners and users.
- *Step 6. Select a Pilot Project:* Select a key decision process that involves people across several departments as a pilot.
- *Step 7. Select and Adapt Appropriate Technology:* With the selected pilot project acting as a focal point, now is the time to start detailed consideration example of the computer solution. The choices are bewildering, and are proliferating daily.
- Step 8. *Nurture the Intelligence Processes:* This requires encouraging interaction across departmental boundaries and subcultures. Therefore, the creation of events and forums to encourage this interchange is often a useful starting point.

- *Step 9. Focus Dissemination:* Issue weekly or monthly bulletins of key developments; it should be short and focused. They give organisation relevant and specific information that no external newsletter, with its generic coverage, can provide.
- *Step 10. Market the Capability:* Create two way interactions with library clients. Use all the techniques of marketing to reach the library's internal audience and consider carefully the incentives the library can offer to encourage the regular inflow of useful information.

AS TRAINER

Ben regard managing technological change is somewhat akin to the Queen's concept of progress in Through the Looking Glass. He claimed *"It takes all the running you can do, to keep in the same place. If you want to get somewhere else, you must run at least twice as that."* Thus to 'manage' this frenetic running pace, training is critically important. Trainers have to be very philosophical people, very adaptable, too. MacKellar claimed that two million anecdotes of unhappy and unavoidable crisis situations, however, do not replace the necessity of thorough preparation and competent training coverage, especially with basic tools such as Internet, CD-ROMs and other electronic sources.

He added, in the documentation manual for Folio VIEWS, the following four statements are listed, emphasising the fact that trainers have to train users to do more than simply be able to push the right buttons:

- *Information* does not equal knowledge.
- Use of *information* can lead to knowledge.
- If you can't find the *information* you need, gaining knowledge can be difficult.
- If you can't use the *information* once you find it, gaining knowledge can be impossible.

So, what can trainers do to move users from button pushing to knowledge gathering? They can be patient, teach some underlying technology, and explain some basic search rules. Erlendsdottir consider training in libraries as in other organisations, is divided into two main categories:

1. *Maintenance training*—that enables the library to maintain its existing procedures and include induction training for new entrants to the library system or particular parts.
2. *Basic updating and improvement training in identified areas*—whereby training should be concerned with the whole person, concepts, skills and behaviour patterns.

As suggested, the technological training needs of the librarians in libraries depend on the IT level of the particular level.

Thus, the librarian must:

- know the Art of the Search.
- know what the systems contain example how the shopping streets of information are laid out.
- know the back alleys as well as the main routes to the information example on the CD-ROMs.
- bargain with the system to get the 'best answers' in the cheapest, quickest way.
- consider using a greater range of visual and auditory challenges in the presentation.
- keep abreast of the ongoing and latest technological advancements.
- able to identify the body of core knowledge and skills required by them to run information and communication technology applications.
- improve and promote the existing and new library services to reach their clients.

Training library users to use these technological resources, and to understand the cultural rules and the new environment such as functional setup, linking, split screens, exporting, cutting and pasting) are the challenges. Trainers are similar in a way to personal shoppers for Westerners who land in Hong Kong and don't know the environment or culture. Thus the trainer's end goal is to see these clients finally doing their own shopping in the information marketplace, hopefully with enough expertise to be able to pick up a few bargains.

Why the Need for Training

The three major benefits are:

1. Appreciate the gaps that may exist between what is currently being done and what needs to be done.
2. Opportunity to make corrections in their systems within a safe environment.
3. Develop 'ownership' and reduce or eliminate staff and users resistance to change, thereby adding longevity to the system.

Training for trainers is regard a necessity in academic libraries and it is the library's responsibility to structure training so as to help librarians clarify both their own expectations and the expectations of their clients and the organisation itself.

ROLE OF STORAGE DEVISES IN DIGITAL LIBRARY ENVIRONMENT

Storing documents is one of the foremost jobs of present digital library and it's professional. In order to store a large number of digital collections and to retrieve them at any point of time, the necessity for having a computerized system in this regard was felt; digitalization of printed material was the result. It is highly valuable for storing the information in an organized manner and retrieves the same quickly. Managing documents in the proper order is very much necessary in library to provide better services to the user community and some permanent solution to preserve the library material was needed. The permanent solution will be digitalizing the printed materials, which can be transmitted and received anywhere in the world where the infrastructure to send and receive is in place. This new access of technology will help to preserve the information in digital form for future use for future generation.

WHAT IS DIGITAL LIBRARY ?

Although Metrics for traditional libraries such as precision and recall can be directly applicable to some aspects of a digital library and have been widely accepted, the digital library is much more complex and there is much more to be considered.

Matrices are required to deal with issues such as the distributed nature of the digital library, the importance of user interfaces to the system, and the need for systems approaches to deal with heterogeneity among the various components and content of the digital library. The main activities of users can be classified into five categories:

- Locating and selecting among relevant sources
- Retrieving information from them
- Interpreting what was retrieved
- Managing the filtered-out information locally, and
- Sharing results with others

Definition of Digital Library

Digital Library can be define as "Computer-based information system for acquiring storing, organizing, searching, distributing and displaying digital materials for end-user access; not necessarily network-based but designed and constructed so as to be capable of attaching or being attached to a network" It means it is clear that fundamental mission of libraries for the users are not changed, *i.e.*, easy access to knowledge and information but the processes tools, techniques are totally changed.

Digital Libraries are viewed as systemic providing a community of users with coherent access to a large, organized repository of information and knowledge. This organization of information is characterized by the absence of prior detailed knowledge of uses of the information.

The ability of the use to access, recognize, and utilize this repository is enriched by the capabilities of digital technologies. More people are recognizing that digital library is not a topic only computer and information science, but advances in digital library also depend on efforts from legal community. Digital libraries are libraries extended and enhanced through digital technology. Important aspects of a library that may be extended and enhanced include:

- The collection of the library
- The organization and management of the collection
- Access to library items and the processing of the information contained in the items
- To communicate information

PURPOSE AND FUNCTION OF DIGITAL LIBRARY

Purpose of Digital Library:

- To speed up the systematic development of the means to collect, store and organized information and knowledge in digital form, and of digital library collection
- To promote the economical and efficient delivery of information to all parts of society
- To encourage cooperative efforts which leverage the considerable investment in research resource, computing and communications network
- To strengthen communication and collaboration between and among the research business, government and educational communities
- To contribute to the lifelong learning opportunities of all people

Function of Digital Library:

- Provide access to very large amount of information resources to the users wherever they are and whenever they need.
- Focus on providing access to primary information apart from the secondary sources
- Support multimedia content along with the text makes the information more useful and understandable to the users.
- Network accessibility in an Internet and Intranet environment
- Provide user-friendly interface to enable the users for access information comfortably
- Provide hypertext links for navigation through the required reference
- Support client server architecture
- Support advanced search and retrieval for better output to the users
- Integration with other digital libraries

WHAT IS STORAGE TECHNOLOGY

Computer technology may conveniently be grouped into: processor technology, storage technology and software aspects. In storage technology considering advances in devices for digital information storage it may be stated that most of the primary storage in computers is now supplied by semi-conductor circuits. There have been significant developments in memory technology affecting three areas of performance spectrum; the high speed, high performance the midrange and the low speed bulk memory systems. It is now possible that even a small computer system might have cache memory, a small associative memory retaining most recently referenced information and in a readily available place.

In some cases, cache memory may be at the top of a hierarchy of memories having a wide variety of characteristics. Memory management, dynamic memory allocation, and virtual memory schemes, generally found in large computer systems, are now appearing on computers which are small and less costly. The development of *charge coupled devices* (CCDs) and bubble memories have filled the gap which previously existed in the continuum of memory devices such as Fixed-head magnetic disk and these are slower than other semi-conductor memories.

These memories have advantage over magnetic disk in that they contain no mechanical parts and could be used to store significant amount of information and can be treated as a structured file system. There has been continuous improvement in recording densities of magnetic media. Floppy disk and microfloppies provide a convenient media to store data.

The development of video disk has added a new dimension to the information storage technology. Video disks could be used to store large volumes of information in digital form. These kinds of mass storage are believed to be very useful in the development of information storage and retrieval systems. It may be stated that all these innovations in storage technology provide us a variety of alternatives depending on the requirements of speed of operation.

TYPES OF COMPUTER STORAGE

Computers systems include two types of digital information storage: internal storage, within the CPU and the Backing storage on external devices such as disks or tapes. Different types of storage media differ according to a number of criteria such as speed of operation, capacity cost, reliabilities, the degree to which information is immediately accessible, etc. The various types of storage devices are available in computer market like Network Storage, Backup Storage, Internal Storage and PC Storage Products but we think the manufacture wise classification are different.

Internal Storage Devices: Internal storage is also known as main, primary or core storage, or memory. It is used to hold those instructions and data required at any moment while a programme is running, which must be available instantaneously. Silicon semiconductor chips are now invariably used for internal storage; these are categories as either RAM or ROM chips. ROMs are used for data which is never altered for example, a computer's operating system instructions, while RAM is used for data which is liable to change often, and instructions used in the execution of a programme Backup storage: Backup storage, also termed external storage, is used to hold programmes ad data which are read into internal storage when required. The most common form now, as for the last thirty years, is magnetic storage media, either tapes or disks.

With both of these, data is recorded onto a plastic surface, coated with a varnish containing an oxide which can be magnetized in one or two directions; each magnetization representing one bit of data. Data is written or read with the help of read/write heads. Small electromagnets, close to the surface. Magnetic Tapes are very commonly used for storing large quantum of data for which rapid access is not necessary; especially for archival data backup, etc. Tapes are cheap means of storing data but access is generally slow. Small cassette tapes, of relatively low capacity are used with microcomputers. Magnetic Disks are most widely used form of baking storage, suitable for holding information required rapidly for example, data for running programme.

In the type of disk drive in large computer system, data is recorded on the flat surfaces of circular disks revolving on a common spindle, with one read/ write head for each disk. Access times typically 0.01 second, although much faster than tape, are rather slow by comparison with other computer operations and disk access times are one of the main limiting factors in the speed of operation of retrieval system with information stored on disk. Disk capacities have increased greatly, from original values of about 10 MB to present units with 1 GB which is one thousand million bytes.

Smaller computer systems use Winchester disks, with a single hard disk in a sealed unit, floppy disks, which are compact, cheap and convenient for transfer of programmes and data. They are limited in storage capacity, with relatively slow access times, and less movement than a hard disk in day to day use.

Floppy disks are available in two sizes, 1.44 MB and 1.2 MB but now-a-days 1.2 MB floppy are not used. So, we would mention only two types one is Internal Storage and External Storage. In Internal Storage device it may be Network Storage, Internet Storage, Hard Disk Storage, etc. and External Storage devices like Floppy, CD ROM, CD Writer, DVD, USB Port, Pen drive and many more but we discuss only external storage drives. The contents of a digital library get to the readers via direct physical transmission: one person talked to another.

These kinds of transmission have so many disadvantages. The other transmission methods like physical objects computer network technologies can perform the duty in a better way. The mainly used physical objects are books and CD ROMs. Books are the permanent version of information. The economics of scale in modern publishing are such that it is difficult to issue a book today in a small press run. Since so many to the costs of printing a book are incurred before the first copy comes off the press, a small press run means high costs and thus high prices. Scholarly journals are even more affected by the push by authors to see their names in print. Their prices have been raised to levels that no one could have imagined 30 years ago; today a journal subscription can cost as much as a new car. Since the authors are not being paid for their contributions, and since journals do not carry a retailer's mark-up, these prices reflect the very small number of libraries that are still willing to subscribe.

CD ROM

The first product in evolutionary optical storage of information is CD ROM. It is a permanent optical-based storage device that in conjunction with an associated drive becomes a powerful peripheral for the PC. The CD ROM puts multi megabytes permanently store data bases at user front end of a PC. Its only drawback is that the end users cannot put his own information on it. CD ROM stands for Compact Disc Read Only Memory.

A compact disc is a 12cm diameter disc made from polycarbonate substrate and a reflective metalised layer. A disc weighs 16 grammas. A typical CD ROM can store about 650 MB data. One would get a better idea of the size of the data that a CD ROM can hold if we say that a CD ROM can hold about 250000 pages of text of 5000 handling systems and services CD ROM can store full motion video, animation, graphics, text and high resolution audio. One should keep in mind that a floppy drive cannot run a CD ROM. For running a CD ROM one would require a CD ROM drive. The time taken by a CD drive to find and grab a piece of information is known access time. This is usually in milliseconds. The smaller the access time, the better the drive; the amount of data transferred form the CD ROM to the computer in unit time is known as transfer rate.

The basic rate is 150 *kilo bytes per second* (kpbs) and "4x" drive transfers at the rate of 600 (4*50) kbpsz. Today "16 xs" become the normal CD drive. However, in the market "24 xs" is also available. One would require more the 450 high density floppy diskettes to store an equivalent amount of information on CD compared to hard disc or floppy diskettes. Read Only Memory means that the information stored on a compact disc can only be read but it cannot be modified.

As CD ROM stores text, graphic or still images audio and video or moving images, one would need to install a sound card and speaker to enjoy the world of multimedia that a CD ROM offers. The music CDs were followed by CD ROMs. CD ROM can hold a variety of multimedia information. At one point of time, it was called CD-I or compact disc interactively to the user's instructions. Of course, today such terminology has become irrelevant as almost every CD ROM available in the market is interactive. The benefits of storing data in the CD ROM are:

- High storage capacity
- No head crash

- Low error rate, correctable data
- Long life
- Random access
- Early transportable
- OS independent file system
- Low cost
- Reliable medium
- Less shelf space

This benefits that made CD ROM practically attractive in today's competing information environment are:

- Multi-Media: the ability to deliver unlimited end users access to over 600 MB information delivered using ordinary post means. It can be used for text, graphics, data, audio and video in one simple purchase.
- Multiplatform: It is the first truly system independent media with appropriate SWI, CD ROM allows equal access to information regardless of the computer HW or SW platforms used by the end users.
- Multilingual: Sophisticated CD ROM systems today allow the end users to select the operating language at choice and change it on-the-fly.

The technology which will most characterize the nineties is multimedia, Multimedia technology integrates text, images, graphics, video, animation, sound or music. It is interactive on the lines of technological barriers, for examples, extra disk space required to store multimedia formats and broad bandwidth to transmit the text.

PRESERVATION AND NEW TECHNOLOGIES

Preservation in cultural institutions over the past 30 to 40 years has been seen as fairly straightforward, involving specific activities such as environmental control, proper storage, disaster planning, reformatting, and conservation treatment. The increasing presence, however, of digital imaging and digital resources within cultural institutions in recent years has changed the way institutions perceive preservation. Digitization increases the complexity of the relationship between the medium and the message.

Digital preservation must be considered in two contexts:

- Can digital scanning be used to preserve the content of existing collections, and if so, does that mean traditional preservation activities are not needed?
- How should collections that are originally created digitally be preserved? What does it mean to preserve a digital object that can be easily changed without leaving any trace that the change was made?

Collection managers face difficult questions about technology's role in preserving collections. When is it sufficient to preserve just the information in an object, and when is it necessary to preserve the object itself? Is digital scanning of collections solely an access tool and a means of protecting collections from handling, or can it be considered a preservation strategy? Is digital scanning actually an effective means of protecting collections from handling, keeping in mind that the scanning process may involve much more handling of the collection than occasional use would? How does digital preservation fit into a traditional preservation programme?

Reformatting and Treatment, but it is crucial to understand that digital technology does not make traditional preservation unnecessary. Because of the difficulties inherent in preserving digital objects over the long term, digitization of collections is not a substitute for environmental control, proper storage, and other types of reformatting; it is simply another option in the preservation tool box. New technology does, however, make it even more difficult to allocate already-scarce resources among preservation activities.

ELEMENTS OF A PRESERVATION PROGRAMME

Although there is general consensus within the preservation community on the basic elements of a systematic preservation programme, where the emphasis falls will depend on the type of institution, since institutional and user needs will vary. For example, the primary interest of a public library may be to keep materials in good repair so that they can be used until they become obsolete and are withdrawn, while a research library or an archives would emphasize preservation of intellectual content over the long term and/or preservation of original items with artifactual value.

The basic elements of a preservation programme are as follows:

- *Environmental Control*: Providing a moderate and stable temperature and humidity level as well as controlling exposure to light and pollutants. This should be a priority for all institutions, although control will usually be less tight for general circulating collections than for rare books, special collections, or archival materials.
- *Disaster Planning*: Preventing and responding to damage from water, fire, or other emergency situations. Again, this should be a high priority in all institutions. The reasons are obvious for collections of enduring value, but even collections that are not meant to be retained over the long term represent a capital investment for an institution and as such must be protected from loss.
- *Security*: Protecting collections from theft and/or vandalism. This type of protection is needed for both special and general collections, since loss and vandalism of general collections results in unnecessary replacements and expense.

- *Storage and Handling*: Using non-damaging storage enclosures and proper storage furniture; cleaning storage areas; using care when handling, exhibiting, or reformatting collections; educating staff and users in proper handling techniques. Again, this should be a priority for all types of collections.
- *Reformatting*: Reproducing deteriorating collections onto stable media to preserve the informational content or in cases where the originals are fragile or valuable and handling is restricted. This category includes microfilming, production of preservation facsimiles, and duplication of audiovisual collections. These strategies are most appropriate for collections whose intellectual content needs to be preserved over the long term and/or where security copies are needed for unique items. Preservation microfilming is an excellent strategy for unique paper-based collections, but a low priority for institutions with general collections that are duplicated elsewhere.
- *Library Binding*: Rebinding of damaged volumes to provide sturdy use copies. This strategy is used by libraries with general collections in heavy use. It should not be used on any items that have artifactual value.
- *Conservation Treatment*: Treating individual objects using the services of a trained conservator. This may be appropriate for a wide range of institutions, provided they hold unique materials that are of sufficient value to justify treatment.
- *In-House Repair*: Repairing objects that do not have artifactual value using a trained collections conservator or trained in-house staff. In-house book repair is used by public and academic libraries to keep non-unique books in good condition for use, and some institutions use basic paper repair techniques for historical materials. But for special collections libraries, archives, and historical societies, general preventive activities such as rehousing should be given a higher priority than in-house repair.
- *Digital Projects*: Using digital imaging to provide access copies of deteriorated original collections; creating digital objects that will act as preservation copies of original items; and/or preserving objects that are "born-digital". Digital projects may be appropriate across a wide range of institutions; the key in undertaking such a project is for the institution to have a good understanding of the requirements and limitations of digital imaging.

It is helpful to keep in mind that the primary goal of preservation is to ensure that collections survive in good condition for as long as they are needed. Preservation should never be limited to the treatment of a few select items. The most cost-effective way to establish longevity is to prevent or retard deterioration.

SELECTION FOR PRESERVATION

"Preservation" refers to all the activities undertaken by an institution to ensure that its collections survive in usable condition for as long as they are needed. While this sounds relatively simple, the process of deciding what to preserve and how to preserve it can be complicated and challenging. Which materials will be important in the future? What items or collections should be preserved, and how?

Even with a national cooperative microfilming effort, cultural institutions with paper-based collections have increasingly realised that it is not possible to preserve every brittle item. As a result, various strategies have been developed for selecting collections for preservation.

This part will explore the various criteria that you should consider when selecting collections for preservation action. Once you have decided what materials merit preservation, the choice of preservation method will depend on the intellectual content, the physical characteristics, and the condition of the materials. We will learn more about evaluating the condition of your collections and choosing the appropriate preservation method(s).

The key to making effective selection decisions is to realise that:

- You cannot save everything (even with cooperative projects);
- Priorities must be set among collections (*e.g.*, you must define your collection's strengths and concentrate on them); and
- Every item may not need to be preserved (*e.g.*, will a representative sample of certain materials be acceptable?).

SELECTION FOR LIBRARY COLLECTIONS

The selection process for preservation has been discussed and analysed extensively within the library community because of the growing need to develop strategies for selecting collections for repair, replacement, and reformatting.

Identification of damaged or deteriorated materials often occurs in the course of other library activities, although it may also happen as part of a special project. Consistent procedures for the identification of damaged items are necessary. When an item is identified for possible in-house or offsite preservation action, the librarian must indicate in the catalog record that the item has been temporarily removed from circulation and complete a form indicating what preservation action is needed.

This form will accompany the item, which should be placed in a particular area and routed for further review or preservation action. Items must also be placed in a particular area and routed for further review or treatment. In her article "Selection for Preservation," Carolyn Harris summarizes the most common methods librarians use to identify collections whose importance and condition justify preservation action.

Some of these methods are appropriate in the archival context as well:

- *Condition and Use*: Deteriorated items in need of attention are identified as they are returned after circulation or pointed out to staff by users or stack maintenance staff.
- *Condition and Library Processing*: Items in need of attention are identified during acquisition, cataloging, or other processing activities.
- *Condition at the Shelf*: Special projects that require inspection of materials at the shelf (*e.g.,* bar coding, shelf reading) can also identify deteriorated collections. For historical or special collections, a conservator may be needed for further review.
- *Collection and Condition*: An entire collection is identified as important for preservation and individual items within that collection are reviewed to identify materials in need of preservation attention.
- *Scholarly Review*: Faculty, researchers, or scholars identify deteriorated items with particular research value. This may be on an individual basis or part of a special project.
- *Vulnerability to Loss or Deterioration*: Materials that are particularly subject to deterioration, such as newspapers or items to be exhibited, are identified for attention.
- *Value or Uniqueness*: Items that are particularly unique or valuable (in monetary or other senses) are identified for attention.

Decision-making on the Collection Level

While it is easy to identify materials already in special collections as important, a research library may hold other collections of importance as well. In many cases, libraries have chosen to preserve only those collections that are circulated and used. But the library community has also realised that research libraries have a responsibility to preserve collections that may be important for research in the future, even if they are not currently used. Thus, strategies have been developed to select collections for preservation according to their quality and importance.

The criteria used to identify important collections include size of the collection; subject strength (*e.g.,* the depth and extent of the collection as compared to other collections on that subject); past, current, or projected future use; quality and extent of bibliographic control of the materials; available funding for preservation of the collection; media contained in the collection; cooperative responsibilities of the institution; and scholarly interest in the collection.

Decision-making on the Item Level

Before any item is preserved, it must be reviewed to make sure that preservation is the proper action to be taken. How is the item related to others in the collection? Are there additional copies or other items by the same author?

Does the item fit the collecting policy? Are there other copies that are easily accessible in a close geographic area? Has the item been preserved (*e.g.*, filmed or treated) elsewhere? Is a replacement (*e.g.*, reprint, facsimile, microfilm) commercially available?

If these questions do not establish that the item should be discarded or replaced, additional analysis will be needed to determine the item's priority for preservation action and how it should be preserved.

SELECTION FOR ARCHIVAL COLLECTIONS

As in libraries, selection for preservation in archives often happens as part of other activities, such as acquisition, appraisal, arrangement, and description. The process of selection for preservation is closely related to archival appraisal, since it involves identifying the value and importance of collections.

While many of the criteria libraries use to select printed collections for preservation can be used in the context of archival collections, identifying important historical and archival collections also requires consideration of types of value specific to those collections. Since archivists have no more time or resources than librarians, they cannot save everything. Thus, they have developed methods for deciding which records have long-term research value and which do not.

Types of Value for Archival/Historical Collections

Most archivists follow, at least in a general sense, the guidelines for value T.R. Schellenberg established at the National Archives in the mid-1950s. On the most basic level, Schellenberg distinguished between primary value and secondary value.

The primary value of records is their ongoing business value for the organization that created them, to assist in carrying out its administrative, financial, legal, and operating activities; this is referred to as administrative, fiscal, or legal value. Secondary value refers to the value records may have to external organizations and/or private researchers. Schellenberg defined two types of secondary value: evidential value and informational value. Note that these two types of value are not mutually exclusive: a record may be valuable for both evidential and informational purposes.

Evidential value refers to the value of records in documenting the organizational structure and functions of the institution or the activities of the individual that created them. Who created the records? Do they accurately reflect the activities of the organization or person? Do the records provide evidence of the structure and policies of the organization or institution or evidence of the changing interests of the person? In the case of an organization, are these records also maintained elsewhere within the organization? Do the records reflect policymaking or implementation of functions?

Informational value refers to the subject content of the collection.

Types of informational value include:

- *Uniqueness*: The information in the records must be more complete and useful than that found on this topic in other existing sources, whether public or private. The records should also not be duplicated elsewhere, an occurrence that is fairly common in modern public records.
- *Form*: Records that provide concentrated information (*e.g.,* some information about many people, as in census records; or in-depth information about a few people, as in case files) are the best candidates for retention. The form of the record is also important: can it be accessed and understood easily by researchers?
- *Importance*: Value for long-term scholarly and public research is difficult to determine. Archivists generally try to document those subjects, people, and events that are considered important by the society within which the records were created.

Other types of value commonly encountered are:

- *Intrinsic Value*: This refers to records with characteristics that require them to be retained in their original form. They may be valuable because of their age (in general, older records have more significance, but this is not always the case), because the records have a unique physical form or aesthetic quality, because the records are directly associated with people or events of historical significance, because they might be useful for exhibition, etc.
- *Historical Value*: This term is used in many different ways; it might refer to materials that are valuable because of their age or association, or it might encompass both evidential and informational value.

Both value and condition must be considered in selecting archival and other historical collections for preservation. Additional considerations include whether the records are duplicated or maintained in another form elsewhere; whether they are complete (fragmentary materials can be frustrating for research); whether they need to be retained in their original form, or whether they can be reformatted (*e.g.,* onto microfilm); and whether there are donor or other restrictions on the use of the records.

NEEDS FOR DIGITIZATION OF LIBRARY: TECHNOLOGY AND SUPPORTING FORMAT

The Dr A P J Abdul Kalam, President of India, International Conference on Digital Libraries: Knowledge creation, preservation, access, and management on 24-27 February 2004 keynote address conclusion, said that Digital Library is a national mission. We should see that all the schools, colleges, and universities digitize their libraries in their own native languages and connect to the outside world within 4 years. We have to ensure availability of fibre optic cables, satellite communication and wireless infrastructure especially in remote areas. It is also essential to realize high bandwidth technology like Multiple 10 Giga Bits connectivity across the country. The topic of " Digital Libraries" is currently the subject of world wide debate and research. To some simply suggests " Computerization of traditional libraries" to others, who have studied library science it calls for carrying out the function of libraries in a new way encompassing new types of information resources, new approaches to acquisition, new methods of storage and preservation, new approaches to classification and cataloguing, new modes of interaction with and for patrons more reliance on electronic system and networks and dramatic shifts in intellectual organizational and economic practices.

The handling and use of rare books, fragile books and non-book materials are not new problems to libraries. In recent years libraries are acquiring non-book materials and have been developing special collections at an accelerated rate. As a result of this many university libraries have established a separate unit of special collection. This collection covers rare-books, maps, manuscripts, pamphlets, posters, broadsides, newspapers, musics, non-musical recordings, micro facsimile, microfilms, university archives, slides and films, book plates, pictures, painting, graphic materials, coins and currency, stamps, little magazines, clipping files. Etc.

NEEDS FOR DIGITIZATION

Most of India's ancient manuscripts were written on bhurj patras. Ancient India was well developed in the subjects like Astronomy, Mathematics, Space Science, Medicine, Defiance, Political System, Economics, etc. Unfortunately many of these valuable manuscripts were lost due to improper care. Some of them were destroyed due to water, fungus, fire and som were purposely destroyed by foreign invaders. Book is one of the medium which deal with comprehensive knowledge and information. Preserving the books and other reading materials is a burning question which the librarians of past and present are facing. Therefore, it is urgently needed to find out some permanent solutions to preserve the library materials.

OBJECTIVES

The main objectives of the digital library are:

- To capture, store, manipulate and distribute information,
- To introduce and provide new services,
- To provide need-based and retrospective search services to the user,
- To have large number of database in CDs'
- To avoid routine and redundant activities,
- To provide facility for networking and resource sharing,
- To access national and international journals which are being published only in machinereadable form,

- To digitize the documents for preservation and for space saving,
- To support library functions such as circulation, serial control, acquisition control, stock maintenance and other routine office works and developing in house database, and
- To improve the cost effectiveness of library operations.

COMPONENTS

Digital libraries require well-tested and proven information technologies including the multimedia kit. Much of the work in digital libraries is achieved through E-mail service, by participating in Usernet, by accessing the database or servers through network, little Internet. Locally developed databases will contribute a lot to develop digital libraries. In other words, the components of digital libraries are:

- Data-Technical Data: This consist of books and journals stored in digital form in a computer disk store. These are two ways to storing this information. One way is to photograph a page and Scan the image with a scanner. This form of storage is called a bit mapped form. It is practical way of storing old manuscripts, texts and journals. The practical way of storing old manuscripts, texts and journals. The image of the page may be retrieved and displayed on the video screen of the computer. The other way of storing a text is to present each character by its ASCII Code.
- Numeric Data: Consist of tables of various types such as physical property data of various materials from experiments, astronomical table's, etc. Such numeric data stored digitally may be used by curve setting programmer spreadsheet programmes, etc.
- Graphic Data: May be photographs, maps, drawings, etc. The simple way of storing such data is to scan the image and store it as a bit patterns. Data should in this form eases retrieval.
- Photographs: Colour and Monochrome are stored in bit mapped form using compression algorithms to reduce storage space.
- Audio-Data: Autio-data is digitized compressed using a commonly accepted standard comprehension algorithms and stored. A musical scores may also be coded and stored with Audiodata.
- Video Data: Audio-data is digitized compressed using a commonly accepted standard comprehension algorithms and stored. A musical scores may also be coded and stored with Audio-data.
- Indexing: Indexing and inter-linking multimedia data is extremely import and for ease of retrieval. Keywords in textual documents are selected and linked to related words with logical links by appropriate software. This is called hypertext. For materials on other media also related elements are selected and linked in what is known as hypermedia.

- Linking: The information collection of the digital library will normally not be stored in one computer. It will be distributed in may computers known as servers. All these servers will be linked by highspeed communication links. The fact that the information in the digital library is distributed need not to be known to a user as it is not relevant from his/her point of view. A user gets easy access to the information based on his/her request regardless of its geographical location.
- User: Access the library from anywhere using a terminal or a computer connected to the network to which the information servers of the library are connected.

TECHNOLOGY

Until recently, not many people were happy to read from a computer screen. Quality of display was one of the factors behind it. Recent advances in the field of Information technology have improved not only the quality of computer display but also the font displayed on them. Besides, a variety of software are now available which are capable of manipulating and rendering information.

Personal computers are getting cheaper and cheaper not only in the developed countries, out are also available at an affordable cost in the developing countries. With the availability of computers, capable of computing at a very high speed and having large disc storage space, it is feasible to digitize and store information in the form of high quality graphics, colour images, voice signals and video clips at a low cost.

HARDWARE OF DIGITAZATION

In the early years of computing, computers were so expensive that it was difficult to purchase by libraries. Today, computers are cheap and middle-sized libraries in India are having computers. Apart from this, in the past, lack of hardware and absence of proper technology was also a hindrance in creating a digital library. In the present time, however, we have many hardware equipments available for digitization process. Some of these are mentioned below:

- Flatbed Scanner: Till today, the flatbed scanner is probably the most common piece of equipment available having compatibility with any personal computer. The scanner has a glass plate onto which the source document is laid face-down. The *charged coupled device* (CCD), which allows to convert analog to digital, moves beneath the surface of glass and records the reflected light as an array of pixels. Flatbed scanners are both quick and economical to use. In the past their speed is increased and only single pass is required under the document. These flatbed scanners are often bundled with their own scanning software and sometime with *Optical Character Recognition* (OCR) software. The cost of these flatbed scanners have come down dramatically and now available at the rate as low as five thousand rupees. However, the main disadvantage of the flatbed is that it relies on contact scanning, and is thus unsuitable for rare or fragile material. It also requires the document to be placed flat on the glass, so any curvature of the source material will distort the image.

- Sheet feeders – Sheet feeders are very useful in case a library is having loose leaf documents for processing. The benefit of this type of scanner is its remarkable speed and one can leave it churning through the documents unattended. However, one can not load more than 100 pages into the feeder at one time. Yet one more demerit of the sheet feeder is that it is unable to deal with fragile or brittle items. Furthermore, these are not suitable for oversized documents, though various models of these scanner are available in the market.
- Drum Scanners – These are called as drum-scanner because the source document is actually attached to a glass drum. Though these scanners offer the highest resolutions but rarely found outside a dedicated scanning agency because of their high cost. Several other kind of scanners are also available such as slide scanners and Microfilm scanners. Some of these are extremely cheap. Quality of scanning is normally in resolution, measured in dots per inch. For the textual material 300 dpi is a minimum quality of scanning, and 600 dpi is considered a good-quality resolution.
- Digital Camera – The digital camera is particularly useful in case of fragile or brittle items as these items can not bear the pressure of flatbed scanners. Many vendors have launched their products in the market over the past few years, for example, Kodak, DC215, Kontran Progress 3012, Minolta, etc. Some of these are in use in libraries in India and overseas. For instance, the central library of *University of Hyderabad* (UOH) is using a model of Minolta for digitization project of theses and dissertations. Large projects such as those running at the National Library of Scotland, the Arnamagnean Institute in Iceland, British Library, etc also uses high level cameras which are capable of giving an effective resolutions. However, there are some inherent problems with the digital camera in general. For example, the scan time can be quite long meaning there by lighting conditions have to be maintained throughout potentially damaging procedure particularly when using warm lighting on documents. Also the are cumbersome pieces of equipments, which most of the time require some form of stand or cradle. Furthermore, these are not effective in the digitization of books that could not be opened beyond 45 degrees because of delicate binding.

DIGITIZATION SOFTWARE

Software for digital imaging covers three main area.

- Capturing the image
- Processing the image
- Delivering the image

Initially, as suggested, need a piece of software having interfaced with the peripheral device used for scanning such as the camera or scanner. Important point to take into consideration when choosing the capturing software is the type of output file formats. This can be extremely significant particularly when it comes to create master image. TIFF is perhaps the most important image format available at the moment. It is widely used as the cross-platform and archiving format in most digitization projects, particularly as it allows for high-quality images to be saved without any loss in the original capture. Moreover, it is not tied to any particular scanner or display. Conversion from TIFF to other formats is relatively straight forward.

Furthermore, images in TIFF are the best suited for universal accessibility and high resolution archival storage. However, the software should also be capable to produce *Joint Photographic Experts Group* (JPEG) derivatives for display on the World Wide Web. The JPEG and the *Graphical Interchange Format* (GIF) are the most popular image files delivered via the web and are ideally suited for displaying in all browsers. Many digitization projects create JPEG or GIF files format from their TIFF masters for subsequent delivery via the web. This is what know as processing the image and making it suitable for the end-purpose.

Once the actual conversion process over, the most important issue is the eventual delivery of the digital collection. In this step, primary emphasis should be given on what does the user want to see? The catalogues should be searchable and browsable.

Facility for simple and complex searches should made available. Navigation aids should be both intuitive and apparent, and consistency maintained throughout. Additionally, there should be online help. On the one hand, the interface should be aesthetically pleasing while on the other hand, it should be open to accommodate the latest developments in technology.

FUNCTIONS

The primary function of digital libraries is to enable searching of electronic collections distributed across networks, rather than merely electronic repositories from digitized physical materials.

A digital library should have the following five integrated functions:

- Creation and capture of content process of turning: Integrating and importing multimedia objects into digital information – digital library content from many diverse sources different type to format.

- Storage and Management: Process of organizing and managing digital content to ensure that it is available to users whenever they want access to it. Providing stable, reliable storage and management of data in an open environment across a broad spectrum of platform.
- Search and Access: To be able what the user need quickly.
- Distribution: To enable information owners to distribute their material in numerous ways: through existing networks, clients/server business solutions or the Internet.
- Right Management: Providing extensive access control capabilities enabling content owners to capitalize on their protected assets.

DIGITIZATION FILE EXTENSION AND USE

You see a file somewhere on the 'net with a name like "library.*xyz*" and you would like to download it and use it on your computer. Will it work? What does the file extension *xyz* mean, anyway? This paper provide answers to these questions. It is not meant to be read straight through; rather, it is meant to be a reference. An extension may be looked up either with the "find in page" option of your browser or by appending a "#*xyz*" to the "go to" or "URL" field on your browser. There is also a Search Interface that will return not only the specific extension sought but also other entries that reference it. Be aware though that it assumes familiarity with the computer basics discussed in the topic. You may notice that most extensions are three letters long. This is due to a historical limitation of the operating system called CP/M. In fact, the whole concept of file extensions comes from CP/M. Most modern operating systems do not attribute any special meaning to the "."character. Be aware though that there is no standardization to filename extension usage, and many different people have used extensions to apply to many different things.

STORAGE METHODS AND HANDLING

Storage methods have a direct effect on the useful life of material. While proper storage can extend life, slovenly, haphazard, overcrowded conditions soon result in damage to collections. Moreover, poor-quality storage enclosures can accelerate the deterioration of the material they are intended to protect. Handling by staff and users also directly affects the useful life of library collections. Damage to books is cumulative. Repeated poor handling can quickly transform a new book into a worn one, and a worn book into an unusable book that requires costly repair, rebinding, or replacement. By following the guidelines presented here, the library can make significant strides towards improving the welfare of the collection.

Shelving and the Shelving of Books

- Shelving should be designed to provide smooth, secure, clean, and convenient support. Any protrusions and sharp edges should be attended to. Ideally, book cases should be constructed of steel with a baked enamel finish.

- Volumes should be shelved a minimum of 10 cm off the floor to reduce the risk of damage from flooding or passers-by. When possible, use shelving units that have a 'canopy' on top, as this will deflect water, dust, and some damaging light.
- Good air circulation should be maintained in storage areas and around shelving.
- Book cases should be at least 5 cm away from walls and the books another 5 cm away from the back of the book case. This is especially important when book cases are positioned against the outside walls of a building.
- When books are stored in steel cabinets, ensure the cabinets are adequately ventilated. Holes should be in the sides and not on the top of the cabinets to avoid dust and debris falling on the books.
- Books kept on mobile shelving must be shelved carefully to avoid any possibility of them falling off or being crushed when the shelves are moved.

For the maximum protection of books, the following rules should be enforced:

- Shelve books so that they are not difficult to remove or replace. Books which are tightly shelved will soon be damaged when they are removed or replaced.
- Use bookends to support books when shelves are not full. Allowing books to lean will distort and strain the structures and eventually cause their breakdown. Bookends should have smooth surfaces and broad edges to prevent covers from being abraded and leaves torn or creased.
- Do not let books extend beyond the edges of shelves into aisles because they can be damaged by passers-by and trollies.
- Shelve books by size whenever possible. Avoid keeping large books next to small ones because the large book will be inadequately supported.
- Box, or at least separate with a piece of card or board, bindings with metal furniture (clasps, bosses, studs, etc.), which are shelved next to unprotected books.
- Separate paper and cloth bindings from leather bindings. Acidity and oils in the leather migrate into paper and cloth and hasten their deterioration. Furthermore, degraded powdery leather will soil paper and cloth.
- Shelve small, structurally sound books upright.

- Move the books or rearrange the shelves if books are too tall to stand upright. Do not store books on their fore-edges as this will damage the structure of a book and loosen the binding.
- Store oversize, heavy, structurally weak, or damaged books horizontally to give them the overall support they require. Additional shelves may need to be inserted at narrow intervals to avoid having to stack these books.
- When oversize books that are stored flat are removed, the upper volumes should be transferred to an empty shelf or book trolley. The desired volume should be removed by lifting it with both hands, and the removed volumes should then be transferred back to the shelf. Replacing the book on the shelf is done in the same way.
- Avoid stacking books in piles on shelves or tables as the books can easily topple over. Ensure the stacks contain no more than two to three books.
- Take special care to ensure that shelfmark flags or titles of books that are stored flat are visible so the books can be identified without moving them.
- Do not place a large book on a small book.
- When the binding must remain on view, such as in a period room in a historic house, the use of book-shoes (supports that cover the sides but leave the spines of books visible) or placement of a piece of polyester film between the books.

Poor handling procedures can cause irreparable damage to books.

- They should not be pulled off the shelves by the headcap, a practice that causes the headcap to fail, tearing the spine of the binding.
- If there is room above the book, reach over the top of the book to the foreedge and then pull it out.
- If there is no room, push back the books on either side of the one to be retrieved, to expose enough of the spine to allow for a firm grip on either side of the spine with the thumb and fingers.
- The book should be removed, and the remaining books on the shelf and the bookends readjusted.

Carrying and Transporting Books

- Do not carry more books than can be comfortably held firmly in both hands.
- Pack books flat in tough boxes when moving them out of a room.
- If necessary, pad the box with polystyrene or foam so that the books do not slide around.
- Transport individual books in card boxes. Carry the box in a polythene bag when going outside.

- Use water-resistant polypropylene containers with securely fitting lids when moving books out of a building.
- Whenever possible use two people to move containers.
- Avoid leaving library material in vehicles.

Book Trollies and Books on Trollies

Use book trollies that:

- Have large rubber wheels, for this helps stability, and manoeuvrability, and reduces vibration
- Have wide shelves or protective rails to secure the items in transit
- Have bumpers on corners to minimize damage from inadvertent bumps.

When putting books on trollies ensure that:

- They are shelved upright on the trolley and are properly supported as in the stacks
- Volumes do not protrude beyond the edges of the trolley
- The trolley is loaded so that it has a low centre of gravity.

ENCLOSURES FOR BOOKS AND PAPER MATERIAL

Enclosures should be lignin-free, sulphur-free, alkaline buffered, and have a high cellulosic content (above 87 per cent). Enclosures include boxes, envelopes, and folders and are available commercially in a range of shapes and sizes.

Enclosures are crucial to library preservation, for they:

- provide protection from over-handling
- provide protection in transit
- provide protection on the shelves
- provide protection against fire, smoke, and flood damage
- keep out light
- keep out dust
- act as a buffer against fluctuations in the ambient environment
- act as a buffer against atmospheric pollution.

Types of Enclosures for Books

- Tailor-made boxes of bookboard and cloth are ideal but are expensive and require time and skill to make. They can be justified only for extremely rare, unique, and valuable material. They have the advantage of being able to provide all round support and are more robust than other types of enclosures.
- Phase-boxes are a cheaper alternative, which provide adequate short-term (15-20 years) protection, and are much quicker and simpler to construct. They can be made in-house or commercially.

- Commercially made, archival-quality boxes and four-flap folders come in a wide range of sizes and can be purchased in small and large quantities.
- Book-shoes are appropriate for books that require structural support while being displayed on shelves.
- Slipcases should be avoided because they often abrade the surface of the binding and damage the text-block when the book is slid in and out.
- Envelopes are sometimes used for the storage of books. These generally do not provide the support books need and should be replaced with boxes.
- Wrappers of a permanent durable paper or card can be used to protect books that are infrequently used, if enclosures are too expensive or take up too much space on shelves.

Selecting Material to be Boxed

When prioritising books for boxing the following should be considered:

- Books with fragile and important bindings.
- Vulnerable and damaged books – books with loose or torn leaves, and books with loose covers.
- Books bound in vellum or with vellum text-blocks. Vellum responds readily to changes in relative humidity by expanding and contracting. This can result in warped covers and cracked joints. Boxing helps restrain vellum bindings and thereby minimizes warping.

Shrink-wrapping and Vacuum-packing

Shrink-wrapping and vacuum-packing, adapted from the food and packaging industry, are economical ways of protecting material. Both processes involve placing an item between sheets, or into pouches, of polyester/polyethylene film. The film is either shrunk using heat, as in shrink-wrapping, or a vacuum is created around the item and all air expelled, as in vacuum-packing. While they seem to be stable in the short term, further tests have yet to be carried out on the effects of long-term storage. Material which is to be moved and fragile items, in particular those with brittle paper, can be placed between boards and protected in one of the ways; the result is a rigid and strong enclosure. Shrink-wrapping and vacuum-packing are also being used as means of combatting insect and fungal attack and creating a stable micro-environment. Space can be saved as the process expels most of the air, thereby reducing the thickness of the item.

Newsprint

Commercially made, archival-quality boxes and vacuum-packing are both ways of preserving newspapers. However, because much of the newsprint produced after 1840 is made of short-fibred paper that contains lignin and other impurities, its long-term preservation is difficult at best and, consequently, microfilming has become the most common method of dealing with newspapers. Collections of newsclippings are usually important because of the information they contain and not because of the value of the clippings themselves. For this reason, again, photocopying and microfilming are the most practical preservation options. All photocopying should be done on low-lignin, buffered paper using an electrostatic copier with heat-fused images. Newsclippings that must be retained should be treated and then physically separated from better-quality papers in a folder or in an enclosure made of polyester film.

Periodicals and Pamphlets

Periodicals and pamphlets can be stored in boxes, folders, or card envelopes. Several items of the same cover size can be stored together in commercially made boxes. Items that differ in size can be placed in card envelopes and then boxed. If a single periodical or pamphlet must be shelved between books, it should be placed in a card envelope.

Scrapbooks and Ephemera

Many historical collections include scrapbooks and ephemera (*e.g.,* trade cards, valentines, patterns, paper dolls, etc.). These items pose challenging preservation problems because they often contain a variety of components and media. They may have raised surfaces, three-dimensional decoration, or moving parts.

They are frequently unique, fragile, damaged, and of significant associational value. They should never be interfiled with other categories of library and archival material because damage may result from the different sizes, shapes, weights, and materials represented. Scrapbooks that are of special historic value in their original form should be individually boxed. Unbound ephemera should be grouped by size and type (*e.g.,* photographs, printed material, manuscripts, etc.), individually enclosed to protect items from acid migration and mechanical damage, if needed, and stored in a way that will support them structurally.

Single-sheet Material

- For paper collections, only objects of the same size and category should be stored together.
- Differences in bulk and weight are potentially damaging, so it is not advisable to store single sheets in the same box with books or pamphlets.
- Generally speaking, heavy objects should be stored separately from lighter ones, as should bulky objects (which cause uneven pressure inside boxes).

- As acid migrates from paper of inferior quality to any other paper with which it comes into direct contact, it is important to separate poor-quality papers from those that are better. Newsclippings and other obviously inferior-quality papers must be removed from direct contact with historical documents and manuscripts on better-quality paper.
- Documents and manuscripts should be unfolded for storage, if this can be done without splitting, breaking, or otherwise damaging them. If unfolding may result in damage, a conservator should be consulted before proceeding.
- Documents should be stored in file folders. Ideally, no more than ten to fifteen sheets should be placed in each folder.
- Folders should be placed in document-storage boxes.
- All folders inside a box should be the same size and should conform to the size of the box.
- Boxes should not be overfilled because this can cause damage when items are removed, replaced, or reviewed.
- Boxes can be stored flat or upright. Flat storage will give the documents overall support and will prevent crumbling edges, slumping, and other mechanical damage to which upright storage might subject them. Flat storage, however, causes documents on the bottom of the box to suffer from the weight of those above. If boxes are stored flat, they should be stacked only two high in order to facilitate their removal from, and replacement onto the shelves.
- Upright storage is acceptable when documents and folders are well-supported to prevent slumping and edge damage. 'Spacer' boards made out of stable materials can be used to fill out boxes that are not quite full.
- Vellum documents and maps, etc., are highly susceptible to fluctuations in temperature and relative humidity and should be placed in an enclosure. Suitable enclosures include encapsulation, folders, mats, and boxes, or a combination of these.

Fascicules

Rare and unique single-sheet items, such as letters, have been traditionally bound into guard books. These are satisfactory if they are kept fairly thin and allow a support sheet for each manuscript page to ensure that the support and not the manuscript is handled. A simpler method is to make up fascicules. A fascicule is a single-section, pamphlet-sewn binding comprising support sheets of bifolia and hooked leaves (acting as compensation guards) with an acid-free stiff paper cover. Sizes are made to fit commercial boxes. All items are foliated and placed loosely in the fascicules by librarians. The leaves on which the items are to be attached are also foliated. A Japanese paper hinge is pasted onto the edge of the item. The hinges are then pasted and the items attached to the recto of the support sheets.

The fascicules are then boxed. Fascicules have several advantages:

- Each item is kept flat and supported.
- Items can be easily removed and replaced if necessary (*e.g.,* for exhibition).
- Flexing of the object is reduced.
- Abrasion between items is reduced.
- Handling is reduced.
- A variety of materials within a standard format can be accommodated.
- The contents are protected from light and airborne pollutants.

Oversize Single-sheet Material

Oversize material includes architectural drawings, blueprints, maps, large prints, posters, and wallpaper samples. These items are best stored flat in plan chests. They should be placed individually in folders cut to fit the size of the drawer. If several items are placed in one folder, interleaving with acid-free tissue paper is desirable, especially if the items have colours or are of special value. There should be sufficient space between chests to facilitate the safe removal and replacement of oversize material. There should also be an adequate surface on which to place items once they are removed or prior to replacement.

If they are not brittle or fragile, oversize material can be rolled when flat storage is not possible. Some items need to be rolled individually; others can be rolled in groups of four to six similar-sized items, the exact number depending on the size and weight of the paper.

A tube several inches longer than the largest item being rolled and at least four inches in diameter (larger diameters are preferable) should be used. If the tube is not made of low-lignin, pH-neutral materials, it should be wrapped in neutral or buffered paper or polyester film. Alternatively, place the items between two sheets of polyester film or acid-free tissue cut several inches larger in both dimensions than the largest item being rolled. Roll the item or items onto the tube. Wrap the assembly with neutral or buffered paper or polyester film to protect it from abrasions. Using flat linen, cotton, or polyester tape, loosely tie up the wrapped roll. This assembly can be stored inside a larger rectangular box for added protection if desired. Tubes should be stored horizontally.

Handling and Transporting Oversize Single-sheet Material

- Use both hands when handling large items.
- Take care that large pendant seals are supported and turned with the document.

- Consider the route and destination before setting out, even if simply moving items from one room to another.
- Place maps, plans, and large single-sheet material in a portfolio or purposemade folder.
- Use two people for carrying large portfolios.
- Carry portfolios vertically.
- Use waterproof portfolios when moving items outside.

TELECOMMUNICATION CONVERGENCE IN THE INFORMATION

Telecommunication convergence in the information economy has had a significant effect on the delivery of library information resources and services. Convergence promises a 'clean slate' approach, where things are reengineered to provide better, more flexible service to the user. Convergence, according to Fowler can be defined in four major categories of the telecommunications industry that correspond to layers, or sets of layers, in the Open Systems Interconnect (OSI) network model. The categories are transport, switching, and applications.

- *Transport*: The same physical pipes and transport technology carry multiple services, usually of different customers, for example, multipleT1 or T3 links. Convergence at this level is primarily used by carriers to provision their infrastructure; it is largely transparent to users as they continue to see and pay for separate services.
- *Switching*: The same cable plant carries different types of traffic and does appropriate switching. Content and presentation to the user is unchanged, with the possible exception of new features. Historically, this has been the layer about which most discussion has centered. The distinction between services becomes less distinct or disappears entirely under network layer convergence; at the present time, Internet protocol (IP), a switching technology, is envisioned as the common medium for all (or many) types of telecommunications traffic, especially voice and Internet traffic.
- *Application (Content)*: The same end-user device or type of device and network handles and delivers all content; the user does not have separate network interface devices
- *Telecommunications/IT*: There is also a fourth meaning of convergence, which will be considered here, that refers to *blurring.of.the.distinction.between. tele-communications.and.information.processing*. Examples are use of Applications Service Providers (ASPs) and network computing.

With convergence, separate functions are now available through one source or channel, such as an ISP or through a single vendor. Of particular interest to libraries is the technological convergence at the application level. Multiple resources in varying formats, including text, data, images, graphics, audiovisual media, streaming media, games and simulations, and so forth, are now available over one transmission network, through the same user equipment, and through standard, ubiquitous software applications. Previous channels would have included, and perhaps required, delivery via postal mail service or broadcast media, carrying a variety of formats and media. Enterprise systems, interactive video-on-demand, and telecalls/teleconferencing are becoming the norm. What will limit the rapid expansion of these applications will be intellectual property rights issues. As the United States continues to build infrastructure and to recreate how the infrastructure is policed, broadband will undergo a number of changes.

However, increased broadband access will continue to build convergence. The United States Congress has been urged to recognise and "encourage the convergence of voice, data, image and video information into bit streams" to "[e]nsure the greatest possible regulatory flexibility, to allow for unpredictable future service needs, market developments and technological innovation". Congress has also been urged to reduce barriers to competition, restructure the market in the public interest, and increase spectrum efficiency with both licensed and unlicensed models of spectrum use.

Convergence is seen as an evolutionary, rather than a revolutionary process. Initiatives to ensure broadband to the majority of homes in the United States by 2010, if realised, may speed up these trends. Initiatives include the UTOPIA, the National LambdaRail Network, the NorthEast Education and Research Network (NEREN), the Third Frontier Network (TFN), and the hundreds of other Fibre communities in the United States. Integrated media systems that seamlessly combine video, audio, computer animation, text, and graphics into a common digital display medium were noted as a new area of convergence.

Further, Mihram and Mihram predicted that infrastructure installation, product creation, and commercialisation relating to integrated media systems would become areas of research and development for both the public and private sectors. Today, geographic information systems are seen as the next pivotal technology in this convergence, again due to the advances in interoperability and data standards.

Again, we see infrastructure installation, product creation, and commercialisation in GIS becoming areas of research for the public and private sectors. Standards development, in particular, is a crucial area for GIS convergence. Many organisations work collaboratively to promote the advancement of open geospatial standards and specifications, especially as the market expands into domains associated with Internet and telecommunications communications technologies.

These organisations include the Open Geospatial Consortium, W3C, and OASIS, as well as national and international standards associations. Since, much of the data in the contemporary information economy have geospatial or geotemporal components, no applications, systems, or technologies are unaffected. Further, it is through the efficient use of GIS/geospatial technologies that we are able to understand and leverage the value of spatial/location based information and processes in the broader context of ICT and enterprise information systems. Convergence continues through business processes and architectures.

Business architectures are the starting point from which to develop related and integrated functional, information, process, and application architectures. These architectures are aided by the rapid development and deployment of open, standards-based service-oriented architectures. Examples include the development of XML and XML Schema; SOAP; WSDL; and XQuery.

In addition, more Web service tiers are integrated with business logic and workflow. There is increased deployment of mobile devices, communications, and services with even newer new micromobility management schema and technologies.

There are also smarter and richer client tools (especially in the GIS world) with more robust and flexible secure information exchange solutions. Certainly, enterprise systems will "serve as a 'unifying' element through their capacity to manage and utilise geospatial content, capabilities and services in enterprise environments". As the landscape of information technology changes through the convergence in the industry, the public sector, including libraries, is affected as well. As academic disciplines transition to newer forms of working and educational environment, the situation necessitates a commitment that encompasses several objectives: to change basic educational tools, to retrofit installations of school- and campus-wide data networks, and to create affordable networks that would link schools, homes, and communities. The development of new media technologies tends to be spatially uneven, often concentrating in one sector of society while marginalising other sectors.

The process of being marginalised by technology can often be through cultural, socioeconomic, geographic, technological and political means. The uneven distribution of technology, computer networks, and of the information they transmit, has been characterised as contributing to a 'digital divide' between those who do have access to the Internet and those who do not.

E-MAIL REFERENCE SERVICES

Although libraries have offered e-mail reference services for a number of years, they were slow to adopt chat and sometimes developed sophisticated but complex chat software rather than the simpler systems typically used by Net Gen students. Librarians might need to change their mindset of employing the most sophisticated software that enables features they believe could provide improved service, such as permitting the librarian to demonstrate a search or review an information resource in one window while chatting with the student in another, in preference for software that students are more likely to use. In one study where a library did use standard AOL Instant Messenger software, other roadblocks to student adoption were put into place.

The librarians noted in their report on the service that they did not staff it during late-night hours when students were most likely to use the service and that they did not market the service in information literacy class sessions for fear that the response might overwhelm their capabilities.

Instead, the service was not heavily used. They did collect some responses as to why students took advantage of the service, and convenience was the main reason. One student reinforced why this type of service has appeal to the multitasking Net Gen students by replying that he had used the service instead of phoning the library so that he could continue working and browsing while waiting for an answer from the librarian.

VISUAL, INTERACTIVE SERVICES

Students also like self-service, interactive Web sites, and it is surprising that libraries haven't developed visual representations of their services that students could explore. A survey by OCLC found that one of students' top suggestions for libraries was to offer interactive maps, study tips, and guides. An example of that type of environment is a Web site developed by the British Museum as a "student's room" for an exhibit of Mughal, India, an ancient civilization. Students see an office-style room that they can explore by clicking on components such as a globe, file cabinets, book shelves, and so forth. They are then led to museum resources including an atlas and primary resources from the museum's collections on the Mughal period. This type of model could be used for a library reference room and its resources.

Libraries could add value to key pages of their Web sites by including interactive tutorials on how to find information or how to judge quality information resources. Libraries could use part of their home page to highlight a "resource of the week," to better publicise information content that could likely assist students in their assignments. They could use customised mouse pads to advertise URLs for selected information resources. Libraries also need to think about new services using mobile technology such as cell phones.

They might allow students to reserve group study rooms and be alerted to availability via their cell phones, send simple text-message queries to library catalogs or databases, or check library hours via text messaging. Such services might be particularly valuable for students who live off campus. How will we conceive and design these new services? Librarians should consult with students in the design phase of services and incorporate students on teams that make decisions about the implementation of those services. Making use of the imagination, creativity, technical skills, and perspectives of Net Gen students is the best way to ensure that new services will be responsive to both their needs and their style.

To summarise, Net Gen information services will:

- Use students on teams that design new services and environments
- Integrate services into course management systems
- Explore services for mobile devices
- Represent services and instruction visually and in multimedia modes
- Focus on partnership models
- Emphasise how to evaluate information resources
- Emphasise information policy issues.

Although technology has transformed many campuses, physical spaces remain important in most higher education institutions. The library offers a venue where academic work can be carried out in a social context. As libraries renovate facilities to incorporate technology, they are also making them more suitable for student group work, informal socialising, and ubiquitous computing.

Information Commons often provide space, workstations, and software that encourage both access to information and the capability to create new information products. Some Infor-mation Commons offer joint support to users from both the library and IT units. It is less common for libraries to rethink their virtual services to provide a better complement to their physically based services. Libraries have opportunities to alter their marketing strategies and their use of visual representations of information to encourage more and new creative uses of digital information resources.

INTEGRATING PHYSICAL AND VIRTUAL ENVIRONMENTS

Most libraries have not yet learned how to effectively integrate physical spaces with virtual spaces and services. For example, the introductory screen on work-stations in an information commons may have no description of the services or digital information products offered there. Vassar College has remedied this in their Media Cloisters, where entering visitors are confronted with a brightly coloured set of screens introducing student members of the multimedia team and advertising their areas of expertise.

How might libraries market services to Net Gen students, who are often visual learners? One possibility is to literally project information onto the walls of the information commons. In a changing display, libraries could develop programmes to project pages of electronic journals, guides to subject fields or topics that many students are working on during a specific week, quality Web sites with good visual displays (for example, museum Web sites), and student or faculty multimedia information products. Such displays would alert students to the broad array of electronic information resources accessible through the library and could prompt student interaction with a reference librarian to pursue similar sources for their projects.

To summarise, Net Gen information environments will:

- Provide individual and group learning spaces
- Support access to and creation of information resources
- Offer staff and faculty development and training
- Provide staff with a range of technology and information skills
- Effectively market services to all groups of potential users
- Integrate physical spaces and services with virtual spaces and services
- Build community.

LIBRARY PHYSICAL SPACES

As the Leavey Library at USC demonstrates, students will flock to library facilities that offer environments conducive to Net Gen learners. What Leavey offers are hundreds of workstations in configurations that support both individuals and small groups, group study rooms where students can work together on projects, workstations equipped with a wide array of software that can be used for creation of new information products, and staff with both library and information technology expertise who can address subject-information requests and technology hardware or software issues.

Many academic libraries are following the Leavey Library model and are transforming part of their physical space into information commons, multimedia production areas, classrooms, or all three. For example, the University of Arizona's Learning Center has components that include a library information commons where students can work on workstations configured for individual or group work, develop multimedia projects, and get advice from reference librarians.

Adjacent to the information commons are multimedia classrooms and a computer lab with support by Information Technology staff. The Indiana University information commons, developed jointly by the library and IT and situated on the first floor of the library, incorporates single and multiuser workstation areas, group study rooms, and classrooms and offers a wide range of services supported from a circular central desk staffed by library and IT staff.

While there is no one widely accepted definition of an information commons, generally it is a physical space, not always in the library, that incorporates many workstations equipped with software supporting a variety of uses, offers work-space for individuals and groups, provides comfortable furniture, and has staff that can support activities related to access to information and use of technology to develop new products. While information commons are usually developed for student use, some incorporate centers for teaching excellence or instructional technology support services for faculty.These new types of library spaces communicate a welcoming attitude to Net Gen students. They are the opposite of old-style formal reference rooms where students were expected to sit on straight wooden chairs and work individually and silently, without access to technology. Instead, these spaces project a comfortable, relaxed environment, a celebration of technology, and an invitation to communicate.

Library physical spaces continue to be valued places for building community in colleges and universities. Importantly, they also provide an atmosphere in which social and academic interests can easily intersect.

When students were asked what they desired in an upcoming renovation of Teachers College at Columbia University Library, they replied that they wanted "a social academic experience." Libraries can promote community by providing comfortable spaces for informal gatherings of students. Many libraries are adding coffee bars to their lobby areas or a building adjacent to the library; such spaces encourage students to continue conversations on topics of academic interest. Libraries might develop new ways of promoting community among students, related to course activity. For example, they may develop a message board or online mechanism for students to identify who else in the library building might be working on an assignment for a particular course if they need help from a peer or wish to study as a group.

INDIAN SCENARIO

The Indian libraries also have realised to give web based services to users and they have recognised that working together can accomplish for more than they can do individually. Many Indian libraries in India are not geared up for accessing e-journals due to various reasons including user ignorance, infrastructure and initial funds. The library and information networks in India were initiated in early eighties. The growth during this period can be linked to some of the policies that Government of India pursued. Some institutions like CSIR, ISRO, DRDO, DAE, ICAR, SIRNET, NICNET, NISSAT, INFLIBNET, MHRD and IIM libraries are actively working continuously to improve the present situation. They spend annually a huge amount of money towards library acquisition, especially towards journals, e-journals and e-databases.

Some initiative include, Indian Institute of Management for accessing bibliographic databases, CSIR laboratories for Science Direct, FORSA for accessing Astronomy and Astrophysics journals, Hyderabad Knowledge park members of J-gate, INFLIBNET (UGC–INFONET) initiative for full text and databases like BIOSIS and CAS and INDEST for a host of full text sources and few bibliographic databases for the benefit of IITs, IISc, NITs and Engineering colleges. In India, library consortia are emerging as one of the important service to users. The Indian consortiums will help the library to provide better services to the users by investing Meagre amount. To expand the access for more number of e-journals, e-books and other eresources, we have to develop the digital library infrastructure as a platform for e-learning.

FUTURE OF WEB BASED SERVICES

Library Web services will continue to spread out, offering more full-text electronic journals and indexes that do not now include full text will begin to do so, or link to external resources. Bibliographic access to full-text periodicals either through cataloging, databases, or vendors will be in improved form. There will be more Web forms for user feedback, and perhaps a virtual librarian who interacts in real time chat or video conferencing. More Document delivery services to distance education or users and Savings on Interlibrary Loan and user convenience are incentives. Information resources through creative consortia purchasing will be popular. A well-developed user education modules or tutorials, especially to support independent exploration of library and Web resources. Somebody will have to figure out how to keep Word users from saving print documents as XML, without thinking in terms of Web, not print, space. XML will be embraced as a way to control page appearance and Behaviour, but it will take a while for people to figure out how to use it well and there will be trends we haven't thought of yet.

5

Collections and Organizations of Digital Libraries

INTRODUCTION

The term digital library is diffuse enough to be applied to a wide range of collections and organizations, but, to be considered a digital library, an online collection of information must be managed by and made accessible to a community of users. Thus, some web sites can be considered digital libraries, but far from all. Many of the best known digital libraries are older than the web including Project Perseus, Project Gutenberg, and ibiblio.

Nevertheless, as a result of the development of the internet and its search potential, digital libraries such as the European Library and the Library of Congress are now developing in a Web-based environment. Public, school and college libraries are also able to develop digital download web sites, featuring eBooks, audiobooks, music and video.

A distinction is often made between content that was created in a digital format, known as born-digital, and information that has been converted from a physical medium, *e.g.*, paper, by digitizing. The term hybrid library is sometimes used for libraries that have both physical collections and digital collections. For example, American Memory is a digital library within the Library of Congress. Some important digital libraries also serve as long term archives, for example, the ePrint arXiv, and the Internet Archive.

Academic Repositories

Many academic libraries are actively involved in building institutional repositories of the institution's books, papers, theses, and other works which can be digitized or were 'born digital'. Many of these repositories are made available to the general public with few restrictions, in accordance with the goals of open access, in contrast to the publication of research in commercial journals, where the publishers often limit access rights. Institutional, truly free, and corporate repositories are sometimes referred to as digital libraries.

COLLECTIONS OF RESOURCE DESCRIPTIONS

Digital libraries are collections of resource descriptions that actually describe the catalogue data. In general, these metadata are stored in diverse sources distributed on the Web. One of the main challenges for the digital library community is the integration of such metadata sources in order to provide users with a common vocabulary for searching and browsing them. The Semantic Web offers relevant approaches and standards that can handle these problems. More precisely, RDF can be used as a common framework for expressing the information by providing a semantically rich representation language for metadata.

In this context, a SW integration middleware should be employed for the integration of the heterogeneous and distributed sources. In particular, we propose a SWIM that provides a useful, comprehensive and high-level access to library metadata that reside in relational databases (RDB) or XML sources, by offering a virtual, mediated RDF/S schema. There are many issues involved in the functionality of a SWIM. In particular, a SWIM should facilitate users to formulate queries against the mediated RDF/S schema using declarative languages, as well as, support further abstraction levels using declarative view definition languages. In a nutshell, SWIM should offer the following services:

- Establish mapping rules between XML and RDF and between RDB and RDF,
- Verify the conformance of these mappings w.r.t the semantics of the employed schemas,
- Reformulate RDF/S queries against RDB or XML sources, and
- Combine these queries with RVL views.

In order to address effectively and efficiently the requirements, we should choose a uniform and expressive logic framework to define SWIM integration services. This framework should exploit background theory on conjunctive queries and query containment and minimisation. An architecture based on mediators is highly beneficial for deploying a SWIM. There exist two main approaches for integrating data sources using mediator- based architectures: Global-as-View (GAV) and Local-as-View (LAV). The former provides descriptions of the global schema in terms of the views of local sources and relies on simple query reformulation techniques. The latter considers local sources as materialised views specified in terms of the global schema.

LAV supports easily the evolution of the data integration system by just adding or removing the descriptions of local sources. In our work we advocate a hybrid approach called GLAV, which combines the previous advantages and exceeds the expressive power of both GAV and LAV.

A MOTIVATING EXAMPLE

Let's assume an XML source whose content is described by a DTD or an XML Schema. XML data from this source contain information about Museums, exhibiting some artifacts for which we want to know their creator. Data stored in such sources can be queried using an XML query language like XPath, or XQuery. Now suppose that we add on top of this repository an RDF/S schema from the cultural domain. This mediated RDF/S schema can be queried using RQL and it can be used for defining personalised views with the help of RVL. However, since there are no actual RDF data, we need to reformulate the RQL queries expressed against this virtual RDF/S schema into queries appropriate for our XML source. For example, the following RQL query:

Select X

From {X}exhibits{Y}, {Y}denom{Z}

Where Z = "Louvre".

This reformulation involves several challenging issues. First of all, the schemas employed by our XML sources and the RDF/S mediator are different. Their discrepancies, usually called heterogeneity conflicts, can be classified under three axes: syntactic, structural and semantic. As we can see in our example, we need to view the XML data through the RDF data model, to resolve categorisation conflicts, given that in RDF/S there is a class hierarchy while in XML there isn't, as well as address naming mismatches; for instance the 'name' of a Museum in XML is called 'denomination' in RDF/S.

In order to reconciliate the heterogeneous represent-ations of our data we need to define appropriate mapping rules. Choosing an expressive but tractable logical framework to map data from XML to RDF/S is crucial for the success of a SWIM. These mappings are used for reformulating queries issued against the virtual RDF/S schema into queries acceptable by our XML sources. However, more complex mappings render query re- formulation harder. Query reformulation becomes more complex if we take into consideration the presence of constraints capturing the semantics of both the RDF/S and XML data models, as well as, application-specific constraints coming from the schema of XML sources. So, there is a need for a sound and complete reformulation algorithm. Since reformulated queries are evaluated to remote sources and mediator queries resulting from automated manipulation/generation may entail redundancies, their optimisation is crucial. In particular, optimisation tries to eliminate redundant queries and to simplify queries by removing redundant predicates.

MEASUREMENT OF USE AND PERFORMANCE INDICATORS IN THE DIGITAL LIBRARY

INTERNATIONAL STANDARDS FOR PERFORMANCE MEASUREMENT

The ability to monitor use and interpret the results is essential if any information resource or service is to be deemed a success or otherwise. Internationally standardised performance indicators have been developed for traditional library services.

However, recent studies of usage measurement and performance indicators for digital libraries have found no evidence of standardisation and continue to recommend that international standards be developed and applied.

An initiative in this direction has been taken by the ICOLC who have published guidelines for statistical measures of usage of electronic resources. An eLib supporting study published in 1997 investigated Management Information Systems and Performance Measurement for the Electronic Library. The authors described a three-fold approach to library management with regard to performance measurement:

- The day-to-day needs of library managers;
- The need for information that can be used by planners for forecasting;
- The need for indicators of value for strategic review.

Although they found that some indicators used in traditional libraries can be adapted, it was necessary to devise other 57 new indicators. For example, the number of documents accessed was considered not to be important in an electronic environment; the range and depth of resources available was deemed far more important.

Furthermore, Brophy and Wynne identified a number of issues which must be addressed if progress is to be made in this area. While acknowledging the significant contribution of the eLib programme in this regard, they called for a clearer definition and understanding of what is meant by the term 'electronic library'.

Non-standard Usage Measurement

A requirement for international standards is clear but development of such standards is a lengthy process. While this process is ongoing, each individual digital library initiative requires feedback to inform development and, thus, must unilaterally adopt an approach to performance measurement.

Electronic library projects in the UK, Europe and the USA have used a variety of different definitions and methods of usage measurement and analysis. Thus, neither analyses nor data from different projects can be compared.

Most Internet usage analysis tools are applicable to digital library activities and WWW server log file analysis programmes still predominate. In 1997 the eLib supporting study referred to above found that most work in the electronic library field relied on transaction logging for management information.

If users are authenticated (*i.e.* have usernames and passwords), it is possible using these tools, to monitor individual use by logging the username alongside the URL. Hits can also be time stamped. In this way, an individual's progress can be tracked from page to page. It is possible also, using cookies, for a service supplier to track an individual's movements on the Internet beyond that supplier's site. However, this is likely to be considered a breach of privacy and librarians 58 make it an issue in negotiation with content suppliers.

To comply with the library ethos, performance indicators should not rely on information about individuals' reading habits. Many academic subscription services authenticate whole sites by registering and restricting access a list of IP addresses.

Not only does this overcome privacy issues related to individual users as names and time stamps cannot be recorded on accesses, but it also removes the need for costly password management. An alternative means of reducing the cost of authentication in the UK is use of the ATHENS service which provides an individual with a username and password which may be used to access a variety of services.

Unfortunately, use of ATHENS greatly reduces the management information that can be gathered by individual service suppliers. This is deliberate to protect the privacy of individual users. For example, it is not possible for a supplier to monitor use of her service within a specific discipline if neither individuals nor even whole classes are identifiable by user ID.

Limitations of Current usage Measurement Tools

It is important when designing performance measurement activities that they be justified in terms of the benefits derived. Because it is automatic, transaction logging is a cheap way of gathering data in an electronic environment.

Unfortunately, the type of data that can be collected is often restricted by the delivery format. In 1996, when Michigan University intended to test economic models during the TULIP Project, it was unable to do so because 'the Web does not support the kind of data collection required to test economic models'.

Project MUSE is still unable to distinguish between downloading/printing and browsing as the Web is a stateless environment. SuperJournal know that although users claim to prefer HTML documents for onscreen viewing, given a choice of formats, a large majority 59 chooses PDF over HTML. As most users print documents if they intend to read more than a few lines, it can be assumed that they select PDF as a superior format for printing.

Unfortunately, SuperJournal cannot verify this assumption by monitoring use as it is not possible to differentiate downloading from printing. Thus, although data gathering is cheap, as yet, it is also limited. Furthermore, analysis of such data tends to be time consuming and thus expensive and interpretation is not always straightforward.

For example, it may be assumed that more hits indicate a better service, as a high number suggests that users return and that they recommend a site to others but, of course, this may not always be the case. A subject-based gateway which generates search results that closely match a users needs will record very few hits before that user leaves the site satisfied with the result.

If the search results supplied are poor and include a number of extraneous links or if the user is required to conduct several searches before she retrieves useful links, the gateway will record many more hits before the user leaves.

However, if a subject-based gateway offers not only access to a database of catalogue records but also holds a local archive, it should record a larger number of hits as users are likely both to search the database and to retrieve local resources. Furthermore, attempts to make more efficient use of internet bandwidth by caching and mirroring can subvert attempts to monitor use. Access to resources from site A from a cache or mirror held at site B will not be included in usage measurement unless site B informs site A about the cache and agrees to supply site A with use data. This type of shortfall makes WWW statistics unreliable or, worse, misleading.

Inferring user Behaviour from Transaction Logs

Use of transaction logs for performance measurement requires digital library practitioners to infer meaning from specific types of user act in a digital environment. For example, A. Dawson of the BUBL service (http://www.bubl.ac.uk) suggests that to view a list of journal issues with dates and contents is the equivalent of browsing a library shelf. He also asserts that searching is a deliberate activity which is not easily mistaken and that to access full-text is a likely indication that the user is reading the article.

The latter assertion is qualified by the acknowledgement that the reader may access text to scan for relevance rather than, necessarily, to read the article. However, Dawson argues that this ambiguity need not influence the accuracy of any performance measure as it applies to all journals.

This type of inference helps digital library practitioners to make sense of quantitative data. However, knowledge of user behaviour in the digital environment is limited and it can be dangerous to base inference entirely on assumptions and prior experience.

For example, Dawson's assumption that the frequency with which a reader accessing full text is in fact scanning for relevance will apply equally to all journals is contradicted by the findings of the SuperJournal project.

SuperJournal found evidence that the way in which scientists and social scientists use journal elements differs. For example, scientists are more likely than social scientists to identify a relevant article from its title and to print it on that basis. Social scientists more often read the abstract to establish relevance because article titles in the social sciences can be more ambiguous. There may be similar differences in the way that scientists and social scientists approach full text.

It is clearly difficult to derive qualitative research findings from quantitative information. Qualitative methods such as interviews and 61 observation should be used to inform assumptions about the meaning of quantitative information and for triangulation.

Training and Awareness

Some of the eLib projects in the Training and Awareness programme area have now migrated to a service model and offer training courses in the use of new technologies for teaching and learning. HEIs are likely to continue to pay for this type of training from staff development budgets.

Training of users in the use of IT is unlikely to fall within the remit of libraries although libraries will probably continue to offer training in information skills and the use of specific resources.

It is beyond the scope of this project to explore the economics of this activity and compare the costs and benefits of training academics and students in the use of electronic and print resources. Clearly, the transition from a traditional to a digital or hybrid library involves dramatic changes in the infrastructure that supports the production and use of information resources. At present people prefer not to read on screen so they print articles from electronic journals.

As resources for teaching, learning and research are increasingly delivered in electronic form there is likely to be a mass shift from photocopying to printing; the latter is more expensive than the former but the total opportunity cost of an individual operating a photocopier is not incurred so costs are probably very similar.

As people become more familiar with technology, users may no longer need print copies.

This could lead to a net reduction in the cost of using information. The report of a recent study on the impact of electronic journals on networked printing suggested that one of the reasons for printing material from the Internet is to ensure future access; networked access is not always reliable.

In effect users create a personal print cache of networked resources. The report predicted that improved access to networked resources would 62 reduce the need to print but suggested that it may also increase use of the network, which in turn would increase the print load. The net effect of a combination of such changes is virtually impossible to predict.

Another factor impacting on the economics of digital information is the pace of technological change; new technologies become obsolete at an alarming rate, making it expensive for organisations to meet the changing needs of users. However, technological advances are reducing some costs, for example the cost of storing digital resources. It is not possible within the scope of this project to estimate the infrastructure costs associated with delivering electronic resources in such an unstable and unpredictable climate. Investment in infrastructure that effectively enables all stakeholders to conduct much of their business electronically will be required. The models described here will be based on the assumption that the HE sector will invest in sufficient infrastructure to support digital/hybrid library activities.

At present there is no coherent model of the digital library, nor is there yet any developed model of the hybrid library. Furthermore, economic issues tend to be tested after solutions have been found to the more pressing technical, cultural and legal issues. Many specific digital library activities are insufficiently mature to have generated economic models. Where a model exists it has been evaluated and where alternatives exist these have been compared.

It is clear that a great deal of progress has been made over the last decade towards a greater understanding of how digital library activities may be integrated in HE. Nevertheless, a considerable amount of work remains, specifically in the areas of preservation and archiving and in standardisation of usage measurement and performance indicators. Conclusions regarding specific issues relating to digital library activities are outlined in the remainder of this report.

DOCUMENT REPRESENTATION OF DIGITAL LIBRARY

Before describing the process by which collections are built, we will show how the collection-building process is configured, and how documents are represented internally within the system. In we described our "plugin" mechanism and showed how it provides great flexibility for such varied tasks as ingesting both document files and metadata files, extracting text and metadata from different file formats, and expanding compressed files.

It has proved so successful that we have adopted it in the new framework. However, we depart radically from our earlier system by using the METS framework (which postdates that system) throughout for internal document representation.

CONFIGURATION

Collections are designed individually, and the structure of a collection is encapsulated in an XML file called the "collection configuration file." Its contents include build-time configuration options such as:

- The document types that the collection should recognise
- The metadata access structures or "classifiers" that are to be provided for users to browse the collection, such as by Titles A–Z
- The full-text indexes to build for searching the collection. The configuration file also contains run-time information about the collections, for example display options.

The bulk of an example configuration file can be seen in Figure—all that is omitted is the part concerning the purely runtime configuration. It defines a simple collection of HTML pages and plain text files, along with XML files that define metadata that is to be associated with these documents.

A document may consist of several separate files—for example, in this collection any images associated with the HTML pages will be contained within the HTML document rather than being identified as documents in their own right. Or a document may comprise complementary pairs of files—like a Word file and matching PDF version.

A collection configuration file

```
<documenttypes>
<document type="HTML">
<document type="Text">
<document type="MetadataXML">
</doctypes>
<search type="mg">
<index name="dtx" level="document" field="text">
<displayItem name="name" lang="en">entire documents</displayItem>
<displayItem name="name" lang="fr">documents entiers</displayItem>
<displayItem name="name" lang="es">documentos enteros</displayItem>
</index>
<index name="stx" level="section" field="text">
<displayItem name="name" lang="en">chapters</displayItem>
<displayItem name="name" lang="fr">chapitres</displayItem>
<displayItem name="name" lang="es">cap?tulos</displayItem>
</index>
<index name="stt" level="section" field="title">
<displayItem name="name" lang="en">section titles</displayItem>
<displayItem name="name" lang="fr">titres des sections</displayItem>
<displayItem name="name" lang="es">t?tulos de las secciones</displayItem>
</index>
<format>
<gsf:template match="documentNode"><td valign="top"><gsf:link><gsf:icon/></gsf:link>
</td><td><gsf:metadata name="Title"/></td></gsf:template>
</format>
</search>
<browse>
<classifier name="CLSubject" type="Hierarchy" file="subject.xml"
```

```
field="Subject"/>
<classifier name="CLTitle" type="AZList"/>
<classifier name="CLOrganization" type="Hierarchy"
file="organization.xml"
field="Organization"/>
<classifier name="CLKeyword" type="List" file="howto.xml"
field="HowTo">
<displayItem name="name" lang="en">HowTo</displayItem>
</classifier>
</browse>
```

The search block in Figure defines the full-text-searchable indexes that will be built. In this case the MG indexer will be used to build document-level and section-level indexes of the main text, and a section-level index of Title metadata. The browse block defines the metadata-based browsing mechanisms through which users can access the collection.

This configuration file specifies a hierarchical subject browser by defining a Hierarchy-type classifier of each document's Subject metadata, and the file that defines that hierarchy is named.

Other browsing classifiers are also defined. Run-time configuration items can be seen in both the classification and indexation parts of the file. For example. the "displayItem" nodes give names for the indexes (in English, French and Spanish) and for one of the browsers.

The Greenstone 3 building programme reads this file and configures the components to be used by the collection-building process. Many default options are implied. For instance, this collection would automatically expand Zip files—because the Zip expansion plugin is enabled by default. The process followed during building will be described later.

METS and Document Representation

We were eager to adopt an open, standard form for modelling the content and metadata of a document. The METS framework supports a free selection of metadata formats and avoids duplicating data that is already stored in constituent files. Using this standard, open framework should facilitate interoperation with other digital library systems. These are the METS Header, Administrative Metadata, Descriptive Metadata, File lists and Structural lists.

The structural content is the only required section, and the content of the remaining sections is mapped onto the encoded structure. For the sake of clarity, this example shows only the connections between sections and the descriptive metadata and files.

A document is encoded into METS form by a plugin that corresponds to the type of the document. Each such plugin extracts any appropriate metadata from the document files (*e.g.* title), catalogues the files that comprise the document, and extracts the document text in subsequent phases. In other words, it encapsulates the document content and acts as a standard gateway to its METS representation. This means that other phases of the building process are able to access data without having to understand the particulars of each file format—even if the data is stored as a binary object.

Document text can be provided in one of three ways, as the processing component requires. Plain Unicode is a simple baseline recognized throughout the system. At a higher level of sophistication, an XML representation is supported.

Finally, indexers can use the underlying binary files if they so desire. A complete document plugin provides all these formats, though the XML representation is optional. In any case, a document may have no textual content whatsoever (in which case all forms are empty).

For example, a PostScript file can be translated into an XML format. The PostScript plugin allows a plain-text reduction of this, but if an indexer wishes to treat PostScript files in a special way, it can access the original files directly. METS documents are partitioned into several components, the most common elements being structure, files, administrative metadata and descriptive metadata.

A given document may form part of a single file, or be an agglomeration of individual files and parts of files. Metadata can be associated with a document as a whole or with any part of its structure. A document may also have more than one structural form.

For instance, it may have both a page based structure and a logical chapter-and-section based structure. Metadata may be provided in several different formats and standards, and this allows for the native coding of metadata on the document in different formats—for instance RFC1807 and Dublin Core.

When a document first enters the library, it is given a unique identifier. That identifier will remain with the document throughout any subsequent revisions, and is recorded within the METS framework. Having described the configuration controls and document representation that underpin the new collection-building architecture, we now describe the building process itself.

Building Digital Library Collections

In our new architecture, collections are built in several distinct phases, which occur in sequence.

- *Expansion*: Compressed files such as Zip archives are expanded, and links to web sites are expanded into lists of constituent web pages.
- *Recognition*: All files are sent to the Recognition Manager, which identifies groups of files as documents.
- *Encoding*: All the recognised documents are catalogued for the subsequent phases of building.
- *Extraction*: Every document is passed through extractors, which use

special processing algorithms to extract information from the document (*e.g.* title, keyphrases) or add metadata stored in special files.

- *Classification*: Documents are assigned to classifiers (*e.g.* topical classifiers, ordered list classifiers) depending on their inherent and extracted metadata.
- *Indexation*: Documents are sent to indexers to build indexes that support later searching.
- *Validation*: Post-building checks are carried out on the collection as a whole, and on its constituent documents.

Expansion

Before any individual documents are identified, any files that are compressed, or refer to external sources, are expanded. The case of a Zip archive has already been mentioned; other cases include OAI repositories, and links to web sites via a file of URLs.

The purpose of this phase is to create a complete list of all files that are available for building the collection. These raw files are then passed to the next phase for grouping into documents.

Recognition

The relationship between files and documents is complex. A file of e-mails may be seen as one file that contains many documents. Conversely, a JPEG image and a plain text file that describes it may constitute a two-file document. Our architecture uses special "recogniser" plugins to address the problem of distinguishing documents from files.

When the building process is initialised, all plugins listed in the collection configuration file are registered by a "Recogniser Manager." When the Expansion phase terminates, this Manager is handed each file in the collection in turn. It sends these files to each plugin.

For some simple cases—like a plain text document comprising a single file—the plugins are trivial. However, in other circumstances conflicts can emerge, and the Recogniser Manager includes a scheme for resolving these. For example, suppose a collection includes both web pages and digital photographs. A single JPEG file may be a document in its own right, or form part of a web page. By default, JPEG files that are referred to by web pages, being constituent parts of a larger whole, are not treated as documents in their own right, while JPEGs that do not appear in the web pages are identified as separate, discrete documents. This default behaviour can be adjusted, if desired, to allow all JPEG files to be treated as documents, even ones that also appear in a web document.

The same issue arises with any image file on a web page. Furthermore, such a file (for instance a logo) could well be part of more than one document.

In this case it is treated as a subcomponent of all the documents in which it appears. A web page and associated files cannot form a strict subset of another web page, because the.html files must necessarily differ. The same strategy is used in other cases.

Once the Recogniser Manager has taken a pass through the entire inventory of files and identified the documents, it resolves any conflicts that occur and hands the output on to the Encoding phase.

At this stage all that is known of a document is the list of files that constitute its content. No metadata has yet been assigned—even that found within the document itself. The content and representation of any metadata internal to the document is identified in the next phase.

Encoding

Documents appear in a wide variety of forms, textual encodings and file formats. The Encoding phase creates the document framework that is used throughout the remainder of the building process.

This framework supports the retrieval of the full text of the document. It contains metadata defined within the document, and will also contain any metadata added to it. Finally, it binds the document, with its representation, into the classification and indexation structures.

The METS document framework is used to encapsulate the files, metadata and structure of each document. At the end of the Encoding phase, documents are ready to be processed by extracting further metadata, indexation and storage.

Extraction

The Extraction phase is controlled by the Extraction Manager, which filters the documents through a series of extraction plugins. These can have one of two origins:

- Metadata-only files identified in the recognition phase above
- Explicit mention in the collection configuration file

The former method is typically used for files of descriptive metadata that are provided with the documents. The latter is used to invoke automatic extraction tools such as the KEA Keyphrase Extractor.

At the conclusion of the Extraction phase, all metadata has been collected and stored in the METS document representation. The next two phases place the documents into the context of the collection as a whole.

Classification

The Classification phase uses each document's metadata to site it within the browsing structures, or "classifiers," that are supplied by the collection to access the documents it contains. Each classification is represented by a plugin specified in the collection configuration file.

There may be more than one instance of any given classification type, achieved by initiating a separate copy of the plugin for each classification. Classifications are stored in a database, and when a document is matched to a node in a classification, this fact is recorded in both the document and the classification node.

Indexation

Indexing follows classification. To support the widest range of indexing systems, indexers are also treated as plugins. Again, the indexer—or indexers—used when building a collection are determined by the collection configuration file. For each indexer, parameters can be supplied that control its behaviour.

Indexers can build several different indexes, each with its own parameters. In the case of MG, for example, the structure level (*e.g.* document, section) and field (full text, title, etc.) can be controlled.

Validation

Validation plugins are used to control the quality of the collection by checking the final form of each document, and the collection as a whole. For example, a collection may insist on a complete metadata set—that is, all compulsory fields must be present. Or the databases may be checked for empty classification nodes, which may be suppressed. Validation could be done in earlier phases, but we separate it into a final phase for architectural clarity.

DIGITAL ARCHIVES

Physical archives differ from physical libraries in several ways. Traditionally, archives were defined as:

- Containing primary sources of information (typically letters and papers directly produced by an individual or organization) rather than the secondary sources found in a library (books, periodicals, etc);
- Having their contents organized in groups rather than individual items;
- Having unique contents.

The technology used to create digital libraries has been even more revolutionary for archives since it breaks down the second and third of these general rules. In other words, "digital archives" or "online archives" will still generally contain primary sources, but they are likely to be described individually rather than (or in addition to) in groups or collections, and because they are digital their contents are easily reproducible and may indeed have been reproduced from elsewhere. The Oxford Text Archive is generally considered to be the oldest digital archive of academic physical primary source materials.

LEADERS IN THE FIELD

Project Gutenberg, Google Book Search, Windows Live Search Books(shutdown), Internet Archive, Cornell University, The Library of

Congress World Digital Library, The Digital Library at the University of Michigan, and Carnegie Mellon University's Million Book Project are considered leaders in the field of digital library creation and management.

The Future

Large scale digitization projects are underway at Google, the Million Book Project, and Internet Archive. With continued improvements in book handling and presentation technologies such as optical character recognition and ebooks, and development of alternative depositories and business models, digital libraries are rapidly growing in popularity as demonstrated by Google, Yahoo!, and MSN's efforts. Just as libraries have ventured into audio and video collections, so have digital libraries such as the Internet Archive.

Searching

Most digital libraries provide a search interface which allows resources to be found. These resources are typically deep web (or invisible web) resources since they frequently cannot be located by search engine crawlers. Some digital libraries create special pages or sitemaps to allow search engines to find all their resources.

Digital libraries frequently use the Open Archives Initiative Protocol for Metadata Harvesting (OAI-PMH) to expose their metadata to other digital libraries, and search engines like Google Scholar, Yahoo! and Scirus can also use OAI-PMH to find these deep web resources.

There are two general strategies for searching a federation of digital libraries:

- Distributed searching, and
- Searching previously harvested metadata.

Distributed searching typically involves a client sending multiple search requests in parallel to a number of servers in the federation. The results are gathered, duplicates are eliminated or clustered, and the remaining items are sorted and presented back to the client. Protocols like Z39.50 are frequently used in distributed searching.

A benefit to this approach is that the resource-intensive tasks of indexing and storage are left to the respective servers in the federation. A drawback to this approach is that the search mechanism is limited by the different indexing and ranking capabilities of each database, making it difficult to assemble a combined result consisting of the most relevant found items.

Searching over previously harvested metadata involves searching a locally stored index of information that has previously been collected from the libraries in the federation. When a search is performed, the search mechanism does not need to make connections with the digital libraries it is searching - it already has a local representation of the information.

This approach requires the creation of an indexing and harvesting mechanism which operates regularly, connecting to all the digital libraries and querying the whole collection in order to discover new and updated resources. OAI-PMH is frequently used by digital libraries for allowing metadata to be harvested. A benefit to this approach is that the search mechanism has full control over indexing and ranking algorithms, possibly allowing more consistent results. A drawback is that harvesting and indexing systems are more resource-intensive and therefore expensive.

DISTRIBUTED SERVICES ARCHITECTURE IN DLIBRA DIGITAL LIBRARY FRAMEWORK

The dLibra Digital Library Framework has been developed in Poznan Supercomputing and Networking Center since 1999. The first dLibra-based digital library (DL) was the Digital Library of the Wielkopolska Region (WBC). It was started in October 2002 and now it consists of over 3000 various publications grouped into four thematic collections: cultural heritage, regional materials, educational materials and music notes.

Such number of publications makes from WBC one of the largest Polish digital libraries. In the end of November 2004 the second dLibra-based digital library was deployed – the Wroclaw University of Technology Digital Library. There are also four other test dLibra installations academic libraries, and in the nearest future three new regional digital libraries will be started. Due to the diversity of mentioned digital libraries, many different aspects must be taken into account during the dLibra development.

Each DL has its own specific publications – for example the majority of WBC publications are relicts of writing and old documents associated with social life of the Wielkopolska Region. Such resources are mostly stored in a graphical form, in formats like DjVu, PDF or JPG scans. All that publications consist of quite large files and their content is often not searchable. On the other hand, there are academic DL systems, like one of test dLibra installations in AGH University of Science and Technology, where a typical publication is an academic script stored as a set of HTML pages or small PDF file with searchable text content. Such differences requires support in many areas – from format dependent publication structure analysis during the publication upload process, to sophisticated mechanisms for content indexing and searching, to different publication view and download possibilities. Another important element is the amount of stored publications.

When there are many gathered resources, and a large number of readers accessing it, the overall system performance becomes a crucial parameter. We want to show the way in which we designed the internal dLibra architecture and its basic mechanisms to create an efficient, flexible, distributed and error-resistant digital library system. The structure of distributed services architecture developed in the dLibra Digital Library Framework. We also show an overview of these services functionality. We try to demonstrate our approach to improving the dLibra stability in some extreme situations, like very heavy user requests load or network communication errors. Those mechanisms are an integral part of dLibra services and service management system.

dLIBRA ARCHITECTURE

The initial dLibra architecture and design was based on experiences from previous PSNC projects. We assumed that the dLibra environment should consist of a number of portable, distributed services. Portability was achieved by choosing Java™ as the programming language. Further works and practice from dLibra deployments formed the current dLibra structure.

This structure is based on a set of cooperating remote services. All these services together create the complete dLibra-based digital library. Each service can be started on a separate computer, but they can also be connected into service groups running on the same machine.

When services are started on different hosts, they use Java RMI technology to communicate with each other. Six of dLibra services give together the entire dLibra server functionality.

These services are:

- *The Metadata Server*—gives a possibility to define, modify and remove metadata attributes that are used to describe digital library publications. It also gives access to dictionaries and thesauri with values of all attributes. It is responsible for managing digital library directories and collections. In addition, it allows adding, modifying and deleting publications, and it has possibilities to manage lists of languages defined in the DL system. Moreover, it has a module for performing periodic metadata consistency test.
- *The Content Server*—gives access to all gathered digital content. Before sending content to the client, this service is able to compress it or encrypt and send securely. The Content Server is also used to store the publications content. Resuming is supported during both publication upload and download.
- *The Search server*—allows users to search through all gathered content and metadata. It also contains indexing functionality, which prepares indexes used during search.
- *The Distributed Search Server*—is used to harvest remote dLibra instances by means of the OAI-PMH protocol. It also gives the user a possibility to search through gathered remote metadata. In fact, any OAI-PMH-enabled repository can be harvested and searched using that service.
- *The User Server*—contains all user-related data and allows users authentication and authorisation. It is also used to create groups of

users and to grant users different digital library rights, from library administration to simple publication view.

All the services give together the entire dLibra digital library functionality. However, at least two more elements are required to create a fully functional system. There must be a possibility to connect all these services and create an entry point to the system for both external applications and users.

The first of them is a service called the System Services. It can be treated as a broker of services for single instance of the distributed digital library. It allows inter service communication and handles services addresses resolving, connecting and authorisation. For example, when the Search Server wants to refresh its indexes, it asks the System Services for the Content Server and the Metadata Server. The System Service checks if such services are registered, if they are available and if the Search Server is authorised to access them. If all those conditions are met, as a response the Search Server receives references to the requested services. In order to become available to other services, each service must register itself in the chosen System Services. Services registered in one System Services create a digital library. The second additional system level service is the Event Server. It allows services to communicate with the event messaging system. It is very useful when one service wants to notify some other services about a particular event. A good example of this mechanism can again be a process of refreshing search indexes.

Just after start, the Search Server registers in the Event Server for events related with the modification of gathered content and metadata. When a new publication is added, modified or removed, the Metadata Server sends an event notification to the Event Server. Next, the Event Server forwards this event to all services registered for this event type. After receiving such event, the Search Server can decide if index refreshing is required or maybe just some data should be removed from the index.

This corresponds to two additional parts of the dLibra Framework. One of them is WWW Service and the second is the Editor/Administrator application. The WWW Service is designed as a read only entry point to the system. It can be used by readers to access gathered resources. Content browse and searching are the main functionality of this service, but it is also an OAI-PMH data provider, and it has many user-friendly features like RSS feeds with information newly added publications, publications ranking etc. This functionality is realised with the use of all other dLibra services reached through the System Services. The Editor/Administrator Application is an application for librarians and library administrators. It allows adding and modifying library resources and managing all library items.

IMPROVING SERVICES AVAILABILITY IN dLIBRA FRAMEWORK

The distributed architecture of the described dLibra services requires additional mechanisms for improving system reliability and availability. When one of the services stops responding, the library may become less functional or may not be functional at all - when the User Server or Metadata Server fails. To prevent such situations, a number of mechanisms were introduced. The first of them is the way of service resolving done by the System Services. There is a possibility to create such services configuration, in which multiple instances of the most crucial services are started.

Before the System Services gives one service access to another service, it tests the requested service functionality. When the tested instance of a given service fails, the System Services can return reference to other instance. Such instance switch is transparent to other services. With addition of services load monitoring functionality, this mechanism can also be used for load balancing between service instances. The second mechanism is internal services monitoring.

Each service is periodically checked if it is responding or has enough processor time for its tasks. This check is performed by a special service wrapper based on an open-source Java Service Wrapper project. The Wrapper can restart or shutdown the service when, for some reason, it stops responding or when host processors are overloaded for a longer period of time. This service monitoring is done locally so it is independent of the state of network connections. Another reliability improving mechanism is implemented in events sending and receiving parts of the dLibra framework. When service generates an event, it is not directly sent to the Event Server, but it is stored in a persistent storage. This storage is implemented with Hibernate, so it can be based on many types of relational databases.

All stored events are read by a specialised Event Sender thread. This thread tries to send events to the Event Server. If connection to the Event Server is lost, all events stay in the storage until there is a possibility to send them again. On the other hand, when the Event Server retrieves an event, it also stores the event before trying to send it to registered services. Each service, while registering for events, gives the Event Server special timeout parameter. This parameter describes how long the events should be stored in the Event Server, if the registered service becomes unavailable. If the registered service becomes available again, all events stored for this service will be passed to it.

FUTURE WORKS

We think that next dLibra development stages will bring this distributed digital library framework closer to grid technologies. In order to do so, it will be necessary to extend our services model. Each service should gain the ability of describing itself with metadata. On top of the System Services there must be some kind of a new, much more advanced service – a dynamic distributed digital library services broker. This should allow automated service discovery and creation of virtual DL organisations. Such active organisations of services could be used to create distributed digital collections from resources gathered in heterogeneous DL systems. We can also imagine Information Retrieval Grid services based on different distributed digital libraries. By creating an environment for advanced cooperation of computational grid services, grid data management systems and digital libraries we want to give an opportunity for advanced usage of digital libraries in sophisticated grid scenarios.

SEMANTIC QUERY ROUTING AND PROCESSING IN P2P DIGITAL LIBRARIES

The digital library community envisions the availability of digital content on a global scale through Digital Libraries (DL) that can be accessed, integrated and individualised for any user, anytime and anywhere. A key point in such a vision is the interaction with multiple DL nodes to support integrated access. We believe that such interaction is far beyond the traditional information integration technologies, which impose restrictions on representation and communication languages used at both the semantic and the structural levels, since:

- DL nodes should be autonomous. Ideally, a node must not have restrictions on how to organise its data and what kind of query capabilities to offer.
- DL services should support decentralised sharing and management of data through a network of DL nodes. In such a network, a DL node must be able to provide data to other DL nodes and, at the same time, to have access to data of other DL nodes.
- The diversity of DL nodes in terms of availability, processing power and interface options, makes a DL network a highly heterogeneous environment in terms of hardware/software setup in addition to the data being provided.
- Finally, the system needs to be evolving in the sense of DL nodes joining and leaving the network at their own will. DL node arrivals and departures affect the data that is available.

Our work explores the application of the peer-to-peer (P2P) paradigm in DL technologies. In particular, schema-based P2P systems exploit schema information to specify what kind of data is provided by the involved peers. The advantages of this approach lies to the fact that:

- More sophisticated than keyword-based queries can be posed and
- More efficient approaches can be developed for identifying peers that are capable of answering the queries.

A natural candidate for representing descriptive schemas of information resources is the Resource Description Framework/Schema Language. RDF schemas offer rich semantics. The primitives of RDF schemas are classes and properties. Classes describe general concepts or entities. Properties describe the characteristics of classes or the relationships between classes. RDF/S:

- Enables a modular design of descriptive schemas based on the mechanism of namespaces;
- Allows easy reuse or refinement of existing schemas through subsumption of both class and property definitions;
- Supports partial descriptions since properties associated with a resource are by default optional and repeated and
- Permits super-imposed descriptions in the sense that a resource may be multiply classified under several classes from one or several schemas.

These modelling primitives are crucial for schema-based P2P systems where monolithic RDF/S schemas and resource descriptions cannot be constructed in advance and DL nodes may have only incomplete descriptions about the available resources. The advanced structuring and retrieval functionality of schema-based P2P systems raises new challenges for view integration, query routing and processing over autonomous, distributed and dynamic networks of DLs. The main contributions of our work presented in this paper are:

- The design and implementation of effective and efficient query routing in P2P DLs, exploiting intensional indexing of DL node views and
- The study of interleaved query routing and processing algorithms in P2P DLs in order to produce as quickly as possible the first query results.

Related Work

Several projects address query processing issues in general P2P systems. However, they require a priori knowledge of the relevant to a query peers. Mutant Query Plans (MQPs) implement efficient query routing. Unlike our approach, MQP reduces the optimisation opportunities by simply migrating possibly big XML fragments of query plans along with partial results of sub- queries. In indices are used to identify peers that can handle containment queries.

However there are no details on how a set of semantically related peers can actually execute a complex query involving vertical and horizontal distribution. RDFPeers is a scalable distributed RDF/S repository which efficiently answers multi-attribute and range queries. This approach ignores RDF/S schema information during query routing, while distributed query processing and execution policies are not addressed.

In, a P2P architecture is introduced, based on the extension of an existing RDF/S store. Although schema information is used for indexing, RDF/S class and property subsumption is not considered. A schema-based P2P infrastructure for the Semantic Web is described in. Their approach involves exact matching of basic class and property pattern and does not consider run-time adaptability of query plans.

P2P DIGITAL LIBRARIES

In order to design an efficient P2P DL infrastructure we need to address the following issues:

- How DL nodes advertise their bases?
- How DL nodes formulate queries?
- How DL nodes route queries? and
- How DL nodes process queries?

Advertisements of DL Nodes

A schema-based P2P DL infrastructure requires that each DL node advertises its local base content to other DL nodes. Using these advertisements, a DL node becomes aware of the bases hosted by other nodes in the DL. In our approach, we assume that there are global RDF/s schemas for various communities, in which DL nodes have access through the mechanism of namespaces. However, a global RDF/S schema may contain numerous classes and properties not necessarily populated in a DL node. Therefore, we need a fine-grained definition of schema-based advertisements. We employ RVL views to specify the sub- set of a community RDF/S schema(s) for which all classes and properties are populated in a DL node base. These views may be broadcasted to other DL nodes, thus informing the rest of the P2P DL of the information actually available in the DL nodes.

Query Formulation in DL Nodes

In this work, queries and views in a P2P DL are formulated by nodes in the RQL/RVL language. RQL is a typed functional language in the form of OQL. It uniformly queries both RDF data descriptions and schemas. RVL ex- tends RQL by supporting views on RDF/S. In RQL/RVL, class and property path patterns allow users to navigate through the RDF/S schema of a DL node to retrieve resources. RQL queries allow us to retrieve the contents of any DL node base, namely resources classified under schema classes or associated to other resources using schema properties. It is worth noticing that RQL queries imply both intensional and extensional filtering conditions.

Query Routing in P2P Digital Libraries

Query routing is responsible for finding the relevant to a query DL nodes by taking into account data distribution of their bases committing to an RDF schema. The query-routing algorithm takes as input a query and the available DL node views and detects which DL nodes can actually answer the query as a whole or fragments of it. The latter is important, since there might be answers that can be received by joining partial answers from different DL nodes. Our approach exploits query/view sub- sumption algorithms to check whether the classes or properties of the view are subsumed by the respective classes or properties used in the query. In this way, query routing takes into consideration semantic information from the RDF Schemas of the involved DL nodes. Specifically, a fragmentor breaks the given query into subqueries, whose number is bounded by an input variable. The query/view subsumption algorithms of are employed to determine which part of a query can be answered by a DL node view. For maintaining a distributed catalog of views published by the DL nodes in a P2P DL, appropriate DHT structures have been designed.

Query Processing in P2P Digital Libraries

Query processing is responsible for generating query plans according to the results returned by the routing algorithm. If more than one DL nodes can answer the same query fragment, the results from each. "The results obtained for different query fragments that are connected at a specific domain or range class are rejoined".

The generated query plan reflects the data distribution of the system and uses it for obtaining at execution time both complete and correct results. The resulting query plan can be optimised. Compile-time optimisation relies on algebraic equivalences and heuristics allowing us to push, as much as, possible query evaluation to the same DL nodes. Additionally, cost-based optimisations based on statistics about the DL node bases enable to reorder joins and choose between different execution policies for the query plans.

A key feature of our approach is that query routing and processing are interleaved in several iteration steps. This leads to the creation and execution of multiple query (sub)plans that when 'unioned' offer completeness in the results. Specifically, starting with the initial query, at each iteration step, smaller sub- queries are considered in order to find the relevant DL nodes that can actually answer them. The routing information, *i.e.*, remote DL node views, is acquired by the lookup service offered by the system on top of intensional DHT structures. The interleaved query evaluation terminates when the initial query is decomposed into its basic class and property patterns.

The main advantage of the interleaved query routing and processing algorithm is that the query results are collected as quickly as possible since they require fewer intra-DL node joins. More precisely, each query fragment is looked up as a whole and only DL nodes that can fully answer it are actually involved in each query processing iteration step.

PUBLISH/SUBSCRIBE FUNCTIONALITIES FOR FUTURE DIGITAL LIBRARIES

We are interested in the problem of *distributed resource sharing* in future digital libraries. We adopt a pure P2P architecture but our ideas can be easily modified to work in the case of hierarchical P2P networks, as in. *Information providers* (DLs) and *information consumers* (users) are both represented by peers participating in a peer-to-peer (P2P) overlay network. There are two kinds of basic functionality that we expect this architecture to offer: *information retrieval (IR)* and *publish/subscribe*. In an IR scenario a user poses a *query* and the system returns information about matching resources. In a pub/sub scenario a user posts a *subscription* to the system to receive notifications whenever certain events of interest take place. In this extended abstract we concentrate on the latter kind of functionality and sketch how to provide it by extending the distributed hash table Chord. *Distributed Hash Tables (DHTs)* are the second generation *structured* P2P overlay networks devised as a remedy for the known limitations of earlier P2P networks such as Napster and Gnutella.

We present a set of protocols, collectively called *DHTrie*, that extend the Chord protocols with pub/sub functionality. We assume that resources are annotated using a well-understood attribute- value model called *AWPS* in. Thus publications and subscriptions will also be expressed in *AWPS*. *AWPS* is based on *named attributes* with value *free text* interpreted under the Boolean and vector space (VSM) models. The query language of *AWPS* allows Boolean combinations of comparisons $A \; op \; v$, where A is an attribute, v is a text value and op is one of the operators ‘equals’, ‘contains’ or ‘similar’. The following is an example of a publication in *AWPS*:

{ (Author, “John Smith”), (Title, “Information dissemination in P2P...”), (Abstract, “In this paper we show that ...”) }

The following is an example of a query:

$$(Author = \text{“John Smith”}) \wedge (Title \sqsupseteq P2P \wedge (information\ [0.0]\ alert)) \wedge (Abstract \sim_{0.7} \text{“P2P architecture have been...”})$$

This query requests resources that have *John Smith* as their author, and their title contains the word *P2P* and a word pattern where the word *information* is immediately followed by the word *alert*. Additionally, the resources should have an abstract similar to the text value *‘P2P architectures have been...’* with similarity greater than 0:7.

THE DHTrie PROTOCOLS

We implement pub/sub functionality by a set of protocols called the *DHTrie protocols*. The DHTrie protocols use *two levels of indexing* to store queries submitted by clients. The first level corresponds to the partitioning of the global query index to different nodes using DHTs as the underlying infrastructure. Each node is responsible for a fraction of the submitted user queries through a mapping of attribute values to node identifiers.

The DHT infrastructure is used to define the mapping scheme and also manages the routing of messages between different nodes. We use an extension of the Chord DHT to implement our network. The second level of our indexing mechanism is managed locally by each node and is used for indexing the user queries the node is responsible for. In this level, each node uses a hash table to index all the atomic queries contained in a query by using their attribute name as the key.

For each atomic Boolean query the hash table points to a *trie*-like structure that exploits *common words* and a hash table that indexes text values in equalities as in. Additionally for atomic VSM queries an inverted index for the most 'significant' query words is used as in. In this abstract as suggested, focus on the first level of indexing and present the sub- scription, publication and notification protocols that regulate node interactions. Protocols for query updating and removal are omitted due to space. The local indexing algorithms we use and their experimental evaluation are thoroughly discussed in.

The Notification Protocol

Once all the matching queries have been retrieved from the database, *P* creates notification messages of the form Q NOTIFICATION (*l*(*c*)*r*) and contacts all the nodes that their queries where matched against *p* using their IP address associated with the query they submitted. If a node *P'* is not online when *P* tries to notify it about the published resource, the notification message is sent to the *successor (p')*. In this way *P'* will be notified the next time it logs on the network. The modifications to the join and leave protocols of Chord to achieve this functionality originally presented in the non-DHT system P2P-DIET are omitted due to space considerations. To utilise the network in a more efficient way, notifications can also be batched and sent to the subscribers when traffic is expected to be low.

Frequency Cache

In this part, we introduce an additional routing table that is maintained in each node. This table, called *frequency cache* (FCache) is used to reduce the cost of publishing a resource by storing the IP addresses of the nodes responsible for frequent words contained in published documents. FCache is a hash table used to associate each word that appears in a published document with a node IP address. FCache uses a word *w* as a key, and each FCache entry is a data structure that holds an IP address.

Thus, whenever *P* needs to contact another node *P'* that is responsible for queries containing *w*, it searches its FCache. If FCache contains an entry for *w*, *P* can directly contact *P'* using the IP stored in its FCache. If *w* is not contained in FCache, *P* uses the standard DHT lookup protocol to locate *P'* and stores contact information in FCache for further reference. Using FCache the cost of processing a published resource *p* is reduced to $O(v + (h - v) \log N)$, where v is the number of words of *p* contained in FCache. FCache entries are populated as follows. Each time a resource p is published at a node P, P contacts the nodes responsible for storing queries with words contained in p. After this process is over, P knows the contact information of those nodes, and stores it to FCache along with the word each node is responsible for. After that, for each publication taking place at P, P maintains this routing information for the most frequent words contained in resources published to it. Notice that the construction and maintenance of FCache is based only on local information and that the only extra cost involved is FCache misses and the routing information discovered is also cached for further reference).

6

Development from Traditional to Digital Libraries

INTRODUCTION

With the introduction of new technologies in libraries, traditional techniques and tools have been replaced by the new ones. Most of the libraries have started providing an Online Public Access Catalogue (OPAC), access to CD-ROM, Internet and digital documents. Many of them have created their homepages on the Web form where users can have access to a variety of services from their workplaces or homes. The transition of the traditional library to digital library is well reflected in a number of digitisation projects going on at the national and global levels. The libraries have started digitising their resources and making these available over the World Wide Web and providing online services to the users. But in spite of numerous digitisation projects, electronic media by no means have completely replaced the printed material. There is still a lot of paper in our libraries and we expect this to be the case for a long time to come. The paper-less library will exist with the digital library for the foreseeable future. The situation necessitates the librarian to acquire, give access to, and safeguard carriers of knowledge and information in all forms and to provide instruction and assistance in the use of the collection to which their users have access.

ADVENT OF INFORMATION TECHNOLOGY

The advent of Information technology and its invasion almost in all areas of LIS has added new dimensions to LIS by providing avenues to create global network of libraries, offer reference and various other services much better and faster, to open a floodgate of digital preservation and save contents of documents that were on the verge of extinction, to improve house-keeping operations, to make LIS professionals computer literate, and so on. All Information Technology has helped to heighten the status of LIS professionals in the eyes of the authorities. It has taken LIS a long way from a soft discipline towards a hard discipline.

KNOWLEDGE MANAGEMENT

Knowledge management is an old concept, a function traditionally performed by librarians. But, in the digital era, this term has taken on nuances that point to the need to rethink the old paradigms to reconsider who the new knowledge management players in the academy might be. Knowledge management is the process of transforming information and intellectual assets into enduring value. It connects people with the knowledge that they need to take action, when they need it. The prime to knowledge management is capturing the knowledge of process how organisations get their work done and of how various elements of information connect to this process. Two different types of information are necessary to accomplish this: explicit and tacit.

Explicit information is packaged, easily codified, transferable, and communicable. Tacit information, on the other hand, is personal, context-specific, difficult to formalise, and hard to communicate and transfer. Combining these two types of informationusing formal and informal information to guide processesprovides the perceived value of knowledge management. The focus is on unravelling individual know-how and applying it to explicitly driven processes so that the pinpointed knowledge is available to the exact people at the right time.

These concepts are being applied in limited and often modest scale in industrial settings. The commercial world hopes to capture the promised efficiencies of knowledge management in order to gain competitive market advantage. The knowledge management paradigm has even been referred to as the next generation approach that provides organisations with valuable, credible, and insightful informationa tremendous asset and a unique advantage. Thus companies are generating databases, links to Web sites, and portals to facilitate the integration of explicit and tacit information.

The questions to be raised here are whether this change is applicable to higher education? Although academic libraries have focused quite effectively on collecting, organising, and presenting information, the Web adds an entirely new dimension.

Knowledge management in an academic setting must encompass the community of scholars in a given discipline and must be able to integrate publications, data sets, tools for manipulating such data, connections to databases of pictures and images, and much more. Portal technology is being used by corporations to bring together tacit and explicit information in a push technology framework. This also has potential in the academic environment because of its ability to help screen and filter information to the users.

THE CHALLENGES OF DIGITAL PRESERVATION

The purpose of preservation is to ensure protection of information of enduring value for access by present and future generations (Conway, 1990:

206). Libraries and archives have served as the central institutional focus for preservation, and both types of institutions include preservation as one of their core functions. In recent decades, many major libraries and archives have established formal preservation programmes for traditional materials which include regular allocation of resources for preservation, preventive measures to arrest deterioration of materials, remedial measures to restore the usability of selected materials, and the incorporation of preservation needs and requirements into overall programme planning.

Preservationists within the library and archival community have been instrumental in developing an array of tools and methodologies to reduce the decay of traditional materials and to restore books and documents that have deteriorated to such an extent that their longevity and usability are threatened. Provisions for fire protection and adequate environmental controls frequently are incorporated into new library and archival facilities. Rehousing of acid-based paper materials is a common task in many repositories and microfilming is used extensively and cost effectively to preserve endangered materials.

Undertakings such as the brittle books initiative, the American Newspapers Project, and the NEH-funded microfilming programme have saved millions of unique and imperiled items (Preserving the Intellectual Heritage). Many libraries and archives have curbed their voracious appetites for acquisition and collecting in an effort to balance the breadth and depth of their holdings against long-term stewardship responsibilities. The change over from acid to alkaline paper in publishing and much desktop printing counts as a significant victory for preservation. Much remains to be done to preserve cultural, intellectual, and scholarly resources in traditional formats that form the foundation for humanities research and teaching.

An estimated 80 million embrittled books reside in American libraries, 10 million of which are unique; and countless journals, newspapers, photographs, and documents require preservation treatment to survive well into the next century. Thousands of repositories lack the means for disaster prevention or adequate environmental controls to avoid catastrophic loss of their holdings. The success stories and regular use of established preservation methods are found almost exclusively in developed countries, and within developed countries in preservation of print materials in major institutions (Preservation of Archival Materials).

Digital preservation raises challenges of a fundamentally different nature which are added to the problems of preserving traditional format materials. By digital preservation, I mean the planning, resource allocation, and application of preservation methods and technologies necessary to ensure that digital information of continuing value remains accessible and usable. I intentionally use the term “continuing” rather than “permanent” value to avoid both the absolutism and the idealism that the term “permanent” implies (O’Toole). My concept of digital preservation encompasses material that begins its life in digital form as well as material that is converted from traditional to digital formats.

Recording media for digital materials are vulnerable to deterioration and catastrophic loss, and even under ideal conditions they are short lived relative to traditional format materials. Although archivists have been battling acid-based papers, thermo-fax, nitrate film, and other fragile media for decades, the threat posed by magnetic and optical media is qualitatively different. They are the first reusable media and they can deteriorate rapidly, making the time frame for decisions and actions to prevent loss is a matter of years, not decades.

More insidious and challenging than media deterioration is the problem of obsolescence in retrieval and playback technologies. Innovation in the computer hardware, storage, and software industries continues at a rapid pace, usually yielding greater storage and processing capacities at lower cost. Devices, processes, and software for recording and storing information are being replaced with new products and methods on a regular three-to five-year cycle, driven primarily by market forces. Records created in digital form in the first instance and those converted retrospectively from paper or microfilm to digital form are equally vulnerable to technological obsolescence. Another challenge is the absence of established standards, protocols, and proven methods for preserving digital information.

With few exceptions, digital library research has focussed on architectures and systems for information organization and retrieval, presentation and visualization, and administration of intellectual property rights (Levy and Marshall). The critical role of digital libraries and archives in ensuring the future accessibility of information with enduring value has taken a back seat to enhancing access to current and actively used materials. As a consequence, digital preservation remains largely experimental and replete with the risks associated with untested methods; and digital preservation requirements have not been factored into the architecture, resource allocation, or planning for digital libraries.

My assigned topic "mass storage and long-term preservation" offers fertile ground for discussing conceptual and methodological challenges facing digital libraries and archives. The two terms "mass storage" and "long-term preservation" embrace a contradiction in the current state of affairs of digital library development, representing a time bomb that threatens the long-term viability of this new type of library. New technologies for mass storage of digital information abound, yet the technologies and methods for long-term preservation of the vast and growing store of digital information lag far behind.

Strategies, methods, and technologies for long-term preservation of digital information that already exist or are being discussed, designed, and developed today have yet to demonstrate the technological or economic feasibility of operating on a mass scale. Our ability to create, amass and store digital materials far exceeds our current capacity to preserve even that small amount with continuing value.

DIGITAL PRESERVATION REQUIREMENTS

In order to preserve digital materials on a scale commensurate with mass storage capabilities and in formats that are accessible and usable, it is necessary to articulate some basic requirements. There are two ways to examine digital preservation requirements: from the perspective of users of digital materials and from the view of libraries, archives, and other custodians who assume responsibility for their maintenance, preservation, and distribution. Libraries and archives will not accomplish their preservation missions if they do not satisfy the requirements of their users by preserving materials in formats that enable the types of analyses that users wish to perform.

At the same time, libraries and archives are unlikely to be able to satisfy all requirements of all potential users primarily due to resource constraints. By making explicit preservation requirements from both the users' and custodians' perspectives, libraries and archives will be better able to integrate digital preservation into overall planning and resource allocation.

The potential uses of digital materials are varied, unpredictable, and almost endless (Gould). Any generalizations, even if restricted to one community of users such as humanities scholars, run the risk of overlooking and understating potential user needs. Precise requirements for presentation and analytical tools vary among disciplines, yet some basic requirements are likely to transcend fields and disciplines.

The ability to establish the authenticity and integrity of a source is critical to users, whether it is generated by an individual, created in the conduct of institutional business, or produced through a formal publication process (Lynch). Mechanisms that will enable users to establish authenticity require archives and libraries to store much more than the content of digital documents. Attributes such as formal document structures, metadata that document the maintenance and use history of the document, time and date stamps, and a series of references among documents are essential for determining authenticity and for understanding the provenance of sources and placing them in a larger context (Graham).

Michelson and Rothenberg (1992) argue that networking and access to digital sources will change all dimensions the scholarly work process, including identifying sources, communicating with colleagues, interpreting and analyzing data, disseminating research findings, and teaching. If their projections are correct, digital preservation programmes must support a high degree of integration of source material into analytical processes by coupling research sources with the tools necessary to analyze them; by maintaining linkages between research results and the sources on which they are based; and by providing a means to incorporate primary sources into teaching. Users will seek documents that are easily retrieved and manipulated, transmittable, and transportable from a repository to the sites of research, presentation, and teaching. It seems safe to assume that humanities scholars will need the capability to search through and select relevant sources from large bodies of heterogenous materials, to compare sources to each other, and to view specific documents at high levels of granularity.

Digital preservation will add little value to the research process if it serves only as an alternative form of storage from which analog replicas are produced for use with conventional analytical methods. Preserving digital materials in formats that are reliable and usable, however, will require long-term maintenance of structural characteristics, descriptive metadata, and display, computational, and analytical capabilities that are very demanding of both mass storage and software for retrieval and interpretation.

Digital preservation requirements may be expressed differently by archives, libraries, and other types of repositories that are struggling to meet escalating user expectations with limited financial and technical resources. Storage systems should be capable of handling digital information in a wide variety of formats, including text, data, graphics, video, and sound. Digital storage is not only an alternative means for storing print formats because many types of digital objects do not have print equivalents and cannot be preserved in non-digital formats.

Ideally, storage media will have a long life expectancy, a high degree of disaster resistance, sufficient durability to withstand regular use, and very large storage capacities. Conversion from analog to digital formats and migration to new generations of technology will be rapid, accurate, and inexpensive enough to permit very large scale transfers of heterogeneous materials. Storage space requirements will be minimal and not demand highly sensitive environmental controls. To make digital preservation affordable to the widest possible range of organizations and individuals, equipment, media, and maintenance costs must be modest.

Current Preservation Strategies and Their Limitations

Most librarians and archivists have accepted the basic wisdom—for now at least—that digital preservation depends upon copying, not on the survival of the physical media (Lesk). But copying, also referred to as "refreshing" or "migration" is more complex than simply transferring a stream of bits from old to new media or from one generation of systems to the next. Complex and expensive transformations of digital objects often are necessary to preserve digital materials so that they remain authentic representations of the original versions and useful sources for analysis and research (Task Force on Archiving of Digital Information).

Current methods for preserving digital materials do not fully support achieving these objectives. When faced with the responsibility for preserving digital materials, archives and libraries face a series of complex and difficult choices based on the format of the original materials, the anticipated uses for it, and the technical and financial resources available to invest in preservation initiatives. I will review some current preservation strategies beginning with the most elementary and established methods and ending with proposals that have not yet been tested.

Probably the most commonly used preservation strategy is to transfer digital information from less stable magnetic and optical media by printing page images on paper or microfilm. It seems ironic that just as libraries and archives are discovering digital conversion as a cost-effective preservation method for certain deteriorating materials, much information that begins its life in electronic form is printed on paper or microfilm for safe, secure long-term storage. Yet, high-quality acid neutral paper can last a century or longer while archival quality microfilm is projected to last 300 years or more. Paper and microfilm have the additional advantage of requiring no special hardware or software for retrieval or viewing. Perhaps this explains why in many digital conversion projects, the digital images serve as a complement to rather than a replacement for the original hard copy materials (Conway, 1994).

Another strategy for digital preservation is to preserve digital information in the simplest possible digital formats in order to minimize the requirements for sophisticated retrieval software. Digital information can be transferred across successive generations of technology in a "software-independent" format as ASCII text files or as flat files with simple, uniform structures. Several data archives hold large collections of numerical data that were captured on punch cards in the 1950s or 1960s, migrated to two or three different magnetic tape formats, and now reside on optical media. As new media and storage formats were introduced, the data were migrated without any significant change in their logical structure.

This approach has the distinct advantage of being universal and easy to implement. It is a cost-effective strategy for preserving digital information in those cases where retaining the content is paramount, but display, indexing, and computational characteristics are not critical. As long as the preservation community lacks more robust and cost-effective migration strategies, printing to paper or film and preserving flat files will remain the methods of last resort for many institutions and for certain formats of digital information.

Libraries and archives with large, complex, and diverse collections of digital materials are only beginning to test strategies that normalize various types of holdings by converting digital records from the great multiplicity of formats into a smaller, more manageable number of standard formats (University of the State of New York). A repository might accept textual documents only in one or a few commonly available commercial word processing formats or require that documents conform to standards like SGML (ISO 8879). Databases might be stored in one or a few common formats or converted to a SQL (Structured Query Language) compliant format, while image files might conform to the tagged image file format (TIFF) with standard compression algorithms.

This approach has the advantage of preserving more of the display, dissemination, and computational characteristics of the original materials, while reducing the large variety of customized transformations that would otherwise be necessary to migrate material to future generations of technology. The strategy rests on the assumption that software products which are either compliant with widely adopted standards or are widely dispersed in the marketplace are less volatile than the software market as a whole. Most common commercial products today provide utilities for backward compatibility and for swapping documents, databases, and more complex objects between software systems. Although this strategy simplifies migration and may lower digital preservation costs by reducing the amount of customized reformatting needed as technology changes, it does not eliminate the need for regular migration of digital materials. Software and standards both continue to evolve and even repositories with structurally homogeneous holdings can expect to be required to migrate their digital materials periodically.

Current methods fall far short of what is required to preserve digital materials. All current preservation methods involve trade-offs between what is desirable from the standpoint of functionality, dependability, and cost and what is possible and affordable with current technologies and methods. Consequently, most repositories are coping by employing interim and less than desirable strategies, if they are addressing digital preservation issues at all. For example, the simplicity and universality of printing to paper or microfilm come at the expense of great losses in the functionality of digital information. Migration strategies that involve reformatting of digital materials to a simple standard format usually eliminate the structure of documents and relationships imbedded in databases. Computation capabilities, graphic display, indexing, and other features often are lost, thus limiting future analytical potential. Normalization to standard formats is not always technically feasible and it usually is quite costly.

Archives and libraries must also contend with entirely new forms of electronically-enabled discourse and new forms of artistic and cultural expression that do not have predecessors in the analog world. No current preservation method is adequate for preserving dynamic data objects from complex systems. There are no established conceptual models or technical processes for preserving multi-media works, interactive hyper-media, on-line dialogues, or many of the new electronic forms being created today. The archival requirements to preserve content, context, and structure and to maintain the capability to display, link, and manipulate digital objects only heighten their software dependency.

The preservation community is only beginning to explore possible alternatives to storing digital information in "software-independent" form. Rothenberg (1995) proposed an approach for maintaining the content of digital materials intact without losing the ability to retrieve meaning-rich sources. He recommended retaining the original document in its original format encapsulated in a virtual "envelope" that contains software instructions for retrieval, display, and processing of the message in the envelope. The envelopes would contain contextual information and the transformational history of each object. Execution of the instructions would rely on an archive of hardware and software emulators or on instructions in the envelope with specifications to construct emulators. Important research is underway to define standards for data interchange that can support electronic commerce and satisfy business requirements in a variety of environments.

A major research project at the University of Pittsburgh is defining metadata requirements for evidence that will support the need for integrity, authenticity, reliability, and archiving through standards for "metadata encapsulated objects" (Bearman and Sochats). Archives, libraries, and other institutions with preservation responsibilities will benefit if systems are built to implement such metadata standards. Wide scale adoption of data and communication standards by the originators of digital information to support current business needs will also facilitate long-term preservation. Rapid implementation of electronic commerce depends on widespread development and adoption of standards for EDI (electronic data interchange) transaction sets under auspices of the ANSI X.12 committee, and many organizations are adopting standards for format and definitions to enable exchange, reuse, and sale of digital information and to reduce conversion and maintenance costs.

Standards initiatives that address business needs for the secure and reliable exchange of digital information among the current generation of systems will impose standardization and normalization of data that ultimately will facilitate migrations to new generations of technology. Yet to benefit fully from the synergy between business needs and preservation requirements we have to move beyond simply paying lip service to cultural heritage concerns and recognize that equally critical social goals, such as long-term genetic research, monitoring global environmental change, locating nuclear waste sites, and establishing property rights are also dependent on long-term access to reliable, electronic evidence.

Much remains to be done in research, development, and implementation before we can assume that even a small portion of our digital heritage will survive more than a few years. It is fair to say that the state of development in digital preservation remains largely experimental. Only a few libraries, archives, and other institutions have established digital preservation programmes, while most research and innovation comes from pilot projects and prototypes. Tested methods that have proven effective on a small scale in a limited number of repositories are not feasible for preservation of many of the types of digital materials that archives and libraries will confront in their preservation endeavours.

AREAS FOR RESEARCH AND DEVELOPMENT

The current state of digital preservation suggests several fruitful areas for research and development. I will discuss four areas: storage media, migration, conversion, and management tools. These four domains are often mutually dependent and ultimately must to be integrated into an infrastructure for digital preservation. Yet better solutions are necessary in all four areas before such integration can occur. Finally, I will share some observations about the issues of scale and cost that must be considered if we are going to achieve any degree of systematic preservation.

Storage Media

The limited life of magnetic and optical media pose a significant problem, although this is not the primary limiting factor for digital preservation. Recent research on the longevity of magnetic media indicate a useful life span of 10 to 30 years if they are handled and stored properly. Some optical disk technologies promise life spans of up to 100 years. Most authorities argue that enhanced media longevity is of little value because current media outlast the software and devices needed to retrieve recorded information.

Nevertheless, improvements in the stability, capacity, and longevity of the base storage media are needed to drastically reduce the vulnerability of digital materials to loss and alteration and to lower storage costs. Ample research and experience provide evidence of what can go wrong with magnetic media as a result of binder degradation, magnetic particle instabilities, and substrate deformation (Van Bogart). Optical media are susceptible to damage from high humidity, rapid and extreme temperature fluctuations, and contamination from airborne particulate matter (U.S. National Archives and Records Administration).

To prevent these problems, it is imperative to store magnetic and optical media under strict environmental controls that are not always available, affordable, or convenient. Even modest improvements which produce storage media with larger per unit storage capacities and greater tolerance to variations in temperature and humidity will lower preservation costs by lessening the need for strict environmental controls, reducing the frequency with which digital media must be "refreshed" through recopying, and decreasing the number of storage units that must be handled.

This raises the question, however, of whether research on incremental improvements in current storage technologies will benefit preservation in the long run or whether we should seek alternative approaches to digital storage that more adequately meet archival requirements. As a frame of reference it is worth remembering that microfilm, which is considered the only acceptable archival storage medium, lasts at least 300 years with minimal maintenance if stored properly. Last June, the Los Alamos National Laboratory announced the invention of a High-Density Read-Only Memory (HD-ROM) technology that uses an ion beam to inscribe information on pins of stainless steel, iridium, or other materials.

The HD-ROM is capable of storing 180 times more information than current CD-ROM technology at roughly one-half per cent of CD-ROM costs. According to the release about this technology, the HD-ROM is impervious to material degradation and it requires no bit stream interpreter because the technology can describe in human-readable form all of the instructions needed to interpret the data (LANL Ion Beam Storage). Such an approach illustrates the potential for solutions built on entirely new storage technologies.

Migration

Better methods for migration of digital materials to new generations of hardware and software are much needed for digital preservation regardless of breakthroughs in mass storage technologies. Planning for migration is difficult because there is limited experience with the types of migrations needed to maintain access to complex digital objects over extended periods of time. When a custodian assumes responsibility for preserving a digital object it may be difficult to predict when migration will be necessary, how much reformatting will be needed, and how much migration will cost. There are no reliable or comprehensive data on costs associated with migrations, either for specific technologies and formats or for particular collections, and little research underway on methodologies that would reduce the costs and burdens of migration.

The preservation community as a whole would benefit tremendously from the development of backward compatibility paths that would be included as a standard feature of all software. Backward compatibility or migration paths would enable a new generation of software to "read" data from older systems without substantial reformatting and without loss of retrieval, display and computational capabilities. Although backward compatibility is increasingly common within software product lines, migration paths are not commonly provided between competing software products or for products that fail in the marketplace.

Stewards of digital material have a range of options for preserving digital information. One might preserve an exact replica of a digital record with complete display, retrieval, and computational functionality, or a representation of the record with only partial computation capabilities, or a surrogate for the record such as an abstract, summary, or aggregation. Detail or background noise might be dropped out intentionally through successive generations of migration, and custodians might change the format or storage media. Enhancements are technologically possible through clean-up, mark-up, and linkage, or by adding indexing and other features. These technological possibilities in turn impose serious new responsibilities to present digital materials to users in a way that allows them to determine the authenticity of the information and its relationship to the original record. Methods to document changes in digital objects during their life span need to be incorporated as an integral part of improved migration methods.

There are few well developed methods for preserving and migrating software so that it might be used to recreate digital documents that have the "look and feel" of the original sources. Maintaining repositories of obsolete hardware and software has been discussed periodically, but usually dismissed out of hand as too expensive and not demonstrably feasible. This approach deserves more serious consideration as a strategy for maintaining continuing access to certain types of digital materials. Feasibility studies and cost/benefit analyses should be conducted to determine the technological, economic, and commercial feasibility of maintaining selected legacy software systems and performing specialized migrations or, alternatively, of building and maintaining software emulators. Such an approach would support replay of original sources and contribute to the preservation of software as a significant cultural and intellectual resource in its own right.

Conversion

Faster, cheaper, and higher resolution conversion technologies are another critical element needed to make digital preservation feasible on a large scale. Most archivists and librarians accept the fact that we live in a hybrid environment where paper, microfilm, video, and magnetic and optical media need to interoperate in a more integrated and transparent manner. The vast majority of primary sources today still reside on paper and/or microfilm with little chance that we will see the mass conversion of existing archival and library holdings to digital formats. Research and planning for digital preservation must recognize that we will be dealing with conversion for a long time and that investments in improving capture rates, accuracy, resolution, and verification will have long-term benefits.

Moreover, improvements in conversion technologies may support hybrid solutions to preservation and access problems by permitting repositories to store certain formats of digital material on stable media, such as microfilm, with on demand conversion to digital form for analysis and reuse. Efforts to capture and store descriptive mark-up on film for subsequent conversion are hampered by unacceptable error rates in OCR technology and cumbersome conversion processes (Giguere).

MANAGEMENT TOOLS

A fourth area for research is in the development of management tools for digital libraries and archives that integrate descriptive control and maintenance with storage technologies.

Dynamic digital objects, such as those found in hypertext systems, pose special management problems for both current and future retrieval and reuse. The boundaries of hypertext sources, like those found on the World Wide Web today, are difficult to ascertain because no single party or institution controls changes in the nodes and links that make hypertext objects live and highly responsive information resources.

A high degree of volatility accompanies these objects because the contents of nodes change, the sites where information resources are stored change, and the links between nodes change, move, and vanish. Some recent tools, such as the MOMspider (Multi-Owner Maintenance Spider) and Web:Lookout are capable of traversing a portion of the Web and noting maintenance problems such as broken links, moved documents, modified documents, and objects that have exceeded their expiration dates (Ackerman and Fielding). While tools such as these are useful for current maintenance, they do not address long-term preservation concerns. If further developed to address preservation problems, tools such as these have the potential to serve as filters, identify similar or identical objects, and monitor for maintenance problems.

Research and development of tools that would imbed more intelligence about the preservation status of digital material into the objects themselves would make monitoring and maintenance of large digital collections more automatic. Current methods for monitoring the physical status of digital materials are labour intensive, unreliable, and potentially damaging to the materials themselves. Recommended procedures for monitoring physical deterioration of magnetic tape, for example, involve reading a small sample of tapes periodically to determine whether any data losses have occurred (Eaton). The potential exists to build monitoring and reporting mechanisms into digital objects, storage systems, and network architectures that could support self-reporting of physical status and initiate automatic maintenance procedures.

Despite differences, some lessons from traditional preservation are transferable to the digital environment. In order to avoid commitments that far exceed available resources and costly rescue and restoration efforts, preservation must become an integral part of the planning, design, and resource allocation for digital libraries and archives. Integration of preservation requirements and methods with access and maintenance systems is essential to fully and efficiently support the processes of migration, regeneration, and documentation of the life of digital objects.

Planning for preservation must become an integral part of the design and management of digital libraries and archives. If left as an afterthought, there is little reason to believe that long-term preservation of digital information will be any more affordable than preservation of conventional formats has been.

Some Concluding Comments

In closing, I would like to mention three issues that I discussed only in passing. One concern is the question of scale and scalability. The preservation community has at its disposal a variety of tactics for digital preservation that appear to work effectively for certain types of materials in certain restricted environments, but we have not yet developed solutions that are scalable to the general problem of digital preservation.

This is not to suggest that there is or should be a single solution to digital preservation. The methods used will vary depending upon the complexity of the original data objects, the extent to which the functionality for computation, display, indexing, and authentication must be maintained, and the requirements of current or anticipated users. But any solution must be scalable from the laboratory, prototype, or pilot project to the wide range of individuals and institutions who have a need to make digital materials last longer than the current generation of technology permits.

Another closely related issue is the question of affordability. Regardless of how the responsibility for digital preservation is distributed, societies only allocate a small and finite amount of resources to preserving scholarly and cultural resources. And in the digital environment it seems likely that more preservation responsibilities will be distributed to individual creators, rights holders, distributors, small institutions, and other players in the production and dissemination process. Therefore, it seems imperative that digital preservation technologies become affordable and accessible to the wide range of individuals and institutions that will attempt to preserve digital materials.

Finally, it would be beneficial to both the preservation community and to those conducting research on issues of longevity, migration, and conversion if there were more venues for exchange of ideas, requirements, and recent developments. Without a continuing dialogue between humanists, preservationists, and the scientific community it is difficult to include preservation requirements in scientific research endeavours, and it is challenging for those of us outside the scientific community to keep up with and evaluate new products. I hope that the discussion we are beginning at this conference will lead to more regular and formal processes for linking the needs of scholars and preservationists with the research agendas and projects of scientists.

DEVELOPMENT OF IT SKILLS FOR INFORMATION PROFESSIONALS

As a result of Information explosion the libraries and information centers (LICs) have become a necessity. A continuous flow of information in all the sectors of human activity through research and innovation has brought drastic changes in the present society. At present age Knowledge and information are strategic inputs in all walks of life, along with the traditional ones of man, money and materials. Knowledge and information will continue to play a significant role in the socio-economic development. Hence there is expansion of the employment market for library and information professionals. But despite increase in the number of jobs, the total market demand for LISc professionals at present is far less than the total output. Moreover, the quality of output is not fully compatible with the requirements of the expanding job market. Librarianship today has arrived at the information age where the role of information is increasingly emphasised as an economic resource, a marketable commodity and as a social wealth. In this context the role of librarian is very much important. He/ she will have to act as a facilitator, advisor, consultant, instructor, navigator, searcher, researcher, evaluator, organiser, preserver, promoter, communicator, technical expert, as well as a manager, leader, entrepreneur and visionary.

And for the success of library and information centers as effective communication system, the development of manpower to do such work is vital. One of the important aspects of manpower development in this connection is improved education system for library and information science. Mangla 'Library and Information Science programmes should be so designed as to equip the student:

- With knowledge and techniques to handle the immediate job requirements in an efficient manner; and
- "To develop programmes, procedures and services on modern lines in future where the use of various modern techniques, computers etc., could provide better, quicker and efficient service".

Skill in Information Technology (IT) can be gained only when one gets hands-on training and experience in laboratories under simulated conditions or in real life situations. The graduates and post graduates turned out by library schools of West Bengal do not possess adequate skill and expertise to interact confidently with IT specialists, evaluate what is recommended by them and full fill their requirements.

NECESSITY FOR PRACTICAL IT TRAINING

New Information Technology

Technological innovations have given rise to new ideas relating to collection, processing and dissemination of information. These innovations and ideas including Artificial Intelligence, Robotics, Speech Synthesis, Electronic mail, CD-ROM, CD Networking, Barcode systems, Electronic publishing, Hypermedia, Multimedia, Tele facsimile, Radio data paging, Networks etc. share a common technology revolving around electronics, computers, Telecommunication, Printing and Reprography, popularly known as Information Technology.

Futurist Alvin Toffler has rightly predicted that computers will enhance our 'mind power' just as the industrial revolution has enhanced our 'muscle power'. At least complete practical knowledge of computer applications in LICs is essential for a LISc professional. LIS being an information collection, organisation, and dissemination agency, technological innovations especially in the field of IT, have implications both for LIS, and the workforce required to service information users and their needs. Development in educational technology and the changing pattern of education and learning also indicate challenges for the library and information community to upgrade their IT skills.

Revolution Concept of Library

The LIS education aims at providing trained manpower to manage different types of libraries, information and documentation centers which, over a period of time have undergone changes in terms of needs, functions, types and range of services offered, as well as tools and techniques being used when offering the services. Application of information and communication technologies has revolutionised the whole concept of libraries, the system of information storage and retrieval and ways to access the information. Therefore, the objectives of LIS education also need to be redefined. The students need to be more practical oriented and should be equipped with intensive and extensive knowledge on the use of IT in libraries. Application of technology has opened up new vistas and thus, all LIS schools should think seriously in terms of the changing context. Students need to be given adequate knowledge of computers (including hardware), computer and communication technologies, networking, operating systems, Internet concepts, and database management systems, with adequate practical exposure to handle these technological devices.

Table. Traditional Library Concepts and Modern Concepts of Information Science

Traditional Concepts	Modern concepts
History and Development of Libraries	Library Automation, Library Application Software
Preservation and conservation of Library Materials	Multi-media information sources
Cataloguing of Books	Online Public Access Catalogue
Library Systems and services	Design and development of Databases; Database Management Systems
Library Orientation	Computerized Information Retrieval; Online Search and Retrieval of Information; e-journals & e-books
User needs and user surveys	Internet basics etc.
Inter Library Loan	Networking & Resource Sharing; Consortia

Areas of Practical IT Skills Developments in LISc Curriculum

LISc courses offered by Indian library schools in different universities have become partially irrelevant since long. The debate about changing the LISc curricula has been going on for the last few years, but nothing concrete has yet been done at the national level, except for some cosmetic changes.

Dominance of Practice

The issue of the relationship between theory and practice is not properly addressed in the Indian context. An expert once stated that we are drowning in theory at library schools and not giving enough exposure to practice. The dilemma lies in the choice between teaching students the knowledge and skills needed in their first posts to which meet the immediate needs of employers and instilling principles from which they can expand their skills and knowledge base as their career develops. It is also seen that during the challenge of managing the complex and diverse new environment, some of the schools have been merged with different disciplines like information management and technology, information studies and mass communications. Given the pace of change in the nature of library and information services, there is a still need to not only in preparing library professionals but also in establishing practitioners, a commitment to lifelong learning because the circumstances are demanding greater professional and technical awareness.

As professional obsolescence becomes a real and ever present danger, only a systematic continuing education provides a method of combating such obsolescence. In the western countries many schools have made a thorough revision and development of course programmes and also introduced new courses to meet the needs of employers in industries, and the public and private sectors. The introduction of new programmes should therefore be seen too some extent as reflecting the 'Pull-Push Effect' of recognising the increasing need for the professional workforce to match the growth and significance of information industry and the expanding higher education system to provide the appropriate workforce. To design a model curriculum for a dynamic inter-disciplinary subject like Library and Information Science on the national level is quite difficult, and such attempts will raise awkward questions regarding inclusion or exclusion of particular topics and the emphasis to be given to individual topics. Hence, relevant topics, which are already implemented in LIS education emphasis on both theoretical and practical aspects but the information professionals are not getting hands-on training and experience in laboratory under simulated conditions or in real life situations (*i.e* trouble shooting).

Networking

- *Node failure:* In an automated library all the work station should be connected through LAN to the server, if the application is not being accessed from any of the work station then this situation is called node failure.

- *How to detect this problem:* Using of 'ping' command from run, if 'request time error' is coming then there must be an issue with the connectivity.
- *Syntax:* ping 'IP address of the work station' -t
- How to resolve issue:
  - Make sure the computer is turn on
  - Check the local area connection must be enable
  - Check the Ethernet cable must be plug in
  - Check other end of that Ethernet cable should be plug in into a network switch.
  - Check the IP address should be in the same class compare to the server IP if DHCP server is not there.

Database

- *Information retrieving/updating/deleting error:* In a server based library, application library software will be running in which all the information will be stored into the database. Sometimes we face a problem at the time of retrieving, updating and deleting records.
- How to resolve the issue:
  - Make sure the database are running
  - Make sure the database path is correct
  - Make sure that there is no issue with the front end application
  - If needed you can restore the database from database back up taken in every alternative minutes through 'database attachment'

Printing

- *Error:* Printer is not working.
- First needs to check the type (network/desktop shared) of printer, if it is a network printer then the following steps are:
  - Check printer is properly connected to the LAN switch through an Ethernet cable. RJ45 connector is working or not.
  - Check Power is turned on
  - Check the IP address, Subnet and default gateway of that printer by using network command in the printer's display. Also check the port details.
  - Check Printer's IP is pinging or not.
  - Check that is there any issue like paper jam, no paper in the tray etc.

- Make sure that work station's 'printer spooler' service is running by using a command 'services.msc' from run.

Therefore, it is right time to inject some practical IT training with proper resources *i.e* Library Open Source Soft ware, Database, Servers and Network equipments etc. and fine tune the LIS courses accordingly. It will make the LIS courses consistent with the Job market.

7

Digital Library Evaluation

INTRODUCTION

When an animal bred in captivity runs, flaps or slithers into the wilderness for the first time, scientists do not simply wave goodbye, wish it well and move on to the next project.

Usually the animal is tracked and observed for a long time thereafter—the point of release is where the research really begins. However, this has been less true for grant-funded digital library projects. Administrative and institutional barriers tend to confine evaluation to the funding period when the system is being designed, and when its uses and effects can only be guessed at.

In this short paper I will discuss a digital library project in environmental science where some of these evaluation issues arose, the value of eliciting narrative data from users, and some ways to take better advantage of existing but underused mechanisms for long-term evaluation of digital libraries. Viewing information technologies and society as inextricably co-determined makes it necessary to gather data both on the design process and on how the finished systems are used by people—often in quite unexpected ways.

Iterative design and formative evaluation are ways to introduce user feedback into ongoing design, but while these strategies can serve as an effective translation layer between users, designers and builders, the focus is on how an evolving system *might* be used. How it is *actually* used can be more accurately determined when the system is in the wild, when the designers and their formal evaluation instruments have gone away. Digital libraries are social entities. They tell stories about a culture, a science, a place or a time, through the items represented and organized in the collection, and in use, they help generate new stories as well.

Manovich has advanced the idea of database and narrative as two ends of same continuum; both structure information, but where a database aims for access, a narrative aims for psychological immersion in the story. From an institutional standpoint, digital libraries are rarely ends in themselves.

The social missions of the funding organizations—the stories they wish to tell— often drive the creation of digital libraries, but how well a finished system supports the mission can't be fully evaluated until the digital library has had some time to develop a user base. This line of research began with a participant observation of the design of a digital library of environmental science collections. Funded by an Library Services and Technology Act (LSTA) grant, the project involved diverse designers, content, metadata and institutional participants.

As one of the participants in the environmental science digital library noted, "Part of the art of grant writing is interpreting vague language in a way that lets you do what you want to do," or in other words, making project proposals and achievements dovetail with the mission and goals of the funding agency. These goals included outreach and evaluation, so a usability component was included in the grant proposal. My initial role in the project was to develop the instruments and conduct the evaluation.

Understandably, digital library designers tend to create evaluation instruments that demonstrate in a measurable way the work they've done, a tacit statement of the value produced for the grant funds received. For example, the design of the interface, the appropriateness of descriptive metadata, and user success at canned search tasks are classic evaluative measures. However, in an analysis of the Perseus Digital Library (PDL), Marchionini writes: "Operational data are powerful components in a chain of inferences that address impact but the PDL evaluation illustrates the value of anecdotes and "stories" that illustrate new effects, *i.e.*, how DLs augment existing capabilities with new ones. These augmentations garner public support for a DL and should not be underestimated in assessing impact.

Integrating multiple views is more naturally done with narratives than summary statistics and integrating these forms of evidence can aid in assessing complex change." In the evaluation, statistical and demographic data were not hard to come by.

Observation, interviews, document analysis, narrative analysis and social network analysis were effective ways to construct as complete a picture as possible about the interactions of the designers. But the usability component needed to be completed at the same time as the digital library, in time for the results to be included in the final LSTA grant report (though the exact LSTA grant regulations vary by state, most LSTA grantees must submit a final grant report within 15-30 days of project completion).

Participants in the usability study were evaluating a still evolving system, and had to project potential uses into their responses to open-ended interview questions. By the time they might integrate the collections into their professional lives, and perhaps surprise themselves with unexpected dimensions of usefulness, the evaluation would be long over. This is certainly not to say that there is no such thing as continuing evaluation of grant-funded digital libraries. But the mechanisms for long-term evaluation are usually little more than Web forms or e-mail links, not organic components of the digital library. In practice, designers are more concerned with present and future digital library projects than with continuing evaluation of those of the past.

Digital library researchers have an opportunity to conduct this longer-term research, to question and reveal the impacts of digital libraries as social entities, and to apply the resulting knowledge to future projects. The good news is that in some situations, a mechanism for longer term evaluation already exists. For example, the State Library of Ohio's LSTA grant process makes use of a "year-after" evaluation form (http://winslo.state.oh.us/publib/lstayraft.html), which includes questions such as "Did the project produce any unexpected results?" and encourages narrative ("Please provide a success story of how your project has impacted someone's life or had a positive impact on the community.").

This is precisely the sort of openended data collection instrument that can reveal how a digital library is actually being used—but even this document is only the length of a one-page questionnaire. Subsequent research will attempt to evaluate the usefulness of this and other longer-term evaluation instruments, and how they might be expanded. While longer-term evaluation should include quantitative data such as transaction logs and perhaps a list of external sites that link to collection content, evaluation instruments should also be open-ended, designed to encourage narrative expressions of unexpected use, the kind of data that reveal to funding agencies the real impact of their grants.

Iterative digital library design philosophies have always had at their core the sense that user input should feed back into ongoing system design. I propose here simply a wider iterative design circle, one that allows for more naturalistic data about longer-term use to be fed back into future systems.

COLLECTION EVALUATION

Some readers may be surprised to find this article in an issue on collection evaluation. Are online databases indeed a part of the collection, or are they a type of reference service? In actuality, they are both. Databases have become an important part of libraries' reference collections and may in some cases serve as a substitute for the addition of print materials to these collections.

Online databases, both bibliographic and numeric, have been reported to be part of library collections. The literature will be analysed from this point of view. An online database is a machine-readable file of organised information with which the user interacts by means of a terminal connected to the computer housing the file. The terminal may be wired directly to the computer or it may communicate with it via a telecommunications network. The important feature of the online mode is that the user interacts with the information in the computer, sending and receiving messages in an almost instantaneous time frame.

This chapter deals only with those databases which can be accessed directly by a user from his/her own library and does not deal with many available in information analysis centers to which the user cannot be directly linked online. Many information analysis centers receive, analyse and prepare online files. These are, for the most part, accessed only by center personnel or others in the information center's host institution or agency. For the most part dial-up access to the information analysis centre is not available for libraries.

Instead, the library usually submits a search to the centre, which then performs the search and sends back an answer. The emphasis of this chapter is on online access by a library to a database the library staff did not prepare, but which has been made available outside the preparing agency for direct access. It is only recently that databases have begun to be considered a part of a library's collections. No wonder. They only became available in libraries in the 1970s. The first articles on machine-readable bibliographic databases began appearing in the *Annual Review of Information Science and Technology* early in the decade. The first stage on 'Use of Machine-Readable Databases' appeared in the 1974 volume. As online database availability was increasing, library funds for acquisitions were decreasing. This decrease forced libraries to move from the concept of comprehensive collections of all that their users could possibly want to collections of most heavily used items with a dependence on access to others' collections for lesser used items. Online bibliographic databases provided quick and improved access to others' collections and to information about publications which a library might or might not have in its own collection.

The means of access itself, rather than the materials became a component of any individual library's collections. The collection development literature is slowly beginning to acknowledge this change. Although some standard collection development texts such as Gardner now have a section on computer-based materials, Bonk and Magrill does not. Even though databases or tapes may be mentioned as items to consider in the sections on selection, they are nowhere to be found in the sections on collection evaluation. George Bonn's classic *Library Trends* article on 'Evaluation of the Collection' which appeared in 1971 makes no mention of database evaluation.

It was too early. This chapter will focus on developments since, 1974. The ALA *Guidelines for Collection Development* lists datatapes as one form of material collected but the section on collection evaluation gives no specific guidance on their evaluation or the evaluation of any other of the special forms such as newspapers, manuscripts or audiovisual materials. Online files are not mentioned. So, although some sources view databases as part of the collection, few standard sources evaluate them as such.

The new ANSI standard on library statistics does list databases as a part of collection resources and groups them with currently received periodicals in a category titled 'currently renewed resources.' The number of databases to which the library provides access for its users is to be reported. In addition, the standard specifies that database transactions should be reported as a subset of reference transactions.

Databases are viewed in the literature and in the standard as a part of the collections and as a reference service. The nature of databases and their role in libraries are still evolving. A quick scan of the bibliography for this article will indicate that we have not even decided how to spell database yet. Is it one word or two? Earlier usage was primarily *data base,* but the current trend seems to be one word. This author will use *database,* as does the journal of that name which began publication in 1978. The fact is that in a very short ten-year period databases have found their way into library services and collections.

CONTEXT OF EVALUATION

Digital libraries are complex social, institutional and technical systems. No evaluation can possibly address all of these aspects together. Thus, different approaches have been used for different evaluation goals.

Context includes selection of a goal, framework, viewpoint or level(s), basic approach or perspective of evaluation. There are different types of approaches of digital library evaluation on the basis of different aspects.

No single approach can exhaustively evaluate the all aspects of any digital library. Here we try to incorporate most of the approaches as possible.

The approaches are:

- *System-centered approach*: Most prevalent. Involves study of some aspect of performance. Includes assessing effectiveness and/or efficiency of some feature or some specific design or some technological component. Applied in a number of studies with results that may inform specific choices in design or operations.
- *Human-centered approach*: Also widely applied. Involves study of behaviour in respect to given information needs, such as information seeking, browsing, searching including performance appraisal of given tasks, either predetermined or observed in natural settings. Used in a number of studies that illuminated human behaviour, requirements, needs, or difficulties encountered. Provides implications for design, but indirectly rather than directly.
- *Usability-centered approach*: Involves assessment of different features, particularly in respect to portals, by users. It is a bridge between systems- and human-centered approaches. Used in several studies with mixed, or self-evident results.
- *Ethnographic approach*: Involves study of life-ways, culture and customs in a digital library environment. Also involves study of impact of a digital library on a given community. Applied successfully in a few studies, with illuminating results, particularly as to impact.

- *Anthropological approach*: Involves study of different stakeholders or communities and their cultures in relation to a given digital library. Applied in one study with interesting results illuminating barriers between stakeholder communities.
- *Sociological approach*: Involves assessment of situated action or user communities in social setting of a digital library. Applied in one study with disappointing results.
- *Economic approach*: Involves study of costs, cost benefits, economic values and impacts. Strangely, it was applied at the outset of digital library history (*e.g.,* project PEAK) but now the approach is not really present at all.

CRITERIA FOR EVALUATION

Criteria reflecting performance as related to selected objectives. They include:

- What parameters of performance were concentrate on?
- What dimension or characteristic were evaluate?

  Criteria refer to chosen standard(s) to judge things by. Criteria are then used to develop measures. The importance of criteria follows from this truism: there can be no evaluation without explicitly or implicitly having some criterion or criteria first.Since, 1950's evaluation of IR systems uses relevance as the basic criterion for evaluation. Libraries use a variety of (more or less) standardised criteria for evaluation of components, such as a collection, or services, such as reference. Digital library efforts have not as yet developed anything similar as to evaluation criteria. A summary of most often used criteria follows.

USABILITY

Usability has been used widely in digital library evaluation, but there is no uniform definition of what does it cover in digital library context. Usability is a very general criterion that covers a lot of ground and includes many specific criteria – it is a meta term This was pretty much the umbrella under which usability was used in digital library evaluation. Here is a list of specific usability criteria applied in various studies:

- Content (of a portal or site):
  - Accessibly, availability
  - Clarity (as presented)
  - Complexity (organisation, structure)
  - Informativeness
  - Transparency
  - Understanding, effort to understand
  - Adequacy
  - Coverage, overlap,

  - Quality, accuracy
  - Validity, reliability
  - Authority
- *Process*: Carrying out tasks such as search, navigate, browse, find, evaluate or obtain a resource, etc.
  - learnability to carry out
  - Effort/time to carry out
  - Convenience, ease of use
  - Lostness (confusion)
  - Support for carrying out
  - Completion (achievement of task)
  - Interpretation difficulty
  - Sureness in results
  - Error rate
- Format:
  - Attractiveness
  - Sustaining efforts
  - Consistency
  - Representation of labels (how well are concepts Represented?)
  - communicativeness of messages
- Overall assessment:
  - Satisfaction
  - Success
  - Relevance, usefulness of results
  - Impact, value
  - Quality of experience
  - Barriers, irritability
  - Preferences
  - Learning

SYSTEMS FEATURES

As digital libraries are systems, many traditional systems evaluation criteria were used.

Some pertain to performance of technology others to performance of given processes or algorithms using technology.

- Technology performance:
  - Response time
  - Processing time,
  - Speed
  - Capacity
  - Load
- Process/algorithm performance:
  - Relevance (of obtained results)

  - Clustering
  - Similarity
  - Functionality
  - Flexibility
  - Comparison with human performance
  - Error rate
  - Optimisation
  - Logical decisions
  - Path length
  - Click throughs
  - Retrieval time
- Overall system:
  - Maintainability
  - Scalability
  - Interoperability
  - Sharability
  - Costs

USAGE

A number of studies concentrated on use of a digital library, considering this as evaluation.

Usage in itself is a criterion involving studies of:

- Usage patterns
- Use of materials
- Usage statistics
- Who uses what, when
- For what reasons/decisions

ETHNOGRAPHIC AND OTHER CRITERIA

Several ethnographic and anthropological studies used criteria derived from those fields. Among others, these involve determination of conceptions and misconceptions in and between different groups, their practices and environments, their culture, their language and frames of reference, priorities, learning, impacts and similar aspects that provide comparative evaluation in a broader context of a digital library..

ICDL: EVALUATION METHOD

The range of methods used in digital library evaluations is wide. It would be hard to find a scholarly evaluation method that was not used. It involves: What measures and measuring instruments were used? What samples were used? What procedures were used for data collection? What procedures were used for data analysis? In the present study involves mainly limited user study and systematic study of web site of ICDL with respect to Intel Pentium PCs with MS Windows having 14", 17" and 19" monitors.

Actually methodology includes:

- Surveys, including direct questionnaires and online surveys
- Structured interviews
- Focus groups
- Observations
- Task accomplishment
- Think aloud
- Case studies
- Transaction log analyses
- Experimentation
- Records analysis
- Usage analysis
- Documents, meeting, communication analysis (anthropology)
- Economic analysis

FEDERAL INITIATIVES: DIGITAL LIBRARIES AND OTHERS

In May 1995, the Information Infrastructure Technology and Applications (IITA) Working Group, which was the highest level of the country's National Information Infrastructure (NII) technical committee, held an invitational workshop to define a research agenda for digital libraries. The participants described a shared vision of an entire Net of distributed repositories, where objects of any type can be searched within and across different indexed collections.

In the short term, technologies must be developed to search across these repositories transparently, handling any variations in protocols and formats (*i.e.*, addressing structural interoperability).

In the long term, technologies also must be developed to handle variations in content and meanings transparently. These requirements are steps along the way towards matching the concepts being explored by users with objects indexed in collections.

The ultimate goal, as described in the IITA report, is the Grand Challenge of Digital Libraries:

- *Deep semantic interoperability:* The ability of a user to access, consistently and coherently, similar (though autonomously defined and managed) classes of digital objects and services, distributed across heterogeneous repositories, with federating or mediating software compensating for site-by-site variations...Achieving this will require breakthroughs in description as well as retrieval, object interchange and object retrieval protocols.

Issues here include the definition and use of metadata and its capture or computation from objects (both textual and multimedia), the use of computed descriptions of objects, federation and integration of heterogeneous repositories with disparate semantics, clustering and automatic hierarchical organization of information, and algorithms for automatic rating, ranking, and evaluation of information quality, genre, and other properties.

This paper is a short overview of the progress that has been made in the subsequent four years towards meeting this goal of semantic interoperability in digital libraries. In particular, it describes work that was carried out as part of the Illinois Digital Libraries Initiative (DLI) project, through partnership with the Artificial Intelligence Lab at the University of Arizona. Attention to semantic interoperability has prompted several projects in the NSF/DARPA/NASA funded large-scale Digital Libraries Initiative (DLI) to explore various artificial intelligence, statistical, and pattern recognition techniques. Examples include concept spaces and category maps in the Illinois project and word sense disambiguation in the Berkeley project, voice recognition in the Carnegie Mellon project, and image segmentation and clustering in the project at the University of California at Santa Barbara.

In the NSF workshop on Distributed Knowledge Work Environments: Digital Libraries, held at Santa Fe in March, 1997, a panel of digital library researchers and practitioners suggested three areas of research for the planned Digital Libraries Initiative-2 (DLI-2): system-centered issues, collection-centered issues, and user-centered issues. Scalability, interoperability, adaptability and durability, and support for collaboration are the four key research directions under system-centered issues.

System interoperability, syntactic (structural) interoperability, linguistic interoperability, temporal interoperability, and semantic interoperability are recognized by leading researchers as the most challenging and rewarding research areas.

The importance of semantic interoperability extends beyond digital libraries. The ubiquity of online information as perceived by US leaders (*e.g.*, "Information President" Clinton and "Information Vice President" Gore) as well as the general public and recognition of the importance of turning information into knowledge have continued to push information and computer science researchers towards developing scalable artificial intelligence techniques for other emerging information systems applications.

In a new NSF Knowledge Networking (KN) initiative, a group of domain scientists and information systems researchers was invited to a Workshop on Distributed Heterogeneous Knowledge Networks at Boulder, Colorado, in May, 1997.

Scalable techniques to improve semantic bandwidth and knowledge bandwidth are considered among the priority research areas, as described in the KN report: The Knowledge Networking (KN) initiative focuses on the integration of knowledge from different sources and domains across space and time.

Modern computing and communications systems provide the infrastructure to send bits anywhere, anytime, in mass quantities - radical connectivity. But connectivity alone cannot assure:

- Useful communication across disciplines, languages, cultures;
- Appropriate processing and integration of knowledge from different sources, domains, and non-text media;
- Efficacious activity and arrangements for teams, organizations, classrooms, or communities, working together over distance and time;
- Deepening understanding of the ethical, legal, and social implications of new developments in connectivity, but not interactivity and integration. KN research aims to move beyond connectivity to achieve new levels of interactivity, increasing the semantic bandwidth, knowledge bandwidth, activity bandwidth, and cultural bandwidth among people, organizations, and communities.

Semantic Research for Digital Libraries

During the DLI, which ran from 1994 to 1998, significant research was conducted at all six projects in the area of semantic retrieval and analysis for digital libraries. Among the semantic indexing and analysis techniques that are considered scalable and domain independent, the following classes of algorithms and methods have been examined and subjected to experimentation in various digital library, multimedia database, and information science applications:

Object Recognition, Segmentation, and Indexing

The most fundamental techniques in Information Retrieval involve identifying key features in objects. For example, automatic indexing and natural language processing (*e.g.*, noun phrase extraction or object type tagging) are frequently used to extract meaningful keywords or phrases from texts automatically. Texture, colour, or shape-based indexing and segmentation techniques are often used to identify images. For audio and video applications, voice recognition, speech recognition, and scene segmentation, techniques can be used to identify meaningful descriptors in audio or video streams.

Semantic Analysis

Several classes of techniques have been used for semantic analysis of texts or multimedia objects. Symbolic machine learning (*e.g.*, ID3 decision tree algorithm, version space), graph-based clustering and classification (*e.g.*, Ward's hierarchical clustering), statistics-based multivariate analyses (*e.g.*, latent semantic indexing, multi-dimensional scaling, regressions), artificial neural network-based computing (*e.g.*, backpropagation networks, Kohonen self-organizing maps), and evolution-based programming (*e.g.*, genetic algorithms) are among the popular techniques.

In this information age, we believe such techniques will serve as good alternatives for processing, analyzing, and summarizing large amounts of diverse and rapidly changing multimedia information.

Knowledge Representations

The results from a semantic analysis process could be represented in the form of semantic networks, decision rules, or predicate logic. Many researchers have attempted to integrate such results with existing human-created knowledge structures such as ontologies, subject headings, or thesauri. Spreading activation based inferencing methods often are used to traverse various large-scale knowledge structures.

Human-computer Interactions (HCI) and Information Visualization:

One of the major trends in almost all emerging information systems applications is the focus on user-friendly, graphical, and seamless Human Computer Interactions. The Web-based browsers for texts, images, and videos have raised user expectations of rendering and manipulation of information.

Recent advances in development languages and platforms such as Java, OpenGL, and VRML and the availability of advanced graphical workstations at affordable prices have also made information visualization a promising area for research.

Several digital library research teams including Arizona/Illinois, Xerox PARC, Berkeley, and Stanford, are pushing the boundary of visualization techniques for dynamic displays of large-scale information collections.

The Illinois DLI Project: Federating Repositories of Scientific Literature

The Artificial Intelligence Lab at the University of Arizona was a major partner in the University of Illinois DLI Project, one of six projects funded by the NSF/DARPA/NASA DLI (Phase 1). The project consisted of two major components:

- A production testbed based in a real library
- Fundamental technology research for semantic interoperability (semantic indexes across subjects and media developed at the University of Arizona).

The Testbed

The Illinois DLI production testbed was developed in the Grainger Engineering Library at the University of Illinois at Urbana-Champaign (UIUC). It supports full federated searching on the structure of journal articles, as specified by SGML markup, using an experimental Web-based interface.

The initial rollout was available at the UIUC campus in October 1997 and has been integrated with the library information services. The testbed consists of materials from 5 publishers, 55 engineering journals, and 40,000 full-text articles. The primary partners of the project include: American Institute of Physics, American Physical Society, American Astronomical Society, American Society of Civil Engineers, American Society of Mechanical Engineers, American Society of Agricultural Engineers, American Institute of Aeronautics and Astronautics, Institute of Electrical and Electronic Engineers, Institute of Electrical Engineers, and IEEE Computer Society.

The testbed was implemented using Soft Quad (SGML rendering) and Open Text (full-text search), both commercial software.

The Illinois DLI project developers and evaluators have worked together very closely on needs assessment and usability studies. The production testbed has been evaluated since October 1997. Six hundred UIUC user subjects enrolled in introductory computer science classes have used the system; and their feedback has been collected and analyzed. We expect to have collected usage data for about 1500 subjects at the end of the study. Usage data consists of session observations and transaction logs.

After four years of research effort, the testbed successes include:

- Willingness to build custom encoding procedures for SGML. This enabled the testbed to succeed in federating journals from different publishers with differing use of SGML, where Elsevier and OCLC failed.
- Canonical encoding for structure tags. The testbed can federate across publishers and journals.
- Willingness to build custom software for searching. The Illinois DLI system is able to show multiple views on the Web and has advanced structure search capabilities.
- Production repositories for real publishers. The project became the R&D arm of several scientific publishers and generated valuable contributions to the scientific publishing industry.
- Changing the nature of libraries with research. The project enables a research prototype to become a standard service capability for engineering libraries.

However, in the nature of research, we also have experienced many testbed difficulties:

For the user interface, the project originally planned to modify the Mosaic Web browser (which was developed at UIUC). When the Web became commercial, Mosaic was quickly taken out of the control of the developers. Custom software is hard to deploy widely: the Web browser interface has widespread support, but the functionality was too primitive for professional full-text search and display.

Several practical difficulties were found in using SGML for this project. Plans to use standard BRS as full-text backend had to be abandoned. It proved essential to use an SGML-specific search engine. Good-quality SGML simply was not available. We had to work with every publisher, since nothing was ready for SGML publishing.

SGML interactive display proved not to be of journal quality. Physics requires good-quality display of mathematics, which is very difficult to achieve.

As the project comes to its end, several future directions are being explored:

- Technology transfer to publisher partners: Several partners have expressed interest in receiving the testbed technologies. A contract has been developed with the American Institute of Physics to clone the testbed software and processing. A similar contract is under development with American Society of Civil Engineers.
- Testbed continuance by university library: An industrial partnership programme has been established between the UIUC Library and publishers. A UIUC spin-off company has been formed to provide software and future services.

Semantic Research in Illinois DLI Project

The University of Illinois DLI project, through the partnership with the Artificial Intelligence Lab at the University of Arizona, has conducted research in semantic retrieval and analysis.

In particular, natural language processing, statistical analysis, neural network clustering, and information visualization techniques have been developed for different subject domains and media types.

Scalable Semantics become Feasible

Statistical and neural network clustering proves useful and feasible interactively and for large-scale collections. Specifically, the AI lab has developed a noun phrasing technique for concept extraction, a concept space technique for building automatic thesauri, and a self-organizing map (SOM) algorithm for building category maps. More details are provided below.

Semantic indexes for large collections

Two large-scale semantic indexing simulations were performed in 1996 and 1997, respectively. We analyzed 400,000 Inspec abstracts and 4,000,000 Compendex abstracts to generate about 1,000 engineering-specific concept spaces (automatic thesauri) using the NCSA supercomputers (Convex Exemplar and SGI Origin 2000). Results of such computations could be used for semantic retrieval and vocabulary switching across domains.

EVALUATION OF DIGITAL LIBRARIES AND THEIR SERVICES

Evaluation data of digital libraries and their services are not yet widely available. In fact, very few evaluation studies of digital libraries have taken place so far. The most prominent publications reporting some digital library evaluation experiments appear in *Library Trends.* Saracevic discusses a number of issues related to the methodology and criteria for evaluation of digital libraries. Arguing that digital libraries were still at the stage of research and evolution, he commented that the best practice standards have yet to develop against which the performance levels are to be measured. Carter and Janes reported a study that analysed the log of over 3,000 reference questions asked of the Internet Public Library (IPL), which is one of the most widely used reference services on the Web.

This study has identified different categories of reference questions, such as common questions, quick questions, regular questions and unanswered questions, which were handled by IPL. The study revealed that users seem to have difficulties in assigning subject categories to their questions, and also in determining whether they are factual or require detailed information searching.

Since, the greatest part of reference and information services in the past has revolved around assisting users in their information search, and because of the fact that in a digital library environment end users need to search information resources all of which are online, it may be wise to take a quick look at some recent studies involving end-users' search behaviour in the online and Web search environment.

Pending any data from large-scale digital library evaluation experiments involving users, findings of these studies may help us assess the users' online information search behaviour.

Gordon and Pathak compared the retrieval effectiveness of eight search engines: Yahoo!, Excite, Magellan, HotBot, AltaVista, Lycos, Infoseek and Open Text, and noted, among other things, that there were no statistical differences in the retrieval effectiveness among users for recall, though there were for precision.

Although this study talks about the performance of the selected search engines, this observation is very important as far as the need for personalised help in digital library searching is concerned.

It shows that the Web search tools differ in terms of search precision, and who can argue that in an online search environment of today, precision is a very important issue since, no one will ever have time to sift through the hundreds of thousands of documents retrieved by an online search tool at any given instant.

One million Web queries to discern how the public searches the Web and had some astonishing findings, as follows:

- A great majority of Web queries are short, not much modified, and very simple in structure;
- Very few queries incorporate advanced search features, and when they do so, half of them are mistakes;

- Despite gathering a large number of Web sites as answers to their queries, users do not view beyond the first or the second page of results;
- Web users are notmuch interested in relevance feedback.

Yet another study reveals similar findings. The usage of the MelvylWeb catalogue at the University of California at Berkeley. During the 479-day study period users conducted about 2.5 million search sessions, during which about 7.4 million search statements were executed.

The findings of this study reveal that:

- The length of time research searchers spent at a session grew from six to ten minutes during the 16 month study period;
- During the study period, about 7.4 million database selections were made, out of which the catalogue database accounted for 32 per cent (about 2.4 million uses), Medlars for 22 per cent, magazine database for 10 per cent, periodicals database for 8 per cent, Inspec for 4 per cent and *Current Contents* for 4 per cent;
- The time users spent on each database also varied: about 3 minutes per search in the Medlars database, while 2.2 minutes for the catalogue database;
- Users displayed about four to five citations for each search they performed;
- The length of time users spent displaying results was 30-40 seconds.

The observations of these studies are very useful for designing digital library services. One of the major problems of a digital search environment is the absence of human intermediaries who play a major role in traditional online search services. Appropriate online support for query formulation and modification may improve digital library search results. Again, since, most users do not look at more than a handful of records, appropriate mechanisms have to be developed for filtering retrieved output.

PRESERVATION MICROFILMING

Despite increasing interest in new technologies, preservation microfilming remains an established and valued strategy for producing copies of deteriorated paper-based collections. Since the late 1980s, a national Brittle Books Programme, funded through the National Endowment for the Humanities (NEH), has been in place, using preservation microfilming to produce master microfilms of deteriorated books.

Overall, microfilm is an important preservation strategy for collections that have greater informational value than artifactual value and for those with such tremendous artifactual value and/or fragility that they should not be routinely handled by researchers. While microfilm is no longer the most user-friendly medium for access, it is the product of a tested technology governed by clear standards and guidelines. It provides a master copy from which relatively inexpensive duplicates can be easily made. And unlike digital media, which cannot be read without computer access, microfilm can be read by the naked eye with only a light source and magnification.

STANDARDS/GUIDELINES

Microfilming is governed by a variety of standards, but it is important to keep in mind that most of these standards were developed for commercial microfilming applications, where the microfilm being produced only needs to be retained for a limited time. Thus, certain practices may be acceptable in the production of commercial microfilm that are not appropriate in the production of preservation microfilm.

General Microfilming Standards

Preservation microfilming of paper-based collections makes up only a small fraction of the micrographics industry, so addressing preservation filming is not a high priority for standards-making organizations. The American National Standards Institute (ANSI) issues various standards pertaining to imaging materials, including microfilm, and the Association for Information and Image Management (AIIM) also issues standards for micrographics. These standards can be useful in providing general information, but it is up to the individual institution to decide what level of quality is acceptable.

Guidelines for Preservation Microfilming

For specific guidelines for preservation microfilming geared towards libraries, archives, and other institutions that hold paper collections, the Research Libraries Group (RLG) has produced three publications that have come to be considered de facto standards. The *RLG Preservation Microfilming Handbook*, the *RLG Archives Microfilming Manual*, and the *RLG Guidelines for Microfilming to Support Digitization* should be consulted by any cultural institution planning a preservation microfilming project. Another basic resource is the Association of Research Libraries' *Preservation Microfilming: A Guide for Librarians and Archivists*. All of these publications are referenced in Additional Resources.

These guidelines specify materials and procedures that must be used to ensure the permanence of the film that is produced:

- *Film Type*: All preservation microfilm must be produced on a polyester base. Types of film include silver gelatin (the most stable); diazo and vesicular (less expensive, but not as stable); continuous tone microfilm (a silver gelatin film that can be very stable and is used for filming photographs and similar materials), and colour microfilm (Ilfochrome colour film, which likely has a lifetime of several hundred years in dark storage).

- *Film Format*: The RLG guidelines are based on the 35mm roll film format, which provides a larger, better-quality image than microfiche or 16mm film.
- Film generations: Three generations of microfilm must be produced: the camera negative (*e.g.,* the film used in the camera); a duplicate negative; and one or more positive service copies for researcher use and interlibrary loan.
- *Film quality and processing*: The RLG guidelines specify requirements for reduction ratio (the number of times the original is reduced); orientation of the image on the film; the legibility of the image (background density and resolution); processing of the exposed film; and inspection of the film and correction of mistakes (*e.g.,* number of splices allowed).

THE FILMING PROCESS

For most institutions, contracting out for microfilming services is the most efficient and cost-effective choice, since setting up an in-house lab to produce microfilm that conforms to standards and guidelines for preservation filming is extremely difficult and expensive.

The basic procedures involved in preservation microfilming are as follows:

- *Preparing Collections for Filming*: The materials are examined page-by-page to ensure that they are in the correct order and nothing is missing. Targets are created (informational sheets with bibliographic and condition information that are photographed with the item to assist the user), and reel breaks are determined. During the review process, special instruction for the filmers are noted. The materials are shipped to the vendor.
- *Filming*: A planetary camera (where both the camera and the materials are stationary during filming) is most commonly used. Bound materials may be filmed using a book cradle. Manual exposure is usually necessary for collections with variations in paper colour, texture, and/or ink.
- *Film Processing*: Silver gelatin film processors may be tabletop or deep tank models. They develop, fix, wash, and dry the film. Filmers should use control strips daily to check the performance of the processor.
- *Polysulfide Treatment*: This treatment was developed to combat the formation of redox spots or rings on silver microfilm, which are a result of poor environmental conditions and exposure to pollutants. Polysulfide treatment (which converts the silver to a form that better resists oxidation) can be used during initial processing, it can be provided for the master and duplicate negatives after all quality

control inspections have been done, or it can be applied to older film, as long as it is not yet deteriorated.

- *Quality Control*: Before duplication, the master negative is inspected for proper resolution and density; a methylene blue test (for residual thiosulfate from processing) and a polysulfide test are conducted; and the master negative is inspected frame-by-frame to ensure that each document has been filmed in the correct order and each frame is legible. If necessary, mistakes are corrected using ultrasonic splicing.
- *Duplication*: The choice of film for duplicates will depend on cost and use patterns. Silver film is preferred for duplicate negatives, and should receive a polysulfide treatment. Diazo and vesicular films, which are cheaper and less prone to scratching than silver films, are often used for service copies. Duplicate films are inspected for resolution, density, and completeness as required in ANSI/AIIM and RLG standards and guidelines.
- *Return of Film and Originals to the Institution*: Original materials are generally returned at the same time to facilitate in-house inspection of the film, but master negatives should never be shipped in the same box, or on the same day, with their service copies or duplicate negatives. If possible, master negatives should be shipped by the vendor directly to off-site storage.
- *Post-filming Activities*: You must conduct in-house quality control inspections once the film is returned. These should include a general inspection of the film, packaging, and labeling, as well as a more comprehensive technical inspection that might include testing for density and resolution, as well as scratches, problematic splices, and other problems.
- *Storage*: Once materials have been filmed, house all preservation microfilm in archival enclosures, maintain microfilm readers regularly, and insist that researchers use the microfilm instead of the original materials. Master negatives must be stored off-site, preferably under the proper temperature and humidity conditions.

THE DIGITAL LIBRARIES UNIVERSE: A THREE-TIER FRAMEWORK

A Digital Library is a live organization that comes to existence through a series of development steps that bring together all necessary constituents. Figure presents this process pictorially and indicates three distinct notions of "systems" that are developed along the way: Digital Library, Digital Library System, and Digital Library Management System.

These also correspond to three different levels of conceptualization of the universe of Digital Libraries.

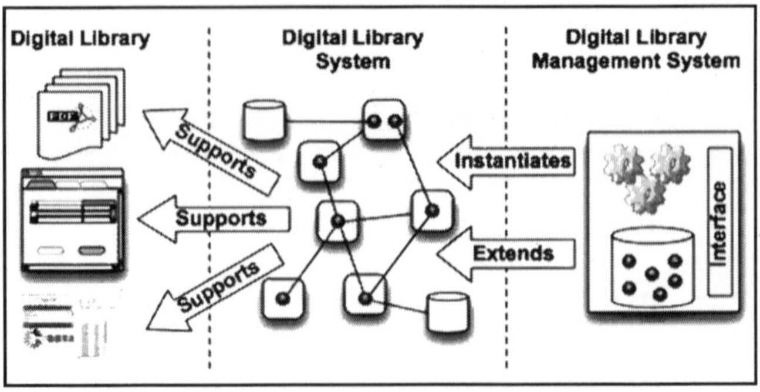

Fig. DL, DLS, and DLMS: A Three-Tier Framework

Unfortunately, these three system notions are often confused and used interchangeably in the literature. Nevertheless, as shown in Figure, they play a central and distinct role in the Digital Library development process. To clarify their differences and their individual characteristics, they are explicitly defined here as follows:

- *Digital Library (DL):* A (potentially virtual) organization that comprehensively collects, manages, and preserves for the long term rich digital content and offers to its user communities specialized functionality on that content, of measurable quality, and according to prescribed policies.
- *Digital Library System (DLS):* A software system that is based on a (potentially distributed) architecture and provides all functionality that is required by a particular Digital Library. Users interact with a Digital Library through the corresponding Digital Library System.
- *Digital Library Management System (DLMS):* A generic software system that provides the appropriate software infrastructure to both:
  - Produce and administer a Digital Library System that incorporates all functionality that is considered foundational for Digital Libraries and
  - Integrate additional software offering more refined, specialized, or advanced functionality.

A Digital Library Management System is what one may call "system software". As in several other domains (*e.g.*, operating systems, databases, user interfaces), such kernel software may be used as a foundation to produce Digital Library Systems. Depending on the philosophy it follows, a DLMS belongs to one of the following three categories:

- *Extensible Digital Library System:* A complete Digital Library System that is fully operational with respect to basic/foundational functionality required. It is based on an open software architecture, so that further software components can be incorporated on top of the ones already there with ease. DelosDLMS is a prototypical example of a system that is based on this philosophy.

- *Digital Library System Warehouse:* A collection of software components that cover all basic/foundational functionality required and a set of tools that can be used to combine these components in arbitrary ways (in Lego-like fashion) to create Digital Library Systems offering diverse sets of functionality. New software components can easily be incorporated into the Warehouse for subsequent combination with those already there. BRICKS and DILIGENT are two prototypical examples of systems that are based on this philosophy.
- *Digital Library System Generator:* A highly parameterized software system that encapsulates templates for a broad range of functionality, which includes all basic/foundational as well as any advanced functionality that has been deemed appropriate. Through an initialization session, the appropriate parameters are set and tuned; at the end of that session, software is automatically generated that constitutes essentially a Digital Library System ready to be installed and deployed.

Note that, while the concept of Digital Library is intended to capture an abstract system that consists of both physical and virtual components, the remaining two capture concrete software systems. For every Digital Library, there is a unique Digital Library System in operation (possibly consisting of many interconnected smaller DLSs in the most general case), whereas all Digital Library Systems are based on a handful of Digital Library Management Systems.

It is also important to note that until now, most Digital Libraries have been created by developing DLSs from scratch without any basis on a DLMS. The notion of DLMS has been recently introduced by the DL community in order to overcome the many drawbacks arising from the current DL development process. When the digital library field reaches maturity, one should expect that only a small number of industrial-strength Digital Library Management Systems will be available on the market.

THE DIGITAL LIBRARIES UNIVERSE: MAIN CONCEPTS

Despite the great richness and diversity one finds among existing digital libraries, there are still a rather small number of concepts that are considered fundamental and essentially characterize all relevant systems and, in fact, the entire field.

These concepts are identifiable in every digital library and should be the starting point for any researcher who wants to study and understand the field, for any system designer and developer who is about to embark in an effort to build a Digital Library, and for any content owner who wants to offer it externally. In this section, we identify these concepts and briefly discuss their roles.

Given that there are three kinds of "systems" in the digital library world, in principle each one may have, in addition to the common fundamental concepts, a number of other related concepts associated with it.

Nevertheless, from the definitions of these systems in the previous section, one may easily derive that there is a natural inclusion relationship on the concepts that refer to these systems: the set of concepts used to define the Digital Library is completely included in that used for Digital Library System, which is in turn completely included in that characterising the Digital Library Management System. This inclusion relationship is depicted in Figure.

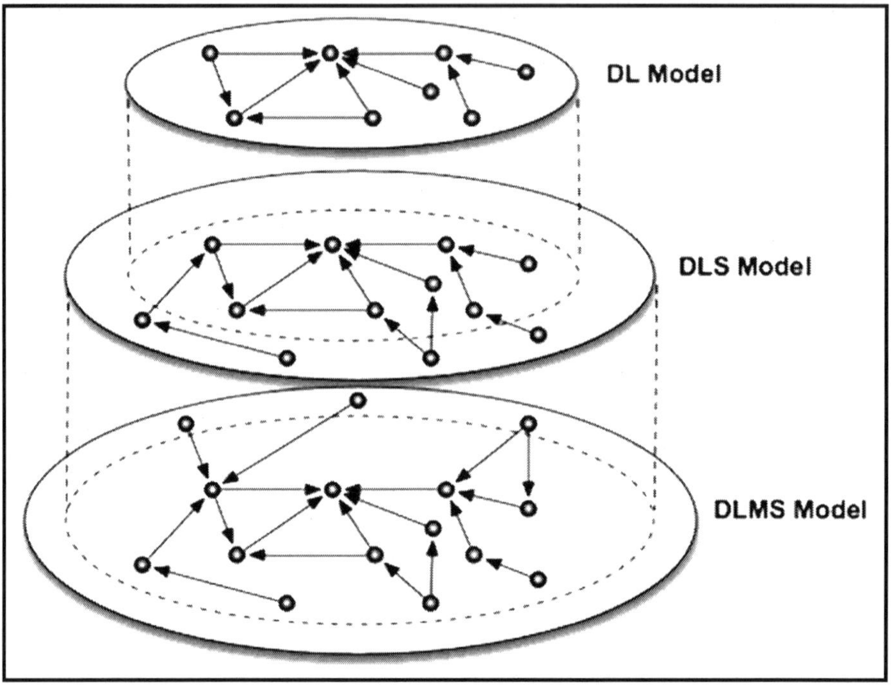

Fig. Hierarchy of Conceptualizations

As a consequence of the above, we introduce below each of these concepts in reference to the highest level of a system (in the three-tier framework) for which it makes sense. All concepts, however, could also be described in reference to lower-level systems, focusing on the characteristics that are of primary concern there. More details can be found elsewhere.

The main concepts that are foundational in the Digital Library world are six. Five of them have been alluded to in the definition of Digital Libraries and are introduced in reference to them: *Content*, *User*, *Functionality*, *Quality*, and *Policy*; one of them has been alluded to in the definition of a Digital Library Systems and is introduced in reference to them: *Architecture*. All six concepts are shown together, influencing the Digital Library framework, in Figure and are defined immediately after that.

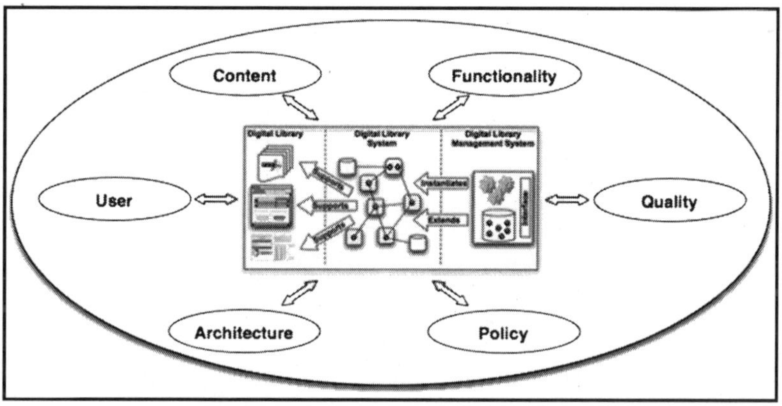

Content

The Content concept represents the data and information that Digital Libraries handle and make available to their users. It is composed of a set of information objects organised in collections. Content is an umbrella concept that is used to aggregate all forms of information that a Digital Library may require to offer its services.

For example, metadata play an important role in the information domain because they describe the contents of other information objects and express their structure.

User

The User concept represents the actors (whether human or not) entitled to interact with Digital Libraries. The aim of Digital Libraries is to connect such actors with information and to support them in consuming already available information and produce new information.

As in the case of the previous concept, User is an umbrella concept that covers all notions related to the representation and management of actor entities within a Digital Library, *i.e.*, the digital entities representing the actors, the rights that they have within the system, the profiles of the actors with characteristics that personalize the system's behaviour or represent these actors in collaborations, and others.

Functionality

The Functionality concept represents the services that Digital Libraries offer to their users. In the most general case, the functionality expected from Digital Libraries is extremely rich. One may not expect, however, that all Digital Libraries must support the complete spectrum. Some core functionality represents the bare minimum that is required by all Digital Libraries, *e.g.*, new information object registration, search, and browse. Beyond that, depending on the particular needs of its community of users and/or the information it is aimed to manage, each Digital Library may offer diverse additional functionality to serve those needs.

Quality

The Quality concept represents the parameters that can be used to characterize and evaluate the content and behaviour of Digital Libraries. It potentially includes several diverse parameters associated with each class of content or functionality, possibly even with each distinct information object or service. Some of these parameters are objective in nature and can be automatically measured, whereas others are subjective in nature and can only be measured through human experiments.

Policy

The Policy concept represents a set of rules that govern the interaction between users and Digital Libraries. Several mechanisms should be available to enable such interaction and the Digital Library should activate those mechanisms in the form prescribed by its policies. The policy concept includes all aspects of system security, digital rights management, system load control, and other similar issues.

ARCHITECTURE

The Architecture concept (which refers to a Digital Library System) represents a mapping of the functionality and content offered by a DL onto hardware and software components6. Having this as a main concept is important due to the following considerations:

- Digital Libraries are often assumed to be among the most complex and advanced forms of information systems;
- Interoperability of Digital Libraries is one of the greatest challenges of the research community. Having a clear architectural understanding of Digital Library Systems offers ammunition in addressing both the above issues effectively.

In addition to the above primary Digital Library concepts, there is one more that is a derivative of them and is also very useful. That is the concept of Resource, which aggregates the concepts of Content, User, Functionality, and Policy, *i.e.*, all concepts that refer to internal entities of a Digital Library and can be sensed by the external world. There are several aspects of all these concepts that are very similar or identical.

Approached as instances of the more general concept of Resource, the Digital Library should treat them in the same fashion. Having described the main concepts characterising the foundation of the digital library universe, we proceed in introducing four main roles of actors that interact with digital libraries at different levels and for different purposes.

THE DIGITAL LIBRARY UNIVERSE: THE MAIN ROLES OF ACTORS

We envisage four different and complementary roles of actors interacting with digital libraries: *DL End-Users*, *DL Designers*, *DL System Administrators*, and *DL Application Developers*.

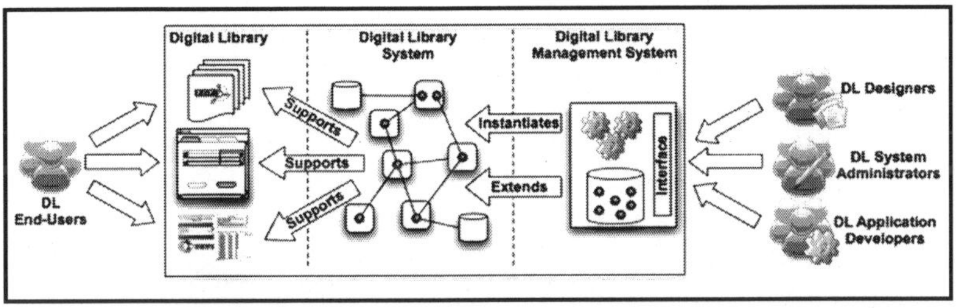

Fig. The Main Roles of Actors versus the Three-tier Framework

As depicted in Figure, each role is primarily associated with one of the three "systems" in the three-tier framework and, therefore, has the view that corresponds to that system. These roles are defined below.

DL End-Users

These exploit the DL functionality for providing, consuming, and managing the DL Content as well as some of its other constituents. They perceive the DL as a stateful entity that serves their functional needs. The behaviour and output of the DL depend on its state at the time a particular part of its functionality is activated.

The state of the DL corresponds to the state of its resources, *i.e.*, it consists of the collections of information objects managed by the DL, its set of authorized users, its functionality, and its set of policies. This state changes during the Digital Library lifetime according to the functionality activated by the users and their inputs. DL end-users may be further partitioned into *Content Creator*, *Content Consumer*, and *Librarian*.

DL Designers

These exploit their knowledge of the application semantic domain to define, customise, and maintain the Digital Library so that it is aligned with the information and functional needs of its end-users.

To perform this task, they interact with the DLMS providing functional and content configuration parameters. The former capture aspects of the DL functionality perceived by the end-users, *e.g.*, the result set format, the query language, the user profile formats, and the document model.

The latter capture third-party resources that are exploited by the specific DL, *e.g.*, repositories of content, ontologies, classification schemas, authority files, and gazetteers. The values of these parameters, which can be modified during the DL lifetime, configure the specific DL perceived by the end-users because they determine the particular Digital Library System instance serving the Digital Library.

DL SYSTEM ADMINISTRATORS

These select the software components necessary to create the Digital Library System needed to serve the required DL and decide where and how to deploy them. They interact with the DLMS by providing architectural configuration parameters, such as the selected software components, the hosting nodes, and the components allocation.

Their task is to identify the architectural configuration that better fits the DLS in target ensuring the appropriate level of quality. The value of the architectural configuration parameters can be changed over the DL lifetime. Any change of these parameters may result in the provision of different DL functionality and/or different quality.

DL APPLICATION DEVELOPERS

These develop the software components of DLMSs and DLSs, realizing the necessary functionality.

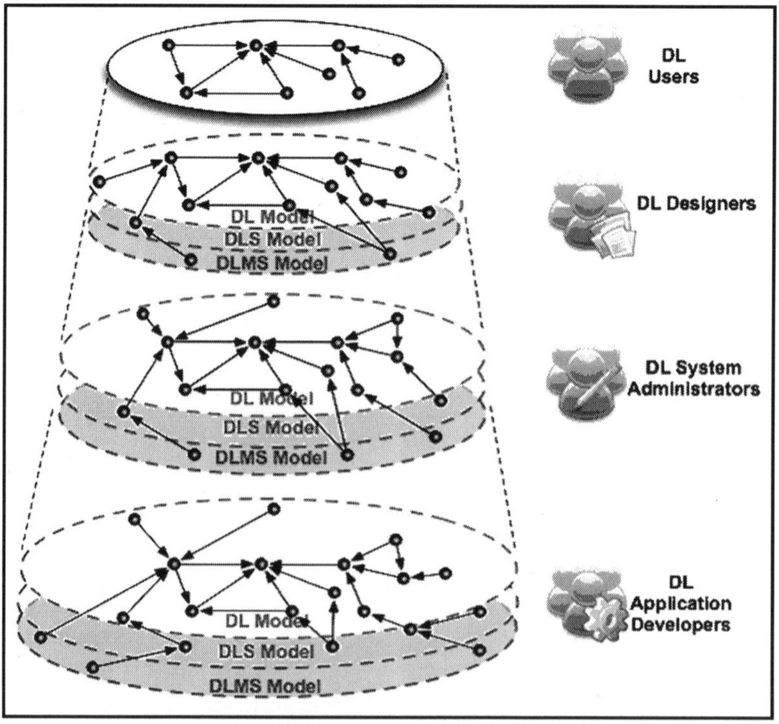

Fig. Hierarchy of Users' Views

These four roles cover the whole spectrum of actors interacting with digital libraries. Their models of the digital library universe are linked together in a hierarchical fashion as depicted in Figure. This is a direct consequence of the above definitions since DL end-users act on the Digital Library, whereas the remaining three roles operate on the DLMS and consequently on the DLS and DL as well.

This relationship ensures that roles designed to directly co-operate share a common vocabulary/knowledge. For instance, the DL end-user expresses its requirements in terms of the DL model and, subsequently, the DL designer understands these requirements and defines the DL accordingly.

REFERENCE FRAMEWORKS

The Digital Library Universe is quite complex and comprises multiple elements. The representation of the details of these elements requires the introduction of several frameworks at different levels of abstraction:

Reference Model

it is a set of inter-related concepts that collectively circumscribe and capture the essence of a distinct part of human knowledge, be it a whole scientific field or an individual idea or anything in between. It is a framework that helps in understanding of the basic elements of its concept(s) of concern.

As stated in, "A Reference Model consists of a minimal set of unifying concepts, axioms and relationships within a particular problem domain, and is independent of specific standards, technologies, implementations, or other concrete details".

It can be established at various levels of abstraction, from very high-level and flexible to very concrete and precise. Although independent of them, it often leads to standards that have to be followed by all systems dealing with the particular parts of knowledge corresponding to it.

Digital libraries need to obtain a corresponding reference model in order to consolidate the diversity of existing approaches into a cohesive and consistent whole and provide a common basis for further advancement.

Reference Architecture

it is an architectural design pattern indicating an abstract solution in implementing the concepts and relationships identified in the Reference Model. Essentially, the reference architecture acts as a blueprint for the implementation of a DLS. There may be more than one reference architecture that addresses how to design digital libraries systems. Each of them proposes an optimal architectural pattern for a particular class of DLSs serving the needs of DLs characterised by similar goals, motivations and requirements. For example, we might have a reference architecture for DLSs supporting federated DLs, *i.e.* DLs built by federating local resources of multiple organizations, and another one for personal DLs, or for specialised applications.

Concrete Architecture

it introduces additional elements making the reference architecture more concrete, *e.g.* replaces the mechanisms envisaged in the Reference Architecture with concrete standards and specifications. For example, it may specify that the run-time environment deployed on the hosting nodes is CORBA or the Web Services Application Framework, and that the Search functional component is implemented by four specific communicating Web Services.

The three frameworks above are shown in Figure in relationship to the general digital library environment. At the top is the most abstract Reference Model, which guides the more specific Reference Architecture and Concrete Architecture further down. In turn, these should constrain the development of any actual Implementation of a system.

The three reference frameworks are the outcome of an abstraction process that has taken into account all the natural Inputs, shown to the left, *e.g.*, the systems already existing on the market, and has taken into consideration all existing Related Work, shown to the right, *e.g.*, best practices and relevant research.

When these frameworks are adopted and followed by the community, the resulting systems will be largely compatible with each other; the interoperability thus afforded will open up significant new horizons for the field.

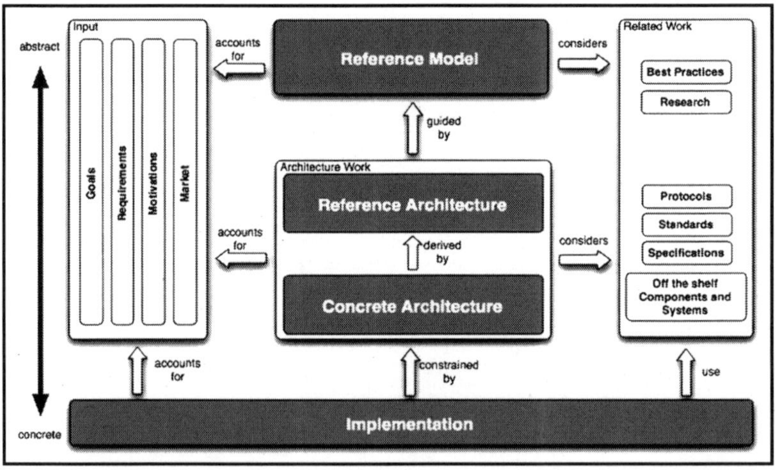

Fig. The Digital Library Universe

The goal of '*The Digital Library Manifesto*' has been to set the foundations and identify the entities of discourse within the universe of digital libraries. It has introduced the relationships among three kinds of relevant "systems" in this area: Digital Library, Digital Library System, and Digital Library Management System.

It has presented the main concepts characterising the above, *i.e.*, content, user, functionality, quality, policy, and architecture, and has identified the main roles that actors may play within a digital library, *i.e.*, end-user, designer, administrator, and application developer. Finally, it has described the reference frameworks that are needed to clarify the digital library universe at different detailed levels of abstraction, *i.e.*, the Reference Model and the Reference and Concrete Architectures.

'*The Digital Library Manifesto*' is accompanied currently by two other documents, which correspond precisely to the aforementioned reference frameworks. These documents come as a first attempt to fulfil the needs of the field in these areas.

Clearly, diversity of needs among different digital libraries will continue to introduce new concepts that will require incorporation into the Reference Model and the Reference and Concrete Architectures. Hence, these documents should be considered as first versions of otherwise dynamic documents that will keep evolving, having the Manifesto as a firm foundation.

The '*Digital Library Manifesto*' has been based on the experience and knowledge gained by many previous efforts that have gone on for the past fifteen years around Europe and the rest of the world. We hope it will serve as a basis for new advances in research and system development in the future.

EXPLORING DIGITAL LIBRARIES THROUGH VISUAL INTERFACES

Libraries are long standing institutions, providing an important service of making information widely available. So it is with Digital Libraries (DL), but this evolution into a computerised format does not come without its own unique challenges. The variety and quantity of information available in the digital space is truly astounding. However, as this growth continues, traditional methods for searching are becoming less effective to support the needs of users to find information quickly and easily.

The conventional library book search system provides several attributes associated with books as a response to the users' enquiry. This includes title, author, publication year, ISBN, page total, and similar information. While considering the increasing volume of data, the current text-based approach to result presentation is not an ideal solution for the modern digital environment. Particularly in the case of comparing a lengthy list of search results, this approach is ill-suited, as it is inefficient and non-intuitive. Assistance, such as ranked results, can aid in such problems but the user will still be relied on to investigate the top results individually.

Additionally, the current popular approach of presenting a summary of content may not accurately reflect what is of value to the user. The advancements and trends that allow for the rapid growth of DL also permit more elaborate interfaces with which to access them. Information Visualisation is one such avenue, which has proven to be an effective approach in acquiring information from a large compilation of data. By making use of users' perceptual cognition for navigating extensive digital workspaces, their ability to understand, and speed with which they review the information space is improved. Previous studies have proven the significance of visualisation in the users' information forage.

One common approach to assist users' search activities uses visualisation techniques combined with information filtering. The users' interaction defines the attributes of interest that easily filter out unrelated data. The following visualisation procedure transforms the remaining data into graphical illustrations. FilmFinder and HomeFinder are interactive visual interfaces which assist the user to narrow down the search scope and easily compare results using the visualisation. Another common approach focuses on presenting the underlying information through visualisation.

A novel text visualisation interface, TileBars, shows the distribution behaviour of a set of query terms. This presentation allows users to compare multiple documents compactly and concurrently. Other visualisation techniques in this category concentrate on showing a portion of the information at a great level of detail while maintaining the overall structure of the information. Information clustering is another method for supporting navigation of a large data collection. Related documents are clustered together, whose notable characteristics are visualised using a mixture of attributes. Visualisation methodologies have shown that the illustration of data has contributed to improving the user's ability to comprehend information quickly.

This, in turn, leads to increased speed and accuracy in finding desired information. We can apply these kinds of visual abstractions to enhance searches on different types of data domains. By presenting information in such a way, a large amount of content can be displayed in a format which is more intuitive. This has the benefit of allowing the user to analyse data more effectively, increasing the user's ability to comprehend results and make better content selections. Periscope, for example, is a visualisation system targeted at web search results.

It provides a series of different visualisations which users can utilise to analyse and explore the result set. A holistic interface can be used to organise documents into various categories, such as language and format, or web related attributes such as DNS domains. An analytical interface allows for up to seven attributes to be relayed at a time, through use of X, Y, Z axes, colour, size, shape, and animation. The search based on the underlying content will increase the accuracy in finding targeted information from the available resources. Think for a moment how one might search a physical book for a topic of interest.

The logical place to start would be the index. Indexes are valuable resources for referencing major terms which appear in a book. The categorical and hierarchical layout of terms in the index allows us to identify associated topics easily, along with their relationships without reading the underlying contents.

The page numbers coupled with each entry makes it possible to estimate the amount information relating to a particular subject. The index will represent the overall layout of entire book contents. Due to a lack of readily available sources, this valuable information has been under utilised. The current trend of digitising books in recent years allows us to exploit content in searches, instead of just depending on superficial book attributes.

The visualisation techniques utilising this information will further enhances the user's search on the DL system. The main objective of this stage is on the utilisation of visualisation techniques for exploring the DL system. The following stage will survey and summarise various visualisation approaches which applied to DL. As suggested, introduce a visual interface which presents general book information through iconic representations. This stage also proposes a novel visualisation which utilises the book index for mimicking the content analysis.

It will allow for detailed comparison of index-based information between selected works. Two different visualisations for this detail view are implemented, each with different strengths. The procedure and analysis of results for a usability test follow, along with discussion and future possibilities, and final conclusions.

RELATED WORKS

The efficacy of visualisation in searching a large information space has been proven in many previous studies. DL are one promising area that should exploit visualisation techniques in searching on various forms of archived information, such as text, imagery, multimedia, citations, and even computer mediated communication.

The 3D Vase Museum is one example applying visualisations for browsing photographs in a digital library collection. A Focus+Context type visualisation displays a set of Greek vases in the Perseus digital library in a simulated 3D virtual museum. By moving around the virtual space, users can appreciate vases with accompanying text data. Christel and Martin introduced visualisation techniques for browsing and navigating another type of multimedia, video documents. Meanwhile, Chen proposed a novel approach utilising a different side view of information in accessing the digital library.

It visualises semantic structures and co-citation networks extracted from a collection of documents. This method displayed the author co-citation networks in a 3D virtual space attempting to reveal the structure of a field of hyperlinks with co-citation patterns of authors. Borner and Chen explained that there are three common usage requirements for visual interfaces to the DL: *First*, to support the identification of the composition of retrieval result. *Second* is to understand the interrelation of retrieved documents to one another. *Lastly*, to refine a search, gain an overview of the coverage of a DL and to visualise user interaction data in relation to available documents.

The goal would be to evaluate and improve DL usage. Clarkson *et al.*, developed a visual interface emphasising on the hierarchy of the repository in presenting the DL search results. They used the hierarchical representation in digital repositories for developing an interface for enhancing query-based search engines. A treemap, a well-known technique, is used to organise results in a space-efficient hierarchical display.

The system, known as ResultMap, maps each document in the hierarchical tree structures to a treemap where items matched with given query are highlighted. ResultMap presents the full contents of a hierarchical dataset while providing a view of underlying levels. The experimental results from two controlled lab studies showed that participants expressed preferences to use ResultMap system and produced comparable performance to a text-only engine. When using physical books, people tend to view multiple at once.

This is to better compare and review information across multiple sources, and to have a better overall understanding of the domain. In their study, Good et al, identify this to be a major weakness in current DL displays. To address related issues, researchers have conducted studies applying visualisation techniques for book searches and presenting various forms of search results for easy comparison. Envision is a visual interface presenting book search results in a rigid matrix. The search results are presented as icons in a 2D grid where the visual attributes represent the characteristics of returned documents. Envision allows the user to organise the visualised output interactively based on their information needs.

The Graphical Interface for DL (GRIDL) and ActiveGraph adopted a similar approach in presenting search results. The GRIDL displays a hierarchical cluster of the relevant data to a query on two-dimensional display. This system provides an interactive grid layout, the axes of which are selectable from a variety of different attributes. Results were displayed within each cell as a collection of different size icons, colour coded by document type. ActiveGraph presented search results based on scatter plots. ActiveGraph also provides similar functionalities to specify shape, colour, and size of nodes representing various forms of digital resources. Because ActiveGraph system results in much more node clustering and overlap, a logarithmic transformation is provided, along with the ability to filter out unwanted items.

Many studies mainly focus on aiding the user in comparing the search results effectively by presenting book properties such as book title, author, publication, year, through various visual attributes, but they don't express in detail the amount of content related to user interest. Citiviz is a visual interface tool kit combining text mining and information visualisation. In order to present the insight of similarity among documents as well as traditional document attributes, this system used two visualisation techniques: an animated 2D scatter plot to represent document attributes and a dynamic hyperbolic tree to show hierarchical relationships among documents. By allowing users to manipulate the manner in which data is displayed, these visualisations provided a better chance to find patterns within the data that may not typically be apparent. Lin proposed another approach through a graphical table of contents (GTOC) that tries to exploit a different perspective of underling information by utilising the table of contents of the book. GTOC showed the dimension of items in the table of contents based on Kohonen's self organising feature map algorithm. The paper introduces how documents can be organised and then visualised to allow the user easy access of underlying contents.

The GTOC prototype describes various interactive tools to assist the user exploring document contents and analysing relationships among terms in the table of contents. Both the attributes associated with documents and its underlying contents are valuable resources finding the relevant information of the users' interest. The increasing computing power and performance of graphics devices make it possible to exercise these information in presenting search results. The following section introduces a newly developed visualisation system that will assist the user's search while utilising the book index, which has been underutilised as a visualisation resource.

METHOD

The Visual Interface for Digital Library Search (VIDLS) system utilizes an Overview+Detail approach for presenting book search results. This is a visualisation technique that uses multiple images to display the entire data space, as well as show an up-close, detailed view of the data. Similar to traditional library searches, the overview will present outline of the book search results through graphical illustration. The user interactively selects a subset of visualised icons that will allow them to execute content level exploration. When a user provides search terms of interests, the Detail view presents a visualisation which relates, in depth, the information presented by the index. For our pilot study, we developed two possible visualisations for this view of the index, each with its own strengths. One emphasises space utilisation, whereas the other is designed to focus on clearly presenting term relationships.

Visualisation

The Overview allows the user to perform a general search on the data space, similar to traditional library tools. This visualisation utilises a tabular layout which offers a familiar spread-sheet style organisation of book search results. The attribute of each axis can be independently selected by the user, allowing for a more targeted display and increasing the users' comprehension of the data set. This functionality will assist the user in customising the search based on their own judgement of which attributes are more important. In the Overview, each book is represented as a circular node, located in the appropriate cell based on the axes.

To deliver the estimated amount of content, node size is determined by the normalised page count of the book compared to the rest. Books with a greater number of pages naturally map to the largest nodes. This will allow users to quickly identify the amount and distribution of content available.

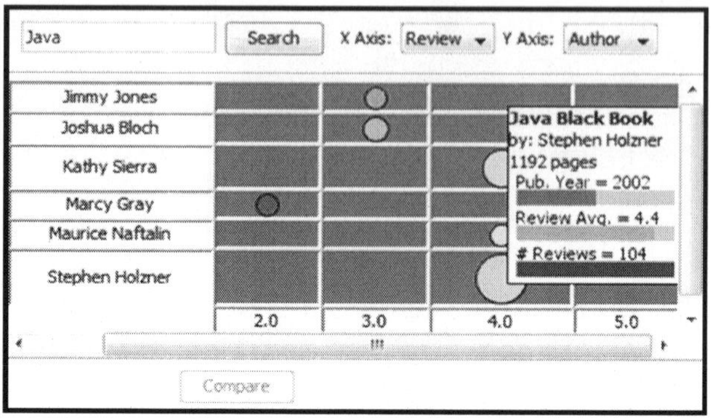

Fig. Overview Interface Displaying Search Results with Tool-tip

The system presents other book attributes through a colour coding scheme. The green component is derived through collaborative filtering. This is a content-filtering technique based upon the opinion of users whom have already evaluated the item in question. This will be a valuable piece of information to know regarding the quality of the book. In the case of VIDLS, collaborative filtering would be done by collecting user reviews, much like you found find at a merchant web site. Higher intensity of the green component would indicate a more positive response from reviews.

The accuracy of the content-filtering is highly correlated with the number of evaluators and their preferences. As an example: the mean score of a book which has a low number of reviews could potentially be misleading and unreliable. To account for this, the Overview associates the blue component with the number of unique evaluations given to a book. The publication year is a valuable attribute to find the most up to date information.

This metric has been represented through the red component. With the utilisation of the RGB colour scheme, the larger more recent books with a solid review will be closer to white in intensity, while older, smaller, poorly reviewed works tend towards black. If the user needs to know more precise information for the components, or other detailed information of the work, the system provides this via a tooltip interface.

Detailed Visualisation

Once a user makes a set of selections from the Overview, the system will provide a detailed view of those items. This display is tasked with presenting visualised index data for each book, allowing the user to perform more refined queries, and compare and contrast each work in detail. Two visualisations were implemented on a data model to present the same information while emphasising different attributes: one a radial graph, and the other a sunburst-like display.

Data Model

The underlying model for the detailed visualisations relies on several important characteristics associated with a term in the index. These are: number of pages, number of occurrences, content density, and location relative to the parent term. Although this information is readily available in the index, it is unintuitive in a text format. Presenting these attributes via graphical illustration, the user should gain greater understanding of the content, and make more informed choices of which books to choose.

The number of pages associated with a term by the index is a potential indicator as to how much coverage a topic receives in a book. A work with a greater number of pages on a subject is intuitively going to have more potential value than one with less. Naturally, this attribute is represented by size in the visualisations. To assist the user in quickly making general comparison between each book, this attribute is further expanded to be a cumulative page total of the term along with its sub-terms. The number of occurrences and content density are related through a colour code.

This is intended to give the user a better understanding of the comparative value of each term being displayed. Term occurrence within the book is related by the green component. Although one work may have more information referenced in a single index entry for a topic, that does not necessarily make it the better choice. If another book contained references of a particular term in many different locations within the index, that may be an indication of a greater breadth or complexity of coverage on that topic.

The number of term occurrences are normalised across the display, with the instances of greatest coverage mapping to the highest green intensity, and the one with the fewest having no green intensity. Although two books may have the same total of pages for a particular topic, this should not be taken to mean they have equal value. Consider the situation in which one index allocates ten pages for a topic, but they are separate and not listed as a single range of pages.

Another index containing the same topic, but listed as a single range of ten pages, such as 152-161 may be more valuable to the user. The first may have fragmented references of the topic, but no detailed coverage, whereas the second may have a full section or stage dedicated to the subject. To relate this information to the user, the content density is mapped to the blue colour component. The value is given by calculating the ratio of page continuity to the total number of pages for a term. This is shown by *equation 1,* where *Cib* is the blue intensity for term i, $\sum_{j=o}^{n} P_j^c$ is the number of individual page ranges for *i*, *Ti* is the total number pages for the term *i,* and *Imax* is the brightest intensity of blue possible on the machine. This gives terms with more concentrated information a stronger representation in the visualisation.

$$C_{ib} = \left(1 - \left(\frac{\sum_{j=0}^{n} P_j^c}{T_i}\right)\right) * \mathrm{I}_{\max},$$

The last attribute represents the relationship between a sub-term and its parent. Similar to the previous attribute, a sub-term which is located close to its parent within the book could be an indication of cohesive coverage of the topic. A user may regard such a case with more value than one where the sub-term is more removed from the parent's location. The value of this attribute is calculated by *equation.*

$$D_j = ABS\left(\frac{NORM\left(\sum_{k=0}^{n} P_j^k - \overline{Root_i}\right)}{N}\right)$$

Dj is a normalised distance between the root node and associated sub-node *j*; P_j^k is the page number contains sub-term *j*; $Root_i$ is the mean page number having the root word *i;* and *NORM* and *ABS* are a normalisation and absolute function respectively.

Visualisations

The two visualisations share several aspects, in addition to the attributes described previously. Each displays the matching term of the search prominently in the center, with the sub-terms radiating outward. Since, each term is sized based on the cumulative page count of itself and sub-terms, the root node will give users a quick guidance as to which book has more content.

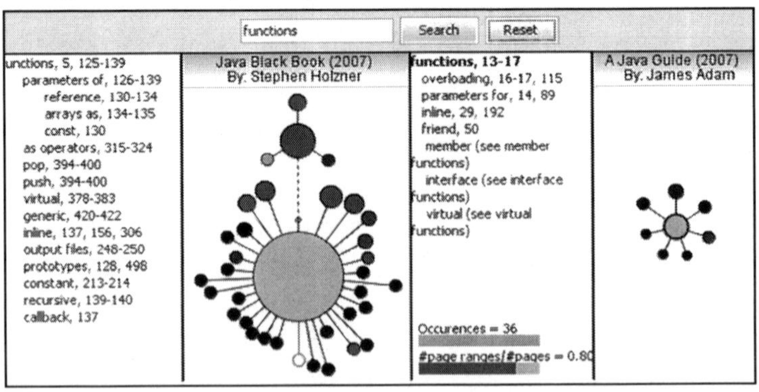

Fig. Diagram shows Two Books being Compared in the Detail View. The Left Shows Expanded Sub-terms and an Overflow Node. Th Right has Context Highlighting of Text List and Bar Display from User Interaction

Additionally, each graph has a context side-bar that indicates which term is currently moused-over, along with a histogram displaying its colour components. The similarities end here for the two visualisations.

The first visualisation approach employs a radial graph layout; with each term presented as a circular node branching off the parent. Sub-terms are sized in the same way as the root, with node size directly correlated to the total number of pages. The largest sub-terms start from the top towards the bottom of the visualisation. This is done to prevent over-crowding of the display. Terms with the fewest pages are considered less important, and are collapsed into a single node, indicated by a red outline, if not enough space is available. Another way in which space is conserved is by displaying only the first level of sub-terms.

A node with hidden sub-terms has a ridged outline. These along with the red 'overflow' node can be clicked show the hidden terms. In contrast, the second visualisation follows a sunburst-like design. Sub-terms are displayed in concentric sections around the center, extending from their parent term. Each sub-term 'slice' is sized as a percentage of its page allocation from the parent's. This has the benefit that all terms can be displayed compactly without hiding any. No additional user interaction would be required to explore the full term hierarchy. One potential downside of this design, compared to the previous one, is that terms are crowded together. This may cause difficulty in picking them out from their neighbours.

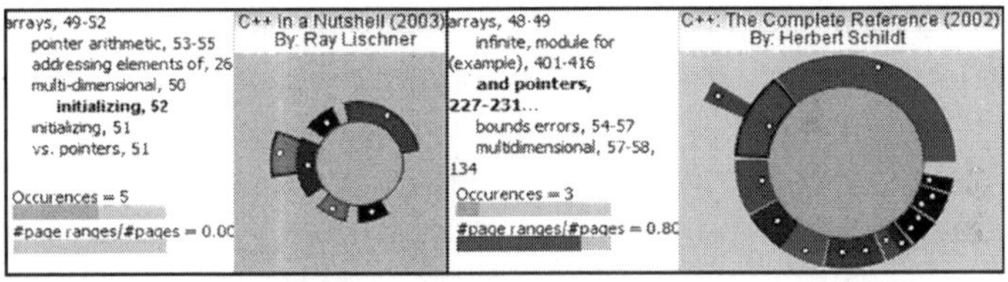

Fig. Alternate Sunburst Detailed View

In the radial graph, the relation between a sub-term and its parent is indicated by the branch length. Terms which appear on pages near those of the parent naturally are drawn with shorter branches. Since, the sunburst approach has forgone branches to conserve space, a different analogue is required. Each slice instead contains a bubble, which will relate this information. As the closeness to parent is normalised, the term with the closest relationship has a bubble at the base of the slice, while the term with the most distant has a bubble on the outer edge of its slice. As was previously noted, the chief difference between the two visualisations is their concern for space conservation.

With its emphasis on the term relation branch, and distinct nodes, the radial graph may have more clarity, but at the cost of poorer space utilisation. This results in the need to hide terms considered less important. The other visualisation puts more value in making better use of space, and is able to display all terms efficiently. However, when many terms are displayed at once, the resultant crowding could make smaller slices difficult to see. The addition of the bubble overlay to each slice can add to this difficulty.

EXPERIMENT

To measure the effectiveness of VIDLS, a series of usability tests were performed to compare it to more traditional text-based interfaces. In this set of experiments the VIDLS system, using the radial graph detailed layout, was used in conjunction with a text-only interface for the same information. Each usability test consisted of a small group of three to five students, comfortable in the use of computers, whom had no prior experience with VIDLS.

Each group was given a brief orientation presentation, and then allowed to acclimate to the functionality of both applications for a few minutes. The tests then began, with each user asked to search for books and information with the text-only application and then with the visualisation based approach. Once the test concluded, participants then filled out a survey to measure their quantitative and qualitative feedback of VIDLS in comparison to the text-based format. The questionnaire has 14 questions which utilise a 5 point Likert scale; 5 indicating the highest level of satisfaction, and 1 the lowest.

Table shows the survey results that summarises the user's feedback to VIDLS over a text-based library search system. Participants overall found the VIDLS system to be satisfactory, with some comments highlighting that unfamiliarity with the visualisations led to preference of the text-based design. The Overview visualisation was well received, with 82 per cent of testers responding that it improved their ability to quickly identify desirable books.

This was supported through the exploratory aspects of the system, which participants indicated positively as giving meaningful result displays, and facilitating better understanding of the information.

The radial graph visualisation of index level information was also seen in a positive light, as 65 per cent found it to be a useful representation, and only 11 per cent preferring the familiar text-only listing of results. As with the Overview, testers considered the Detail View to also be useful in expressing the concentration of information, and improving selection among the results. Table shows a summary of survey results.

Table. 6.3 Post Experiment Survey Results

Question	Pos.	Neut.	Neg.
VIDLS overall was preferable to a text-based search	53%	35%	12%
The Overview improved identification of desirable books	82%	6%	12%
Use of the selectable axis facilitated a better understanding of a set of books.	71%	24%	5%
The Overview helped in selecting a subset of books.	65%	29%	6%

It was easy to discern book attributes based on node colour	53%	18%	29%
The Detailed view was preferable to a text approach	65%	24%	11%
It was easy to discern term attributes based on node colour	47%	24%	29%
The Detail view made relevant book selection easier	88%	12%	0%
The relation between a term and it's child was understandable	65%	35%	0%
The Detail view helped identify terms related to the search	94%	6%	0%

8

Digital Librarians: Safeguard the Past, Looking Advance

INTRODUCTION

Throughout the same eras of upheaval and change, librarians faced similarly daunting challenges. Researcher calls heralding the imminent demise of a proud profession crowded the professional literature of every specialised sector of librarianship for decades. In response, various innovators have explored a mulitiplicity of strategies. Nancy Lemon argues that rethinking traditional roles enables librarians to climb organisational "value chains;" Researchers review the plight of news media libraries and see a history of cyclical renewal, in which existing jobs give way to new opportunities in new locations.

Among corporate libraries, a wide variety of bareknuckle strategies have been put forward, urging librarians to find a competitive edge by offering services that can be demonstrated to boost profits. In the public libary sphere, despite straitened civic budgets and the shock of new media, libraries have achieved a degree of success in staying relevant. Circulation, library card membership and on-site use of services are at an all-time high, countering the idea that community libraries are outdated during the digital era. On the contrary, they are more popular than ever. Therefore even as pessimism about the future became a standard feature in the professional literature, a parallel stream of daring and innovative thinking has run concurrently among a wide spectrum of library specialists.

The resulting intellectual ferment has produced new paradigms and new energy for rethinking library goals in light of the emergence of digital technology. Rather than wait to see what would happen, librarians repeatedly took initiative with new media. They staked an early claim on the crucial issue of intellectual property and copyright, working both with and against publishers as needed to preserve the library's public service mission. As part of this process, librarians became more deeply aware of the publishing industry's travails with digital media. This awareness led to greater strategic knowledge about the marketplace.

Spanning "Online" Eras

Librarians were shaken by the rapid emergence of Web-based information resources, because they had been important players in the previous "online" economy that was dominated by firms like LEXIS/NEXIS and Dialog Information Services. This first "online" era gave librarians the opportunity to cast themselves as experts who conducted mediated searches on behalf of users such as attorneys, scientists and business leaders. As the initial "online" era faded and the Internet exploded into growth, librarians joined the first wave of Internet e-mail "conversationalists", Web content users, Web site producers, and aggregators of high quality information.

They also grasped the importance of creating stable and robust Web portals, which organised and "branded" library-hosted aggregations of databases; such activist strategies stretched scarce budgets while formalising a Web-based library presence. Similarly, the economic upheaval caused by the skyrocketing price of scholarly journals generated energetic responses on the part of research libraries, including formation of the Scholarly Publishing and Academic Resources Coalition (SPARC), as well as active congressional lobbying to protect copyright and "fair use" principles from a runaway marketplace.

The same upheaval also sparked a sustained outreach to faculty, in search of much stronger partnerships with the academy's principle content creators. In general, digital librarians have been agents for innovation over the past 15 years, and have participated in the sweeping process of rethinking scholarly communications. This lengthy process of trial and error has transformed digital librarians' self-perception. Rather than viewing digital media as a force of dislocation that would bring ruin to the profession, digital librarians have instead embraced it. Likewise, constant downward pressure on budgets forced innovative survival plans to the forefront, emphasising new technologies.

Metadata as Enhanced Competency

Perhaps the most significant advance on the part of digital librarians has been the profession's embrace of structured metadata and taxonomy as a reinvigorated core competency. Even as they faced the twin challenges of integrating new technologies and shrinking budgets, digital librarians participated in the formation of international metadata standards such as the Dublin Core.

Libraries became key institutional members of new groups such as the Coalition for Networked Information and the National Digital Library Federation. Academic librarians experimented with diverse forms of preservation, including digital repositories, e-journals, and increasingly, full-scale publishing initiatives that originate within the library. Many metadata platforms and languages have been explored, but Extensible Markup Language (XML) has become a dominant tool for managing digital assets.

XML is a "meta-language of languages," enabling developers to create taxonomies and metadata schema that are customisable, portable and attached to the "digital objects" they describe. The emergence of national and international standards for metadata, the ascendance of digital objects which are transferrable among collections, and a strong focus on systems interoperability have elevated the library profession to a technical status considerably higher than it enjoyed before the advent of the digital era. Although digital librarians are not the only XML developers - many computing firms and other academics are heavily involved—they have left an imprint on the development stream of XML.

XML-based systems have become accepted across many industries beyond the academy, and now play a crucial role in information management and data warehousing by large corporate firms. XML-based information architectures are essential tools for managing text, images and other artifacts, creating new workflows that are based on the principle of "one text, multiple outputs".This kind of workflow would transfer very effectively to the publishing world, yet the publishing industry has been slower to adopt XML workflows at a universal level. The opportunity to manage digital assets using XML is an important leap forward that publishers have not yet fully embraced, and forward-looking commentators have recognised this shortfall.

From Online Repository to Publishing Platform

The turmoil of the Internet's early years also produced solid initiatives to understand the digital library as a publisher in its own right. Thomas provides an early and comprehensive road map that offers large research libraries a template for launching high quality publishing services. She also describes the early emergence of online repositories as a new form of curated information resources. Online repositories grew quickly throughout the early years of the twenty-first century, taking much inspiration from the digital archiving efforts of the computer science and engineering fields.

Librarymanaged repositories also grew up with a strong bias for interoperability, which has led to more dialogue about the need for large-scale "federations" of digital libraries, even at the international level. As these repositories became more accepted, use skyrocted. The University of California's eScholarship repository experienced more than one million downloads in its first two years of operation. "Post prints" and research reports are now also collected in online repositories, and are frequently overseen by digital librarians, or at least coordinated by them.

In late 2009, eScholarship recast itself as a full-scale "publishing platform," which drew strength from the reputation of its source - the University of California system. Although this is not the only example of a library-sponsored publishing service with university imprimatur, it is certainly one of the most high profile experiments. The evolution of library-based online repositories and their current transformation into fullscale publishing platforms is a prime example of how contributors can expand their role and move into new "zones of progressive release". Digital librarians' publishing solutions are guided by two objectives: first, to empower authors, and second, to create robust, collaborative blocs of institutions that share expertise and improve access. These are new "treatments" that address the changing needs of academic publishing. Publishers are rushing to reinvigorate their relationships with authors, but to some degree they are playing a game of catch-up.

CONVERGENCE AND DIVERGENCE: STRATEGIES AND EXAMPLES

Recent events in these two fields reveal several interesting trends, not only in strategic planning but also in the underlying thinking of leading commentators. Although there is considerable ferment and thus many trends underway, there are four areas where publishers and digital librarians face similar challenges. The strategic decisions that each group makes in the coming years will have significant impact on their long-term futures. First, the hurdles to publishing a well-packaged text artifact are dropping rapidly. The result has been that authors, both in the academic and popular literature spheres, now have the option of creating their own digital artifacts without publishers' assistance.

Many already manage online presences and engage in dialogue with readers. In response publishers and digital librarians are testing strategies that reinforce their own roles. Second, the disruptive nature of digital media has forced publishers and digital librarians to evaluate their own native skill sets in a new light. The library profession's core competencies - collection development, information counselling, interpretation and preservation - involve in-depth analysis of information resources. Yet librarians already format, revise, copy-edit and even print bibliographies, scholarly e-journals, festschrift, and full-scale books in many cases.

As these content-intensive roles become more important, research libraries have responded by creating senior management positions with titles such as director of digital scholarly publishing, director of digital publishing, or director of built content. These positions carry responsibility for assessing new opportunities to publish, as well as assisting research faculty in doing so themselves.

Publishers also have the opportunity to review what they do well, re-evaluating existing functions to include new services such content aggregation, developing much-enlarged Web presences, taking on custodial roles and offering services for long-term preservation of their own built content. The technological hurdles to adding new services of this nature are just as low for publishers as they are for librarians who are involved in digital publishing. Both groups are limited chiefly by imagination, by perceived commitments to doing "business as usual," and by the high cost of retraining their already-well-trained workforces to take on new tasks in addition to their existing workflows.

Third, both publishers and digital librarians are looking beyond the boundaries of their own fields of expertise for new ideas and strategies. For example, new social media have carried a heavy impact on the news industry, and both librarians and publishers have studied newspapers as a cautionary tale. News media were one of the first zones where readers began "talking back" to the press and contributing substantive new content. The Blogosphere has also attracted interest, although it increasingly produces voluminous and cyclical "blooms" of creative work that are followed by inactivity and the formation of "dead zones." This pattern suggests that new media are only as vibrant as the minds that are driving them forward. However, over time the Blogosphere has become firmly established as an effective platform for commentary, news, cultural critique and debate.

The Blogosphere's experience implies that longer-term value takes time to emerge as a new technology matures. Fourth, both groups have come to realise that as digital convergence has accelerated, bold action is required. As a consequence, the pace of intellectual thought that is devoted to innovation has also accelerated. There is also greater acceptance that bold actions may succeed or fail, yet they must be attempted to gain new knowledge and expertise. Both groups show evidence of complex responses to the necessity of taking bold action, because both groups believe that they must protect legacy print programmes, whether as book sales or print collections, even as they step into new digital futures. This is a difficult balancing act, because reader and user community loyalty may be challenged as risks are taken. These four trends illustrate the turmoil, and indeed, the excitement of the times for both publishers and librarians. They also illustrate how each group is operating on the knowledge creation continuum, and how they might choose convergent or divergent strategies when compared to each other.

Convergent Strategies

With respect to convergent strategies, publishers and digital librarians are aware that their core competencies must now include a robust and dynamic "conversation" with their readers, collaborators and user communities. Although this may seem obvious during the Internet era, it Nonetheless symbolises a major challenge for established players on the knowledge creation continuum.

New ideas and new technologies, commonly known as "Web 2.0", currently emphasize ubiquitous interaction in a wide variety of locations and via a long list of tools, ranging from desktop computers to "smartphones." Among publishers, this interactive paradigm and the tools it has spawned have caused a seismic shift in thinking.

A book's usefulness is no longer limited to the experience of reading it; it now has a lifespan that can take many forms, involve communities in addition to solo readers, and last for years. In response publishers have launched serious attempts to enter the Web 2.0 sphere. Likewise, digital librarians have seen their print-based mission expand exponentially to include not only the finished works of scholarship and literature, but also the artifacts created by the overall process of creating scholarship, from start to finish. Library responses also include innovative combinations of digital collections and community-building features, such as allowing commentary, running newsfeeds, and adding Wikis to facilitate dialogue. Publishers continue to focus on sales and profits, and they are experimenting with social media to increase revenue.

Two strategies dominate the landscape: narrowcasting and community-subscriber services. Narrowcasting refers to the strategy of discovering discrete markets or user communities who share strong interest in very specific literature, and then offering them targeted products that are based on market analysis.

This approach is greatly assisted by "viral marketing," a common term in the Internet era, which describes how news of events or products can travel very quickly, even circumnavigating the globe in a matter of hours in some instances. Narrowcasting would be paired with general marketing strategies, just as print sales would be complemented by e-book sales, still a small revenue stream. Community-subscriber based strategies also make explicit publishers' new role as their own distribution outlets, joining bookstores, libraries and online firms such as Amazon in direct consumer outreach. Direct outreach is another example of treatment substitution, as it establishes a new zone of service on the knowledge creation continuum for publishers, shifting them further into the zone of distribution and perhaps even preservation.

Recent developments in textbook publishing provide evidence of innovative approaches by publishers and digital librarians, who are exploring classroom teaching aids. It is now possible to print textbooks or sections of them on demand, use e-readers to read them, or purchase printed readers, and the entire idea of how textbooks support teaching is rapidly evolving. Publishers are now perfecting "portal" style learning zones on the Web, which are based on textbooks but include many added features, including unbundled chapters, added teaching aids and accompanying training modules. Interestingly, 55 per cent of students still prefer to buy the textbook in print as part of their study plan.

Meanwhile, digital librarians are also involved in teaching portals, and they have been perfecting e-reserve systems and new formats for class e-readers. Finally, publishers are beginning to show interest in managing their backlists more along the lines of a repository or collection of resources. However, whether publishers will take up archiving and preserving content remains uncertain. Once again, networked information technologies have lowered the hurdles to creating online archives. But in practical terms, taking on an archival role would require publishing staff to learn new skills, or recruit new talent to join the firm. Early evidence suggests that publishers have not fully embraced the link between the process of acquiring, editing and selling books and the long-term value of archiving the material. This further suggests that publishers continue to regard themselves as facilitators of the early stages of a book's lifespan, but not as the custodians of its entire lifespan.

Divergent Strategies

There is a large common ground of shared strategies among publishers and digital librarians, derived primarily from the interactive nature of social media, and how it may be adapted for research or to enhance popular literature. However, the points of divergence between the two groups are pronounced. Divergent strategies flow directly from the history of each group. Digital librarians are working very hard to preserve and advance the role of managed knowledge resources, branded by the library, as part of the teaching process. In addition to experimentation with e-reserves and e-readers, they are now staking a large claim on the full-service teaching Web "portals." Open-source instructional portals now include a variety of added functions, including the ability at attach related files, images and simulations.

They also operate as eportfolios for students that follow them throughout their academic careers, and as information management tools for the faculty. Academic librarians perceive important new roles for information services in these learning spaces. Academic librarians are also brainstorming about ways to enhance "built" content that is created by the faculty—a key zone of knowledge creation where libraries may assume the role of digital publishers. The opportunities are vast, as pre-publication content creation encompasses the supporting information, texts and data sets that lead to finished work. Strategies to preserve this knowledge base are rapidly taking shape, and they are evidence of innovative thinking about librarian core competencies. What is more, the library profession's original core competencies—particularly collection development and classification—gain new relevance and importance as digital publishing moves to the forefront. Metadata schemes are vital tools for managing vast amounts of digital assets. The prevailing scheme, the Metadata Enhanced Technical Standard (METS), has seen heavy involvement by digital librarians; it ensures that metadata are portable and stay attached to a digital artifact, allowing the metadata and the object they describe to migrate over time. In contrast, publishers are in the early stages of harnessing XML to manage content more flexibly.

The most significant divergent characteristic between publishers and digital librarians has been librarians' willingness to enter into collaborative alliances, launching aggressive outreach to faculty authors, building political lobbying groups, and forming consortia that negotiate for better prices. They also have become software developers at their host universities, emphasising open-source computing. Ming-xing Huang envisions even more broad alliances, called "Digital Library Alliances"—which would enable academic libraries and their partners to enhance digitisation initiatives and search capabilities in ways that mimic large commercial firms such as Google. Digital librarians have also sought explicit partnerships with publishers themselves, when a shared goal could be seen. For example, the California Digital Library (CDL) entered into an early agreement with the Berkeley Electronic Press (BePress)—a full service journal publishing solution. Conversely, publishers' efforts to form large-scale collaborations have taken more measured steps.

With respect to libraries, collaborative efforts most often take the shape of advisory committees, which meet with editors and publishers once or twice per year. This has been a useful process, contributing to several significant joint efforts, such as the Wiley Online Library. Wiley's new "learning space" includes extensive links to library services for training and other assistance in using the aggregation of content. Digital librarians could afford to choose a collaborative stance, because they have been able to draw on strong relationships with their user communities. Historically, library patrons would visit a library in person, creating opportunities for a direct, personal relationship with welltrained professional staff. Armed with very good metrics on what library patrons actually need and how they prefer to gain access to resources, digital librarians are exploring how to create "user experiences" that reinforce a bond between the library and the user. Just as important, the library profession conceptualised the digital library as a matrix of content, services and human interactions from the earliest planning process.

In essence they have argued that a digital library is far more than a content platform; it is an entire community. For example, facilitating and teaching how to use of information services, whether print or online, is a measurable core competency for librarians. They have argued that technology should enhance human connectivity, rather than replace it, and they have backed up this claim with solid e-metrics showing how people are using libraries.

This assertion of the digital library as community is not nearly as evident in the professional literature of publishing. However, publishers are beginning to reach similar realisations about digital media, and are examining different approaches. As online publishing creates new synergies between print and electronic artifacts, the book gains a broader venue for discovery: the Web itself. Publishers continue to evaluate reader responses to books and related Web sites; and while print books will continue to exist, new zones are opening up for books to grow via Web sites, as e-books, and as subjects of reader forums. If indeed these trends follow their current course, the digital or Web version of a given book may eventually become the "master copy of record."

COLLABORATE, COMPETE, OR BOTH

Digital librarians possess all of the tools and expertise needed to compete directly with publishers. As universities accelerate their plans to create open-source journals and lend their imprimatur to them, digital librarians may take key leadership roles in managing the new archives and repositories, perhaps even the most central role of content owner. If so, they will be building upon existing relationships with the faculty; the two groups work in close proximity and in many cases share research interests.

Digital libraries also share the advantage of their host institution's imprimatur. This prestige enables them to expand their initiatives and to gain institutional support in doing so. This trend is already underway; if it accelerates, the trend would carry multiple benefits for digital librarians. First, it would cement and formalise their new role as a digital publisher within the academy. Second, the new status conferred by the role of digital publisher will provide digital librarians with a fresh opportunity to argue the value points of their longstanding core competencies.

Third, recognition of editorial work as a library skill will advance the professional status of digital librarians in the eyes of the research faculty and within the university administration. All of these enhancements to the status of digital librarians within the academy are excellent examples of "treatment substitution" as described by Abbott. Not only is the publisher role being offered by a competing group - digital librarians - it is also being used as a springboard to advance the status of the library profession as a whole.

Impetus for Collaboration

Even though digital libraries' enhanced imprimatur strengthens their chances of becoming effective digital publishers, evidence indicates that they remain quite receptive to collaboration, often proposing complimentary services in dialogue with publishers. This suggests that digital librarians could become partners in more ambitious alliances with publishers, structuring them to preserve revenue streams while advancing user access.Such a strategy would serve as a means for using digital media to find solutions to the longstanding problems of the former print-only era, with advantages for both parties. At present, digital librarians are exploring strategies to manage the entire lifespan of knowledge creation and the materials that lead to a finished work.

These include data sets, simulations, and Non-text artifacts of every sort. It is also increasingly common for research libraries to manage their own data functions and image collections, and work closely with other campus organisations that are involved in similar work. The role of data manager is being assumed by many innovators, not only at colleges and universities but also at the Library of Congress and other national-level collections. The digital librarian - as-data manager could be a very powerful ally for publishers who seek to transform their books into extended "dialogues" with readers, including related data resources and coherent and portable metadata management tools.

Collaboration as Revenue Protection

Much is made of the "scholarly journals crisis" and the imbroglios, both legal and rhetorical, that it has engendered; yet the crisis has also revealed how the best minds in both the publishing world and library profession view the economics associated with their mission.

As the difficult issues of pricing academic journals have been addressed, publishers have also learned more about how digital librarians view the future, and digital librarians have gained a much deeper understanding of the travails of publishing. This could lead to shared understandings and strategic alliances that bring both groups together, as they confront changing markets for academic and consumer-oriented publishing. Publisher-librarian collaborations will stimulate fresh perspectives about where value is being generated for both partners.

Revenue protection is vital for publishers, and need not come at the cost of fair use and related user benefits, which digital librarians seek to protect. Pricing models for electronic publishing vary dramatically, and have been the site of much tinkering over the years.

It is unclear at this time which pricing models are going to be the most effective for publishers, as scholarly communications evolve, and consumer behaviour changes. A digital library perspective on value and pricing could be crucial for publishers as they attempt to create new markets and new revenue streams. Finally, evolving perceptions of how markets work in the digital era may encourage knowledge creators and providers to work together.

Long-standing beliefs about how to sell any type of consumer product are in flux, creating new opportunities to reframe markets for particular advantage to particular players. As a result, many thinkers who study organisations and markets are now exploring new models for understanding business practices.

The metaphor of the "supply chain" - which guides how goods or services move forward, from creation to the market - has limited ability to explain how business can operate in a networked and digital environment. In response, researchers are re-imagining the supply chain as a "web" of relationships, which spreads in many directions, and can create new revenue streams even as established revenue streams fade. The print publishing process is quite linear and so publishers continue to find the supply chain paradigm useful, but at the same time, the web of relationships is a useful means for studying the impact of new media. These competing paradigms may influence how each group forms strategies and views collaboration as opposed to competition.

Competition and its Consequences

There are compelling arguments for publishers and digital librarians to join forces in response to the digital era. But at the same time, modern society thrives on competition and the evolution of the Internet has been heavily influenced by innovation, as well as anticipation for the "next big thing."

On one side, a long-term, deeply rooted publisher-library coalition could save both parties considerable time and resources; yet on the other side, if either group devises a matrix of strategies for fully assuming the other's role while preserving its own, that group would gain a whole new level of prestige.

The shape and makeup of digital libraries would be heavily affected by such an outcome, no matter which group were to prevail. Library education provides an example of how core competencies can be repurposed to gain strategic advantage. A career in libraries requires an accredited master's degree, often accompanied by a second subject-area degree. This level of education is comparable to that of most editorial staff. Publishing practices are widely known, further easing the assumption of a publishing role.

Digital librarians who work in large institutions already edit newsletters, bibliographies and even book series. Moreover, digital librarians can partner with academics and administrators who have resources to underwrite publishing programmes at research universities, this trend is well underway. Publishers also may see advantage in taking on roles currently found in the sphere of libraries, for many of the same reasons.

The rigours of publishing require outreach, interpretation of markets, and management of large backlists. With low barriers to the creation of repositories and value-added "collections" of knowledge, it is reasonable to argue that digital librarians' role in collection development could shift to publishers, along with enhanced public service functions via the Internet. Since, publishers understand market dynamics and sales strategies, the arsenal of strategy at their disposal is significant.

CHARACTERISTICS OF A DIGITAL LIBRARY

Assumptions about a Digital Library

There are certain assumptions in discussions of a digital library. Levy and Marshall summarize these as: digital libraries are collections containing fixed, permanent documents which are based on digital technologies and are used by individuals working alone.

Fixity of Content

The concept of a fixed and permanent document is based on the printed book: While a title may be reissued in a revised version, once a specific volume is printed and bound, it remains unchanged. Fixity creates a comfortable environment in which to perform certain library functions. Cataloguing practices have evolved around the largely fixed and permanent document. Fluid or transient documents, such as pamphlets and news clippings have been largely uncatalogued and stored in unclassified areas, such as the vertical file [cabinet].

The perception of lack-of-fixity in fluid digital documents, especially internet-based documents, leads to the assumption that digital items are ill-equipped for cataloguing and other library functions.

This concept of the fixity and permanence of a volume is, itself, flawed. For example, marginalia entered by the reader gives a book some degree of fluidity. Marginalia can contribute error-correction, critique, and even new content to the volume.

Marginalia is viewed as an important addition to certain texts. In addition to marginalia, vandalism— such as removal of pictures or pages from a book— makes it difficult to predict that two books, identical at binding, still contain the same contents on any library shelf.

In classifying books as fixed and permanent, the ways of altering a book after issue have been dismissed. What has, in fact, been catalogued is the pristine just-off-the-press edition. Certainly, many digital-based texts could be archived as a pristine edition, with many fluid copies existing at other sites, and perhaps even linked to and from the archived edition.

While the range of variation from a digital pristine copy would certainly have the potential to facilitate and exceed the variation from a print pristine copy, the practice of cataloging and archiving documents at certain points of development can extend to digital media.

Fluid copies on the internet could be considered manuscripts in progress (just as some authors circulate paper-based working drafts of manuscripts to colleagues for reading, comment and use) and at some point a revised version could be catalogued and archived, not unlike revised editions of print-based texts.

This is a simplistic discussion of fixity in print and digital media, however, it does illustrate the point that fixity is a relative concept and does not necessarily belong exclusively to the print medium.

Technologies of Library Collections

The develop of the concept of a library based on digital technologies has revolved around the concept of a library based on the book. As Levy and Marshall point out, the book is not the only material contained in library collections.

In addition to holdings of books, photographs, unbound and handwritten manuscripts and correspondents, and other ephemera which are adaptable to digital representation, libraries also contain three-dimensional artifacts, such as models, dioramas, toys and games, and realia—for example, a chameleon (for a borrow-a-pet service) or a wooden crate marked with 'Papers of [author].

Do not open until [date]. [Name of custodian or executor].' Realia and certain other three-dimensional items in a library's collection do not easily convert to digital format. Therefore, even if all currently convertible library materials were digitized, not all materials in the library would be in digital form.

The current concept of a digital library, then, is a subset of the larger concept of library, just as a video or a film library is a subset of the concept of library and not a substitute for it.

While it is possible that certain libraries will collect only digital materials, it is more likely that libraries in general will make use of digital material where it best serves their patrons' needs and their libraries' budgets, much like libraries have used microforms and paperback editions.

While some materials will not be suitable for digitalization, representations of these materials, such as the products of indexing and abstracting, will be. At some point in the future when applications such as virtual reality develop sufficiently, we may be able to satisfactorily convert much of the informational content of librariesU 3-D holdings to digital format.

At least for now, a comprehensive library will of necessity be a multiple format collection.

The Act of Information Seeking

The perception seems to be that the work in which the user engages in seeking information and the work in which the practitioner engages in supporting his or her patrons is a solitary act. Contrary to this impression, research finds that the library is a meeting place where collaborative work takes place among patrons, among practitioners, and between practitioners and patrons. For digital libraries to pattern the work capabilities of the traditional library, and to pattern the work habits of the library's patrons and practitioners, collaborative functionality must be included in digital library design. An exceptional example of progress towards this goal, the work of Robertson, Jitan and Reese of the US WEST Research and Information Group, is discussed later.

DEFINITION OF DIGITAL LIBRARIES

In this unit we ask two questions:

- What is a digital library?
- What are its characteristics?

In answering these questions we will learn about digital coherence, discuss the origins of digital libraries, and discover synonyms and metaphors for digital libraries. We will also touch on assumptions about a digital library, technologies of library collections, and the act of information seeking.

Digital Coherence

The term digital library has been applied to a wide variety of offerings from collections of electronic journals to software agents that support enquiry-based education to collections of e-mail to electronic versions of a public library, to personal information collections, and even to the entire Internet. The one property these various entities have in common is their digitization or digital coherence (Daniel Atkins).

Digital coherence means all the objects in a digital library, whether sounds, images, texts, or some other media, can be treated in essentially the same way.

Prior to digital coherence, libraries needed to treat various media, for example, books, journals, videos, and musical recordings, differently.

One could say that digital coherence is the mechanism which permits a form of equality among various information resources. This equality has importance for delivery and integration of information.

Envisioning a World Brain and The Memex

The concept of a digital library is not new. In fact, the concept of digital libraries pre-dates the development of the first computer. H. G. Wells was one of the first authors to write about idea of a world brain that could supplement, add functionality to, and even replace traditional libraries.

It is generally agreed that Vannevar Bush's 1945 article in the Atlantic Monthly, in which Bush conceives of a memex machine, inspired much of the early application of computers to information retrieval. The memex is a mechanical device based on microfilm technology.

The concept of the memex included [a community of scholars indexing and creating] links between pieces of information in a [microfilm-based] research library combined with [microfilmed] personal notes (and classification system) and notes of colleagues, anticipating the ideas of both hypertext and personal information retrieval systems.

Lesk assures us that by 2015 (70 years after Vannevar Bush published his memex dream) "we will have the equivalent of a major research library on each desk. And it will have searching capabilities beyond those Bush imagined".

Synonyms for the Term Digital Library

In the early 1950s computers entered library services in the form of punched card applications in technical services operations and through the development of the MARC (MAchine-Readable Cataloging) standard for digitizing and communicating library catalog information.

The vision of a fully computer-based library began to emerge in terminology in the mid-60s with J. C. R. Licklider's the library of the future.

Over the years, other terms have been coined to refer to the concept of a digitized library, including electronic library, virtual library, library without walls, and bionic library. Library science professor Winfred Lancaster extended this concept beyond the functions of the library, using the term paperless society. The use of the term digital library can be traced to the Digital Libraries Initiative, established through funding in 1994, by the National Science Foundation, the Advanced Research Projects Agency, and the National Aeronautics and Space Admini-stration in the United States. Under this funding, six U.S. universities were granted a total of $24.4 million for digital library research.

Two events motivated this funding: the sudden explosive growth of the Internet and the development of graphical Web browsers.

These two developments significantly increased the viability of extending library resources and services beyond their current walls and communities, facilitating the sharing of scarce resources and the reaching of under-served populations.

Metaphors for Digital Libraries

There is little discussion or agreement in the literature about what constitutes a digital library. Harter juxtaposes two extreme views: the most inclusive view, which takes a digital library to be essentially what the Internet is today, and the metaphor of the traditional library.

The essential differences between these two metaphors deal with their [presumed] properties of location, content, selection criteria, organization, authority control*, authorship, stability, access, and user groups, services and fees. The Internet has no physical or logical location; no quality control and no entry barriers; no organization scheme, authority control, or surrogates; no concept of author; and is fluid and transient.

Everyone has access to the Internet, but access may require payment and purchase of equipment by the individual user. The traditional library is perceived to have their properties and no entry fee for the individual.

*Names of authors, variants of works (editions), and subject headings or descriptors are all controlled and common variants are cross-listed to the designated official form.

DIGITAL LIBRARY PROJECTS ON DIGITAL REFERENCE SERVICES

Some research projects aimed at providing reference and information services as part of the digital library services have recently begun. The most prominent is the Collaborative Digital Reference Service (CDRS) project launched by the Library of Congress.

CDRS

Researcher commented that "by applying the best of what libraries and librarians have to offer to the labyrinthine universe of unstructured and unverified information on the Internet, we can begin to bridge the gulf that exists between providers and users of information". With this end in view, the

Library of Congress has launched the Collaborative Digital Reference Service, the mission of which is to provide "professional reference service to users, anywhere any time, through an international, digital network of libraries".

The CDRS is a library to library network for asking and answering reference questions. It has three main components:

- *Member profiles*: That contain information on member strengths and features.
- *Request Manager*: A software for entering, routing and answering reference questions.
- *Knowledge base*: A searchable database of question and answer sets.

The system is designed to work in a very simple manner. A participating library sends a question to the system on behalf of a user. The system looks into the knowledgebase for a match. If the answer is found, a response is sent to the querying library by e-mail. If the question is not found in the knowledgebase, then it is passed on to the Request Manager, which forwards the query to an appropriate library selected from the profiles of the participating libraries and their collections, expertise, etc. This library receives the query, finds an answer and sends it back to the results store, which then sends the response back to the asking library, and stores the query and the answer in the knowledgebase. Hence, the strength of the system lies in the knowledgebase and the Request Manager. Since, June 2000 CDRS has been a "working" pilot with a current total of 220 active members who are routing real questions and answers. The next generation on CDRS is being co-developed by Library of Congress and OCLC. It will integrate local and global e-reference networks, and will be released as a full production service in June of 2002.

AUTOMATIC REFERENCE LIBRARIANS FOR THE WORLD WIDE WEB

The Automatic Reference Librarians for the World Wide Web, a DLI-2 funded project at the University of Washington. The central objective of this project, according to them, "is to create software agents that posses reference intelligence I a limited understanding of complex technical topics, but a very sophisticated understanding of how and where to find high-quality information on theWorld Wide Web". Etioni and Weld reported the basic working principles of the proposed system, which works on a wrapper technology.

The basic steps involved are:

- The user asks a question;
- The Query Router assigns a topic to the query;
- The topic maps to a number of relevant wrappers;
- The parallel Web search module sends requests via wrappers to the sites;
- Responses from the sites are obtained and sent to the fusion engine for collation;
- User gets the response.

SIFTER is an interdisciplinary research collaboration among faculty and students in the Computer and Information Science Department and the School of Library and Information Science at Indiana University. The broad aim of the project is to develop information agents that would perform a number of functions such as culling information from complex resources residing in diverse locations, and conducting analysis, synthesis and customisation according to the requirements of the user.

The specific objectives are:

- Dealing with heterogeneous information sources that may change over time;
- Handling shifting requirements and interest of users with minimal human involvement;
- Creating a robust agent architecture for reactive, proactive and collaborative filtering;
- Supporting agent collaboration based on natural or artificial economic frameworks for multi-agent tasks.

VIRTUAL REFERENCE DESK

The Virtual Reference Desk (VRD) is a project sponsored by the US Department of Education, and its objective is "the advancement of digital reference and the successful creation and operation of human-mediated, Internet-based information services". VRD defines a digital reference service as Internet-based question-and-answer services that connect users with experts. The basic idea of VRD is that when a given user asks a question that cannot be answered by a participating centre, it is forwarded to the VRD network for assistance.

VRD services include the following:

- *Collaborative AskA Service*: A network of AskA services and volunteer information professionals.
- *The Learning Center*: A Web site for the K-12 community with curriculum-related Web sites, frequently asked questions, and other previously asked questions.
- *AskA+ Locator*: A searchable database of high-quality K-12 AskA services.

VRD also supports research on interoperability standards, metadata and other aspects of digital reference services.

LEVERAGING THE DOCUMENT SELECTIONS OF EXPERT PROBLEM SOLVERS

This is a DLI-2 project at the Oregon Health Sciences University and Oregon Graduate Institute. The goals of this project are "to understand how experts select information in a large and complex information space and to develop tools that assist them in this process", The project aims to capture the trace of information used by experts in the health field, for example medical doctors. The basic idea is that as medical experts traverse the large and diverse collection of documents, they make explicit choices about which information resources to examine more carefully and which ones to ignore.

These choices create a subset of documents relevant to a given problem and this subset of documents may be of interest to other users concerned with the same or similar problem. Thus, by capturing this information that is inherent in the selection of appropriate information resources for problem solving, this project aims to come up with models that may be useful for other users.

The project proposed to develop:

- A trace that describes the path taken by an expert in solving his/her problem by using the available information resources;
- A precis of information about each document, its content, and the history of its use by experts; and
- Navigation tools that would assist subsequent problem solvers using the collection by exploiting the knowledge inherent in the existing traces.

Though the project specifically deals with medical experts and looks into their problem-solving processes, the project team expects that the resulting technology will be scalable, because the value of a set of precis and bundles within a collection should increase as the document collection grows and as more experts use the collection.

QUESTION ANSWERING SYSTEMS

A number of question answering systems (QA) are now being developed that aim to provide answers to natural language questions. Research in this area will have tremendous impact on the future of digital reference services. QA systems often use a variety of natural language processing (NLP) tools and techniques to get the correct answer from the source texts. Breck *et al.* reported a QA system that uses techniques from knowledge representation, information retrieval, and NLP. Research reported in the QA track of Text Retrieval Conferences show quite encouraging results. The goal of research in the QA track is to "retrieve small snippets of text that contain the actual answer to a question rather than the document lists traditionally returned by text retrieval systems".

The basic technology involves analysing user queries in several stages. First, cue words/phrases like "who", "when" are identified to guess what is needed; and then a small portion of the document collection is retrieved using standard text retrieval technology. This is followed by a shallow parsing of the returned documents for identifying the entities required for an answer. If no appropriate answer type is found then the best matching passage is retrieved.

This approach works well as long as the query types recognised by the system have broad coverage, and the system can classify questions reasonably accurately. In TREC-8, the first QA track of TREC, the most accurate QA systems could answer more than two-thirds of the fact finding type of questions correctly.

In the second QA track, the best performing QA system, the Falcon system from Southern Methodist University, was able to answer 65 per cent of the questions. These results are quite impressive in a domainindependent question-answering environment. However, the questions were still simple in the first two QA tracks. In the future, more complex questions requiring answers from more than one document will be handled by QA track researchers. Such robust QA systems can be used to provide reference services in digital libraries.

TEACH ABOUT DIGITAL LIBRARIES

The answer depends, to a large extent, on having a relatively clear idea about what are digital libraries. As mentioned, no agreed upon definition exists, which is fine, because the same constructs can be viewed from a number of viewpoints or perspectives. Let us explore some of these perspectives through definitions offered. Of course, a choice of a given perspective dictates the choice of the content.

Different perspectives about digital libraries, together with competing visions and associated definitions, come from several communities that are involved in digital library work. We are concentrating here on two communities: research and practice.

While they work and proceed independently of each other, they can be considered on two ends of a spectrum, which as yet have not met in the middle. To use another metaphor: the research and practice communities are in the same planetary system, but one is on Mars, the other on Venus.

The research community grounded mostly in computer science, on one end of the spectrum, asks research questions directed towards future vision or visions of digital libraries, or rather of their various technology oriented aspects and components, unrestricted by practice.

On the other end of the spectrum, the practice community, grounded mostly in librarianship and information science, asks developmental, operational, and use questions in real-life economic and institutional contexts, restrictions, and possibilities, concentrating on applications on the use end of the spectrum.

In research, DLIs did not define 'digital library.' In order to incorporate a wide range of possible approaches and domains, the concept is treated broadly and vaguely. Thus, the projects, particularly in DLI-2, cover a wide range of topics, stretching the possible meaning of digital library to and even beyond the limit of what can be considered as being digital and at the same time recognizable as any kind of a library or a part thereof. This is perfectly acceptable for research frontiers need to be stretched. But at the same time, it makes choices for educational content diffuse and difficult.

The closest to the definition applicable to the approaches taken by the research community is the one given by Lesk in the first textbook on the topic:

- "Digital libraries are *organized collections* of digital information. They combine the *structure and gathering of information*, which libraries and archives have always done, with the *digital representation* that computers have made possible." (Emphasis in this and following definitions is added to illustrate possible choices for educational content).

Arms in a newer text on digital libraries, also from a research community and technology applications perspective, provides what he calls an "informal definition:"

- "A digital library is a *managed collection* of inform-ation, with associated *services*, where the information is *stored in digital formats* and *accessible* over a *network*."

The practice community, whose majority is residing in operational libraries, concentrates on building operational digital libraries, their maintenance and operations, and providing services to users. The approach is developmental, operational, and eminently practical, with relatively little or no research involved.

As a result, hundreds, if not thousands of digital libraries have emerged worldwide, with more becoming operational every day. The efforts are diverse. Many approaches are being used. Many types of collections and media are included and processed in many different ways. Many are located in libraries, creating a hybrid library (combination of a traditional and digital library); others are not bound to brick and mortar libraries at all.

In the US, the Digital Libraries Federation (DLF) (formed in 1995) is an organization of research libraries and various national institutions. The stated goal of DLF is "to establish the conditions necessary for the creation, maintenance, expansion, and preservation of a distributed collection of digital materials accessible to scholars and the wider public." The organization represents libraries and practitioners.

After considerable deliberation, DFL agreed on a "working definition of digital library," representing the definition of the practice community:

- Digital libraries are organizations that provide the resources, including the specialized staff, to select, structure, offer intellectual access to, interpret, distribute, preserve the integrity of, and ensure the persistence over time of collections of digital works so that they are readily and economically available for use by a defined community or set of communities.

Borgman provides a more complex definition (including an extensive discussion) of digital libraries, a definition that may be considered as a bridge between the research community definition and practical community definitions:

- Digital libraries are a set of electronic resources and associated technical capabilities for creating, searching, and using information. They are an extension and enhancement of information storage and retrieval systems that manipulate digital data in any medium The content of digital libraries includes data, [and] metadata Digital libraries are constructed, collected, and organized, by (and for) a community of users, and their functional capabilities support the information needs and uses of that community.

Following these perspectives, the content choices fall into categories that are based on: systems, networks, and technology; collection and resources in various media; representation, organization, and operability; storage and searching; functionality, access and use; institutions and services; and user communities and related applications. The educational choices are among technology, resources, organization, access, institutions, and use, or a mix thereof. A balanced and at the same time a comprehensive mix is difficult, if not impossible, to achieve.

SURVEY OF APPLICATIONS

In order to go beyond generalities and into observation of existing educational practices we conducted a survey. The survey consisted of two parts: a *Web survey* of curriculum and course information as posted on the sites of a number of schools and an *E-mail survey* of answers to invited questions posted on several listserves. We report the results of each survey separately.

Each of the survey methods has strengths and definite limitations. Deriving conclusions about the content of education of given institutions through an examination of information provided on their own Web sites is fraught with peril. It is similar to the well-known peril of examination of catalogs.

However, Web listings are more current and inclusive; they provide, by and large, much more information than catalog listings, up to inclusion of syllabi; and they are updated more often. As a rule, general e-mail surveys have a small rate of self-selected returns. But the answers tend to be specific to the questions. Both surveys complement each other. The methodology was considered appropriate for a general (rather than detailed) assessment of the emerging approaches to what is taught and how these approaches are positioned in the existing teaching practice.

Web Survey

Method

In the first part we examined the Web sites of 56 accredited programmes listed in the directory of the Association of Library and Information Science Education (ALISE) as found on their web site.

The schools housing these programmes are generally known as schools of library and information science (LIS), but in reality a good number of them have changed from this designation to several classes of different names. For brevity, we will use the LIS label for the programmes.

The accreditation is by the American Library Association (ALA) and covers the professional degree programme on the master's level. It does *not* cover doctoral or undergraduate education, offered by a number of these schools. Geographically, it covers schools in North America the U.S. and Canada. Thus in this part no other countries were included.

We looked at course titles, course descriptions and syllabi when available. In line with the broad definition of digital libraries (or lack of definition) as discussed above, we cast the net widely. We concentrated on courses where *digital libraries* or *digital librarianship* were mentioned as a term, but we also included courses that used synonymous concepts, exemplified by terms such as *electronic library*, or *library of the future*; we also included *virtual museums*, as having a strong connection with digital libraries.

On a broader level, we included courses that mention processes that are closely related to digital libraries, such as management and preservation of electronic records, electronic text design, metadata for digital collections, production of network multimedia, designing accessible web based materials, and electronic text.

Finally, on the broadest level we included courses that are oriented towards *information technology* and address the technological bases of digital libraries, such as *network architecture, managing networks, digital tool kits, Internet applications*, and the like. We used these gradations and distinctions as tools for classification as incorporated in tables below.

Inclusion

Of the 56 LIS programmes, 47 (89 per cent) include digital library in some form or another or to some degree in their curriculum; for 5 (9 per cent) programmes, this cannot be determined and 4 (7 per cent) programmes show no presence of digital library education.

This analysis shows that digital library education is included in the curriculum of most LIS programmes. However, the degree of inclusion varies widely. When considered closely, the inclusion ranges from a full course or courses on digital libraries to metadata standards being covered in organization of information courses to cases in which digital library focus is relegated to continuing education. Participation of the students in a local digital library project is another way of including the digital library topics within LIS education.

Integration

To what degree are digital library courses offered as independent or full-blown courses? To what degree are digital library topics integrated in other courses? Table addresses these questions.

Table. Course Integration in Digital Library Education in ALA-accredited Library and Information Science Programmes. (N=47 Programmes that Include Digital Library Education from 56 Accredited Programmes).

Digital library content in relation to the curriculum	No. of LIS programmes
1. Independent DL courses	15 (32%)
2. Combination of independent DL course and DL content integrated in other courses	8 (17%)
3. DL content integrated in other courses (without independent DL courses)	23 (49%)
4. Other (DL content integrated with continuing education)	1 (2%)

Note: Two major types of courses are

- Tndependent digital library courses (typically titled "Digital Libraries" or a similar version), and
- Digital library content integrated in other courses.

As shown in Table, half of the schools have significant digital library content in the curriculum. They include schools with specialized digital library courses on the books; we call these independent courses, although we cannot tell to what degree these are also segregated courses, with little or no connection to the rest of the curriculum.

Such an independent course is either an elective or special topics course offered either as the only course with digital library content in the school's programme or a course offered in addition to other digital library topics that appears elsewhere in the curriculum.

The other half of the schools have some level of digital library content integrated in their programme, but no course specifically focusing on digital libraries. The programmes that integrate digital library topics in their courses vary in the level of inclusion and strategies for inclusion.

LIS programmes

LIS programmes at the masters level are *professional* programmes; this defines the context for digital library education in such schools. An examination of digital library course descriptions from Web sites reflects that education for digital librarianship in many cases does not reflect a systematic view or programme of education. Presumably, digital library content is simply an acknowledgment of an emerging field of practice and institutional realities. Even schools with a full course devoted to the problem area of digital libraries show variation in their approaches.

The courses offered under the umbrella term 'digital libraries' range from theoretical and survey courses to project-focused courses. Some are broader and some narrow in focus. A combination of theory (highlighting multiple facets of digital library research) and application (giving an overview of existing practices and providing hands-on experience) seem not to be practiced in such courses.

Weighing one against the other, theory against hands-on experience, it seems that theoretical and survey courses provide a more flexible framework to be expanded with an on-the-job training and apprenticeship in the changing digital library practical environment. An ideal would be the integration of practice-based with survey and theory-based approach to digital library education.

As mentioned, we have been inclusive rather than exclusive in defining what constitutes integrated content. We have considered courses in networking, topics in telecommunications, metadata standards, courses integrating topics on the preservation of electronic-born information as integrating digital library content and digital libraries as developmental form in the history of knowledge records and therefore contributing to digital library education.

In many cases, from brief course descriptions and sparse online syllabi, the degree to which digital library problems were truly addressed is not always clear. In our conservative estimate, in more than half of the schools.

The degree of inclusion cannot be determined with certainty with the methodology used here. The question is whether information technology course addressing the *'library of the future,'* a course dealing with social roles of information organization that includes traditional and digital libraries, archives, network architecture, or the concern with 'structures, processes, dynamics and applications that determine the effective use of motion imagery in multimedia, on-line, and other digital media,' all relate to the problem area of digital libraries.

Together, the approaches represent a pandemonium typical of the general uncertainty towards digital library education. The choices result from an undisciplined mix of the pressures of the libraries as market for graduates, ten years of research and development in the area of digital libraries, and varying degrees of faculty expertise and perceptions of what constitutes a meaningful approach. Multiple and often overlapping approaches in different schools are symptomatic of that general uncertainty.

Because the schedule and frequency of offering is a determinant of impact of specific courses or a mix of courses on digital library education in specific LIS programmes, clearly one cannot make sweeping statements. Several schools that integrate digital library content into other courses, or offer courses that do not have digital libraries in their title but focus on the creation of distributed electronic repositories of information, are taking an integrated rather than independent approach.

The "independent" (segregated) vs. "integrated" approach and the "combined independent with integrated" approaches reveal an underlying philosophy of digital library education. Integration is the ideal, but it may suffer from superficiality. Segregation is also fraught with peril of a different sort of offering a view of compartmentalized technology.

A smaller fraction offers a combination of independent and integrated approach to digital library education (17 per cent). There may be a number of reasons for this, one of which may be a reflection of competing perspectives within a given programme. We did not detect that any school has a organized course of study in digital libraries, such as a specialization or track.

E-mail Survey

We also invited e-mail answers to a list of questions posted on several listserves oriented towards audiences as individuals (rather then institutions) in different areas.

They included: listserve JESSE in library science, the member list of the American Society for Information Science and Technology (ASIST), listserve of the Special Interest Group on Information Retrieval, Association for Computing Machinery (ACM SIGIR), listserve of the Humanist Discussion Group, and ETEXT-L.

We sought answers to the following questions:

- Does your institution offer course(s), seminars or institutes in digital libraries and/or related areas? If so, please provide as much information as possible, particularly including URLs.
- Does your institution teach digital library topics within (or as a part of) other courses, seminars, or institutes? If so, please provide as much information as possible, particularly including URLs.
- In what department or school are the digital library course(s) offered?
- On what level undergraduate, graduate, doctoral, professional development?

While the listserves reach great many recipients, we received only a total of 27 responses, of these 20 were relevant. The small number of responses was very disappointing, but then responses to general surveys are always low. We know that in reality there are many more programmes and courses related to digital libraries, and that this is but a very small sample. We cannot tell how representative it is. Still it is worthwhile to analyse this sample.

Given the nature of the sample and the size of the returns, about all that could safely be concluded is that there is an interesting and broadening array of disciplines other than LIS in which digital library courses are being taught and such courses are at a variety of levels, undergraduate and graduate.

Digital Libraries Taught

To answer the question on how were digital libraries taught we did not look at pedagogy. Instead, we have looked at broader issues: How did various programmes address the basic and connecting areas for digital library education?

What models have emerged? This illuminates the contexts of digital library education within the programmes; more specifically it shows area clusters where digital library education has gravitated.

Method

Here we deal only with 47 ALA accredited LIS programmes that have presence in digital library education to some degree or other. We undertook a detailed examination of presented curricula, course descriptions, syllabi, and other information as provided.

The level of available information differs greatly from programme to programme, thus our conclusions are only as good as the information available on the programs' Web sites. The analysis is qualitative, with all the strengths and weaknesses of such methods.

In a grounded theory approach, we derived classes from data, and then grouped the data in these classes. Subjective? Of course. But the derivative approach also enables to show clusters in the greater body of data, which are otherwise not visible. To provide consistency, we applied the same analysis criteria to all programmes.

Results

We identified several dimensions or models of digital library education emerging in the programmes examined. Various approaches that LIS programmes are taking in conceptualizing the digital library education, with regard to areas of application. Of the 47 LIS programmes that were identified as including digital library education in their programmes, six have digital library content contained within a single course, one programme shows digital library content to be integrated across the curriculum; and for six programmes we could not determine the area of application. The derived classification is divided in two classes. The first or general class identifies four broad areas of application, *i.e.* the general domain of emphasis and orientation for digital library education that could be identified as predominant in a given programme.

These are:

- T-tools (technologies and technology based processes);
- Environments (the context in which digital libraries operate),
- Objects (representation, structure and life cycle of documents in various formats), and
- Combined (several areas of applications present without any one being distinctive).

The second, or specific class, identifies perspectives within the broad areas. It shows a more detailed or specific orientation of programmes.

In the perspectives the'basic' and'advanced' tools refer to the level of technological sophistication. The'compartm-entalized' approach is one in which digital library is conceived as a contained phenomenon.

These models show how digital library education is conceptualized and focused within a particular programme. The approaches are not exclusive and many schools combine several of these approaches. We presume that this is either as a result of competing discourses within the schools themselves or because of the uncertainty that the notion of digital library entails.

PRESERVATION PLANNING

Even in the smallest institutions, a preservation programme needs administrative coordination in order to be effective. If individual preservation activities are undertaken in the absence of an overall plan, one or two preservation activities (such as preservation microfilming or rehousing collections) may be well developed, while others (such as monitoring improvement of environmental conditions) are neglected.

The process of development and ongoing review of a preservation plan helps ensure that preservation is considered an integral part of institutional activities, rather than in competition with other activities (such as collection development) for time and resources.

THE PLANNING PROCESS

- *"Planning Provides a Rational Process to Analyse Needs Systematically to Minimize the Problems and Maximize the Opportunities."* —Jutta Reed-Scott, "Planning for Preservation in Libraries," in *Preservation: Issues and Planning*

In her article, Jutta Reed-Scott sets forth the basic components of the preservation planning process:

- Identify and assess preservation needs (through some type of survey)
- Set priorities among preservation needs according to the institution's mission
- Evaluate existing preservation activities
- decide what preservation functions are needed within the institution and how they will be organized
- Allocate resources for preservation
- Write a plan and determine how the plan will be implemented

Identifying and assessing needs is an information-gathering process: what collections does the institution hold and what is their condition? How are collections housed? What are the environmental conditions within the building(s)? Is there a disaster plan? Are collections protected from fire and theft? Are repair, binding, and/or conservation treatment undertaken regularly? How much funding is allocated for preservation? How much staff time?

Once you have discerned your preservation needs, you must consider potential solutions to the problems you have identified. What answers are most appropriate for your particular institution and situation? What existing activities already have a preservation component, and how should existing preservation activities change to meet the needs you have identified?

As part of this process, you will need to assess your institutional mission and goals and the personnel and monetary resources currently available, as well as potential future resources.

Once all the relevant issues have been considered, you should set preservation priorities and pull together a preservation strategy that includes an action plan and timetable. A systematic preservation plan will allow you to respond effectively to preservation needs and take advantage of preservation opportunities that might otherwise have been missed.

PRESERVATION STRATEGIES

Developing a Preservation Strategy

While the basic elements of a preservation programme are fairly straightforward, the emphasis placed on each of these elements will vary according to the institution and situation. The relative importance of each component for your institution will depend on the type, value, and condition of your collections; the importance of specific collections to your institution's mission; the type of access you need to provide (open stacks, closed stacks, offsite storage); and the amount of use the collections receive.

You will need to develop an appropriate preservation strategy for your institution. In general, preservation programme elements that benefit all collections (such as environmental control, security, disaster planning, and proper storage and handling) should be thought of as the basic "umbrella" components of a programme. Other strategies, such as microfilming, library binding, or treatment would be used for individual (or groups of) items as needed.

Strategies for Different Types of Institutions

Preservation needs and responses are specific to a particular institution and each collection within that institution. Some repositories may see their primary responsibility as preserving unique and/or comprehensive collections over the long term, while others may place more emphasis on serving academic teaching and research needs or services to the general public.

In general, institutions with archival or historical collections assume an obligation to preserve those collections over the long term. These institutions will place a strong emphasis on strategies to stabilize the collections as a whole (*e.g.*, holdings maintenance/collections care, environmental control, security, emergency preparedness), with a secondary focus on preservation reformatting (usually microfilming) and/or conservation treatment for the specific collections that require it.

The primary mission of small- to mid-sized public or academic libraries, on the other hand, is to provide access to collections for as long as the materials are needed. These libraries generally have a high level of use and collect basically rather than comprehensively. In these libraries, reference collections and materials related to current courses receive the most use. These institutions will also need to focus on umbrella issues such as storage and handling, environment, security, and disaster planning-but in addition they will undertake library binding, basic book repair, withdrawal of brittle titles that are no longer needed, and replacement of brittle titles with reprints, photocopies or purchased microfilm. Preservation microfilming and conservation treatment will generally not be a priority, unless the institution also holds historical or other unique collections.

Like smaller academic and public libraries, large research libraries strive to provide users access to collections for as long as the materials are needed.

In addition, they assume responsibility for building and maintaining research collections that are meant to survive over the long term. For these institutions, an even wider range of preservation options will be needed, including umbrella strategies such as environmental control, storage/handling, and disaster planning, as well as preservation reformatting, replacement, library binding, book repair, and conservation treatment.

THE ROLE OF FUNDING IN SETTING PRESERVATION PRIORITIES

Setting preservation priorities involves many cost-related questions. Will you tackle lower-cost preservation options first? How will you plan for higher-cost activities? If your institution needs a preservation survey, will you pay for a professional one or will in-house staff conduct it? If you need to establish an ongoing library binding or book repair programme, how much will it cost, and is your institution willing to bear the charges? Would outsourcing of some preservation activities be cheaper than doing the work in house? How will you fund special projects such as preservation microfilming or conservation treatment? Is outside funding available?

Remember, however, that cost is only one of the factors in setting preservation priorities; you must also consider each activity in the context of the entire preservation programme. Is the activity a critical need? Will it provide a significant benefit for a large number of materials? If it provides a limited benefit, but is also low cost, should it be done anyway? The cost of a preservation activity must also be balanced against the risk of not undertaking the activity; neglecting an activity because of high cost (such as roof repair or installation of fire protection equipment) may have serious negative consequences for all or part of your collection over the long term.

BUDGETING

Budgeting is one of the most challenging aspects of preservation management. You must decide what preservation activities are needed within your institution, how much they will cost, and how you will pay for them. You will also need to decide what work will be carried out in house and what might be outsourced.

Preservation Spending: How Much Is Enough

In an era of declining budgets and staffing, there are never enough resources to address all preservation needs. To determine whether your institution is on the right track in terms of preservation spending, it can be helpful to compare your efforts to those of other institutions.

The Association of Research Libraries (ARL) issues an annual report on preservation statistics in ARL member libraries, which primarily represent libraries that hold two million volumes or more. These reports collect statistics on the organizational structure of library preservation programmes, staffing levels, preservation expenditures, conservation treatment, and preservation reformatting.

ARL statistics gathered over a number of years have shown that research libraries with active preservation programmes spend approximately 5 to 10 per cent of their total budget on preservation (*e.g.,* prevention of deterioration, preparing materials for use, and repairing/copying materials). This statistic does not include costs related to the building and systems that enable the library to maintain a preservation-quality environment. The larger the library, the higher the percentage of total library expenditures that tends to be directed to preservation. While these figures obviously do not apply directly to other types and sizes of institution, they are useful as a general model.

Reallocating Existing Funds

Remember that initiating new preservation activity does not always have to involve allocation of new funds. When planning a preservation programme, review your institution's budget to identify any activities that could be redirected to assist in meeting preservation goals. For example, most archives already purchase folders and storage boxes, and many libraries purchase pamphlet binders or other enclosures. A change in the type of material bought and/or training of staff to use the enclosures properly may greatly improve the overall protection of collections with little or no additional cost.

Since reallocation of existing funds may cross departmental lines, it must be undertaken as part of a cooperative preservation planning process that is coordinated with the institution's overall strategic plan.

Cost Analysis

Cost analysis is crucial to effective budgeting for preservation. In order to decide how best to accomplish a particular preservation goal, a preservation manager must be able to analyse a preservation activity and its associated costs.

A cost analysis might be needed in any of the following situations:

- Submitting a budget proposal for a preservation activity within the institution
- Preparing a response to an institutional request for cost reductions
- Developing a cost estimate for a grant proposal
- Comparing the costs of carrying out an activity in house versus using a vendor

The process of carrying out a cost analysis is explained in detail in *The Preservation Manager's Guide to Cost Analysis*. After identifying the product, service, or other activity to be analysed (for example, to determine the costs of producing book boxes in-house), the preservation manager must gather detailed information on the procedures for carrying out the service or activity.

Costs may include supplies and equipment; services; labour; or indirect costs (*e.g.,* overhead). In each of these categories, the cost of each resource needed to complete the activity should be calculated on a per-item basis. Remember to include "hidden" costs (*e.g.,* supply costs may include not just the cost of the items, but shipping costs or custom order fees).

All assumptions made must be documented (for example, if the cost of staff time is not included in a comparative cost analysis because it is the same in both scenarios), and the effectiveness of the cost analysis must be measured by comparison with actual costs or with similar activities at another institution.

FUNDING SOURCES

There are various potential sources of funding for preservation activities; these include internal sources (your parent institution, or possibly fees for services and/or other income-generating projects) and external sources (federal and state grant programmes, as well as local corporations and foundations). For external funding sources, your primary goal should be to develop a network of funders that matches your goals and ideas, and that can provide regular small grants supplemented by periodic larger grants.

Federal Funders

The three major federal sources for preservation funding of paper-based collections are:

- The National Endowment for the Humanities (NEH) Division of Preservation and Access. NEH has a number of grant categories, including Preservation Assistance Grants, Stabilization of Humanities Collections Grants, and Grants to Preserve and Create Access to

Humanities Collections. Note that the Preservation Assistance Grants are designed specifically for smaller institutions—they provide funding for preservation surveys; purchase of preservation supplies, equipment, and storage furniture; and other activities.

- The Institute of Museum and Library Services (IMLS). IMLS funds the Conservation Assessment programme and the Conservation Project Support programme (both for historical societies, museums, and state/local governments), as well as the Save America's Treasures programme and National Leadership Grants. IMLS also administers the Library Services and Technology Act (LSTA), through which funds are provided to state libraries, which then make re-grants to individual institutions for various purposes, including preservation.
- The National Historical Publications and Records Commission (NHPRC). NHPRC makes Archival and Records Project Grants to archival institutions to preserve records and make them accessible.

Other potential federal funders include the National Endowment for the Arts (NEA) and the National Science Foundation (NSF).

State Funders

There are numerous state preservation grant programmes around the country; these generally provide funding for preservation planning surveys, and subsequently for implementing survey recommendations. The type and extent of these programmes varies greatly, so it is best to consult your state library or archives to determine whether or not a preservation grant programme exists in your state.

Foundations

Remember that private organizations may also be a source of funding. There are several types of foundations: large general-purpose organizations such as the Ford Foundation or the Mellon Foundation; special-purpose foundations; company-sponsored foundations; community foundations (which usually fund within a specific geographic area); and family foundations (which are often informal and unstaffed).

Many small/local foundations or corporations have specific interests and you may be able to find one that matches your needs. For example, if you are trying to preserve a local history collection, you might consider approaching local businesses or others with an interest in the community. As with federal or state funding, you may have to provide funds to match the grant. Also remember that foundations may help in ways other than providing money directly for preservation activities, including providing funding for printing costs, furniture, or equipment.

GRANTWRITING

The key to writing a successful grant proposal is to understand what needs to be included in each part of the proposal, as well as what the proposal reviewers will be looking for when reading the document.

A grant proposal is a written presentation asking for support of a programme, project, activity, or function that an institution wants to undertake in response to a need. The proposal must articulate this need and provide a plan for carrying out the desired activity. The activity to be funded must have a clear relationship to your institution's mission and purpose. Your written proposal should be clear and realistic and should focus on what you can accomplish.

The general components of a preservation project proposal are as follows:

- *Objectives*: This part includes both your goals (a broad-based statement of the ultimate result of the activity) and objectives (a narrowly defined, measurable, time-specific outcome that your institution expects to accomplish as a result of the grant). Be sure to identify the community being served and to state the results of the project, not the activity itself.
- *Plan of Work*: This is a detailed description of the activities and services to be undertaken to achieve your goals and objectives. It should explain why you chose these methods, and it should enumerate what facilities, personnel, and equipment will be used. It should include a timeline for the process and define tasks and subtasks.
- *Budget*: This provides estimated costs for the activities listed in the plan of work. The forms and guidelines of the funder should be followed; government funders usually require more detail than foundations.
- *Evaluation*:This part describes your plans for evaluating the project to determine whether or not it was successful. You may need to measure whether staff members changed or improved their skills, knowledge, etc., or you may need to measure facts such as items rehoused or treated, materials developed, supplies consumed, etc.
- *Sustainability*: This part indicates how you will maintain the project or programme at the end of the grant period. Will the activities continue? If so, how will they be maintained, and what funding/ resources will you provide?

Helpful Hints for Grant Writing

- There should be one writer, even if there are many contributors.
- Follow the funder's guidelines.
- Do your research and get the facts right-be knowledgeable about the most current preservation practices.

- Be aware of related preservation projects.
- All ideas should flow from one central need.
- Avoid jargon.
- Be compelling, but not overdramatic.
- Get an outside person to edit the proposal and review the budget.
- Be thorough, clear, and concise.

Remember that a good proposal doesn't necessarily result in getting a grant; other factors, such as the number of proposals received or the current priorities of the granting agency, may come into play. Ask the granting agency for feedback, and resubmit if necessary.

PREDOMINANT APPROACHES IN LONG-TERM DIGITAL PRESERVATION

In our research we could observe that there are two predominant approaches trying to define the object of preservation. The first is closely related to Archival (including Records Management) and the second is a technical (or merely a technocratic) perspective. We could also observe the lack of an approach based on Information (and/or Information Continuum) perspective.

The Object of Preservation in the Archival Approach

A definition of Preservation Object is given by Dollar as "Preservation Objects are those to be archived. These objects are physically compound by set of files in maybe different formats. The objects logically are compound by data – the content for instance birth date of a person, and metadata – that should describe the context when the birth date of a particular person was used". The Records concept opens another view on the object of preservation. Preservation is a key characteristic for records, which is followed by their creation purpose to be re-used. The preservation also makes the record a vital component in the memory of organizations, individuals and in some cases of society. A record is more than just information, it suppose to be trustworthy *i.e.* being able to serve as evidence, and support accountability. The time for preservation could vary from days or months up to hundreds of years. The International Standards Organization definition of records is: "Information created, received, and maintained as evidence and information by an organizations or person, in pursuance of legal obligations or in transaction of business."

In the Guide for Managing Electronic Records of the International Council on Archives, from an archival perspective, a similar definition of record is given as "recorded information produced or received in the initiation, conduct or completion of an institutional or individual activity and that comprises content, context and structure sufficient to provide evidence of the activity."

Records can occur in different forms and representations.

They are usually represented as logically delimited information objects, for example, as distinct documents. But increasingly we find records in the form of distributed objects, such as relational databases and compound documents.

According to Thomassen a record has four characteristics, which make the record unique in relation to other types of information:

- Records serve as evidence over actions and transactions
- Records support accountability
- Records are related to processes, *i.e.* information that is generated by and linked to some work processes
- Records are going to be preserved, some even for eternity.

Cox stated that the evidential value of a record can only exist if the content, structure and context are preserved. The context is the link between different records that belongs together, and also to the process where the record was created. According to Dollar the electronic record is more of a logical entity, where integral parts can be managed at different places within an information system, or even in different information systems.

The question "What is a record" has been one of the fundamental issues in debates and discussions in archiving and digital preservation over the past twenty years. Attempts to arrive at general definition of an *electronic record* were made in the last decade by several research projects and have by now being replaced by more constructive approach to define properties and functionalities of electronic records that need to be preserved in a given context.

An electronic record can be understood as a package or a set of technical properties and possibilities, and of administrative context where some of these technical possibilities were put to use. In contrast, one approach in Digital Libraries that might have a significant difference is proposed by Nichols.

In this approach the concept of "artifact" is central an defined as "a physical object produced at some time in the past, and attesting to a given set of practices, thinking, and ways of viewing the world, but whose importance will be defined by present and foreseeable future needs and use. The value of the artifact is strongly influenced, but not completely determined by, the document/object's features that are unique". An artifact is then an object with a set of values such as Evidential, aesthetic,

Associational, Market and Exhibition value. An artifact is of value to the extent that it testifies to the information being original, faithful, fixed, or stable. Although, this approach do not mention the term record but "artefact", we interpret this approach to be similar to the Archival Approach.

The definitions of records are to some extent usable in our perspective. Nevertheless the usage of terms as "legal obligations" or "accountability" or "evidential" are strongly connected to Records Management and Archiving. Information is important but not central. We perceive the evidentiallity of records as the major focus of Archiving and Records Management and less focus is given to records as informational source. Thomassen gives emphasis in the need of preservation of records in order to be reused as memory traces.

This encompasses our Continuum perspective which is beyond of just records. The "big difference" is that our perspective is turning the precedence of information in relation to Archiving. Another difference is that our perspective deals with any kind of digitally recorded information as evidence of human activities not just with records as legal evidence.

The Object of Preservation in the Technocratic Approach

A definition of Digital Object is given by Blanchi and Petrone as "a unique identified data abstraction that encapsulates content and access policies while providing a high-level, self-describing, type definition. Digital Objects are described trough the use of an abstract typing mechanism that we refer to as content type".

The concept of Information Package of the OAIS Reference Model states that data is interpreted using its Representation Information (described in metadata), which produces information, that an information object consists of not only data content, but also the information necessary to interpret that content. In order to successfully preserve such a generic Information Object, it is critical for an Open

Archival Information System (OAIS) to clearly identify and understand the Data Object and its associated Representation Information, which together forms what, is called an Information Package.

The PREMIS data model describes intellectual entities, objects, rights, agents and events. Objects, according to PREMIS, can be bitstreams, files or representations (digital objects "instantiation or embodying an intellectual entity") Further, in scientific material the notion Preservation Object can be compared to the approach of Persistent Object articulated by the US National Archives (NARA) in cooperation with the San Diego Supercomputing Centre (SDSC).

The persistent object method presumes that all records can be represented as objects with their specific characteristics and behaviour.

The concept of Significant Properties, proposed by the National Library of Australia (NLA), are functions or characteristics of an object that are essential to its meaning. Preservation of digital objects, in this approach, in some cases will necessitate changes in look, feel, functionality or content if the object is to remain usable at all. Although significant properties may be seen as individual and specific to a given object, most digital archives try to create classes of objects based on common properties.

In the Cedars project, Significant Properties were associated with the Underlying Abstract Form (UAF) of an object. Therefore, objects with the same UAF have the same significant properties. Conversely, if significant properties varied, than objects that were otherwise similar could have different UAFs.

The PREMIS working group, following on the work of OAIS, Cedars and NLA, defined Significant Properties as those "characteristics of a particular object subjectively determined to be important to maintain through preservation actions", noting that "Significant properties may be objective technical characteristics subjectively considered to be particularly important, or subjectively determined characteristics".

Further, the FEDORA architecture describes a content container abstraction, the Digital Object, and the nature of Repositories that provide access to these containers.

They conceptualize a Digital Object as having:

- A structural kernel, which encapsulates content as opaque byte stream packages
- An interface, or behaviour, layer that gives contextual meaning to the data in the Digital Object.

One useful metaphor for a Digital Object is that of a cell. A similar approach is given by Saidis et al. as Digital Object Prototypes (DOPs) which provides the Digital Library (DL) designer with the ability to model diverse types of digital objects in a uniform manner while offering digital object type conformance.

They described a Digital Object that has constituent components, that is to say files, metadata, behaviours and relationships. The derived digital object typing information – that is, which components constitute each different type of object and how each object behaves – is not realized in a manner suitable for effective use by higher level Digital Library application logic including DL modules and services.

A DOP is a digital object type definition that provides a detailed specification of its constituent parts and behaviours. Digital objects are conceived as instances of their respective prototypes.

The approach to Digital Libraries proposed by Arms et al. described the "digital object" in a slightly different manner. The main building blocks in this approach are: "digital objects", which are used to manage digital material in a networked environment; "handles", which identify digital objects and other network resources; and "repositories", in which digital objects are stored.

From a computing view, the digital library is built up from simple components, notably digital objects. A digital object is a way of structuring information in digital form, some of which may be metadata, and includes a unique identifier, called a handle. First lets have a look to the terms and concepts used by this approach.

Very common are the terms of "data abstraction", "data", "bitstreams", "files", "instantiation", "characteristics and behaviour", "functions", "functionality", "objective technical characteristics", "structural kernel", "encapsulates opaque byte stream packages", "interface", "metadata", "behaviours and relationships", "manage digital material in a networked environment", "stored". Looking to the ontology of this approach is quite obvious that the terms utilized comes from computer science in general and at some extent from Object Oriented terminology.

This spokes for data management through information systems making data central. The term object is also important being conceptualization of data (such as files, bitstreams, etc.) having some behaviour (its functionality or implemented functions in as information system). No emphasis is made on information neither on its contents as traces of human activities.

Towards a Definition of Digital Information Preservation Object

Every other approach to define a the object of preservation has focused from different perspectives of preservation and from different characteristics of the digital object using its own ontology. Furthermore, we found that a) there is no existing or established definition of Digital Information Preservation Object, b) existing concepts are context dependent and focuses specifically on object to be preserved. After our study we came to conclusions that research carried out so far do not handle

Digital Information Preservation Object from Information Continuum perspective and do not contribute with any definition of the notion Digital Information Preservation Object. However, the studied research results merely focus on the structure and physical nature of the digital object. Their described abstractions are conceptualizations of the underlying physical level. Nevertheless, although these approaches support our activities to some extent, the definitions provided by these approaches are not suitable for our view, hence; we experienced the emergence of an own definition of Digital Information Preservation Object that specifically focuses on information.

However, this study gave us insights to take another perspective. To define the notion of Digital Information Preservation Object it is needed to take a standpoint. We cannot begin the definition from structure of the object; nonetheless, we will begin definition from a global view. If we start from the structure, we are viewing an object as a delimited entity at structural level, since our focus is on information, not the object itself.

We want to distinguish the conventional view to the object that is a construction, a container or a carrier to hold together the elements (depending on level of conceptualization) from the view that is to see an object from continuum perspective. An object there is a piece or pieces of information that reflects human action in a social context in the continuum.

There is an important remark before we provide our tentative definition of Digital Information Preservation Object (DIPO). We need to state that any for any object is to say that its analysis is made depending on the level of abstraction adopted and due a set of variables at that specific level. The Structure developed at the LDP Centre and the descriptions in section are (technical) conceptualizations of "digital (physical) objects"; they concentrate their efforts in describing or defining (at a very low level) the object to preserve regardless of its continuing information value. Our intention (or level of abstraction) lay merely in the general level or, so to say, we try to define DIPO at an "ethereal" level; we want to define the "thing" DIPO.

We take stand in the philosophy of Dooyeweerd who stated that Meaning rather than Existence is the primary property in created reality. In our perspective, this view encompasses the Information Continuum

Model perspective in which put the continuing value of information (*i.e.* its reconstruction of human social actions) as the meaning (*raison d'être*) of the DIPO. The DIPO is a recorded result of human's action in form of information pieces. This information is categorized in an information type from social context. These information pieces can have relationships to other information pieces either within its own physical carrier or towards other objects.

The vital characteristic of the information object from continuum perspective is that new object can be created through the combination of information pieces that can be a piece of other objects. In that way, the information will be reused in another context and reproducing human social actions. It means that information can be related to processes (that is generated by, and linked to work processes). Furthermore, the information in the object must serve as evidence over actions and transactions as well.

The natural question that arises, should be what is this definition good for? Having a definition of DIPO and a clear perspective of the continuum, long-term digital preservation issues might be easier to tackle. Something we observe is that there is a need of a uniform "aspectual abstraction" of the Digital Information Preservation Object.

Bibliography

A.K. Gupta: *Digital Library and Education*, Pearl Books, Delhi, 2012.

Ajay K. Srivastav: *Digital Library Environment and Networking*, Shree Publications, Delhi, 2006.

Ajay Khatri and Pradip Umdale : *Application of Six Sigma in Library and Information Science*, Ess Ess Publications, Delhi, 2013.

Ajit Singh: *Information Technology and Library Sciences*, Ancient Publications, Delhi, 2011.

Arunima Baruah: *Library Science*: *Prospects in 21 Century*, Kilaso Books, 2004.

B S Aggarwal : *An Introduction to Library and Information Science*, ABD Publication, Delhi, 2005.

Beales, G.: *The Evolving Roles of Information Professionals in the Digital Age*, Long Life Publication, New Delhi, 2003.

Bertozzi, S.: *Special Libraries,* Pune Publication, Maharashtra, 2006.

Bloom, B. S.: *Key Concepts in the Architecture of the Digital Library,* Concept Publishing Company, New Delhi, 2003.

Brook, A.: *Technology and the Changing Role of Teacher-Librarians,* Cambridge University Press, New York, 2004.

C.D. Sharma : *Advances in Library and Information Science*, Scientific Publication, Delhi, 1998.

C.L. Prajapati : *Archivo-Library Materials*, Mittal Publication, Delhi, 1998.

H.R. Chopra, U.C. Sharma and M.K. Srivastava: *Library Science and its Facets (2 Vols-Set)*, Ess Ess Publications, Delhi, 1998.

Harris, J. L.: *Training for Change: New Skills for the Electronic Library,* New Technology, New Librarians?, London and New York: Longman, 2005.

Kusum Verma: *Metadata and Digital Library Systems*, Akansha Publicatins, Delhi, 2004.

Mahendra Kumar Seth : *A Guide to Library and Information Science Jobs*, Abhijeet Publications, Delhi, 2006.

Mahendra Singh Sodhi : *Advancement in Library and Information Science*, Adhyayan Publication, Delhi, 2006.

Menzies, E. P.: *The Electronic Document and its Impact on the Information Chain Professions*, Kogan Page, London, 2000.

Mukherjee, N.: *Digital Libraries: Principles and Practice in a Global Environment*, Concept Publication, New Delhi, 2005.

N.R. Satyanarayana: *A Manual of Library Automation and Networking*, New Royal Book Co., Lucknow, 2003.

Pramod Kumar Singh: *Library Automation*, Shree Publications, Delhi, 2005.

Preeti Batra: *Text Book of Library Science*, Mohit Publications, Delhi, 2010.

R L Sehgal: *Designing and Evaluation of Research in Library Science (2 Vols-Set)*, Ess Ess Publications, Delhi, 1998.

R. K. Krishnan: *The Five Laws of Library Science*, Centrum Press, Delhi, 2013.

Shiv Ram Verma : *Academic Library System*, Shree Publication, Delhi, 2005.

Shri Nath Sahai : *Academic Library System*, Ess Ess Publication, Delhi, 2009.

T C Mohanti: *Research Methodology in Library Science*, Alfa Publications, Delhi, 2008.

T. Nasirudheen : *A Comprehensive Course in Library and Information Science*, Ess Ess Publications, Delhi, 2012.

T.R. Sanjiv Reddy and Shyamgopal Verma : *Library Management and Information Technology*, Pacific Books International, Delhi, 2012.

T.R. Sanjiv Reddy and Shyamgopal Verma: *Library Science and Information Technology Misuse*, Pacific Books International, Delhi, 2012.

U N Singh : *Library Management in Internet Era*, Shree Publication, Delhi, 2007.

V.K. Jain: *Information Technology for Digital Library Management and Automation*, Atlantic Publications, Delhi, 2009.

V.V.V. Satyanarayana: *Modern Librarianship Ushering in Digital Library*, Authorspress Publications, Delhi, 2006.

Index

A

Abbreviated 27
Accession 77
Accommodate 71, 151
Accomplish 166
Adequately 27
Appropriate 31, 130
Archaeological 77
Architectural 159
Artifactual 141, 142, 228, 229
Attributes 79

C

Certainly 254
Citation 243
Clippings 157
Commercial 161, 167
Complexity 21
Consumerism 58
Crontab 105, 107, 108, 109, 110
Cumulative 152

D

Deterioration 142, 144, 152, 153, 281
Dictate 121, 124
Dissemination 68, 80, 125, 133
Dissertations 62

E

Efficiency 208
Encountered 146
Entail 38
Enterprises 5
Extensible 23
Extensively 108
Extent 25, 26

F

Facilitated 250
Fluctuations 155, 158
Fragile 22
Fragmentary 146
Frustrating 146

H

Hierarchical 33
Hierarchy 189

I

Immediately 191
Imperialistic 118
Inadequate 42
Increasingly 98
Infrastructure 87, 90, 160, 161, 166, 167
Ingesting 32
Instantiated 33, 64
Intranets 119, 126

L

Labyrinthine 266

Legislation 45, 49, 50, 51, 54, 55, 56
Librarians 252, 253, 254, 255, 256, 257, 258, 259, 260, 261, 262

M

Mandate 38, 41, 128
Manoeuvrability 155
Metadata 116, 253, 254, 258, 261
Multilingual 140

N

Navigability 119
NEXIS 124

O

Occurrences 76
OrganiSation 89, 90
Oxidation 230

P

Periodicals 76
Perpetual 58
Polyethylene 156
Preservation 253, 255, 257
Primarily 69
Purposemade 160

Q

Quadruple 39

R

Recognition 116, 149
Repositories 31, 32, 33, 244, 253, 254, 255, 260, 262
Representation 169, 187
Retrieval 41, 48, 70, 71, 81, 114, 117, 118, 119, 123, 124, 136, 137, 138, 148, 187, 188, 191, 209

S

Schellenberg 145
Scholarly 253, 255, 261
Semantic 169, 170, 187, 188, 190
Separately 157
Serendipitous 120
Sophisticated 125, 140
Stabilization 282
Subsequent 283
Synonymous 74

U

Ubiquitous 161
UMI 124
Uninitiated 121

V

Vulnerable 156